Transcendent Indi

How might anthropology seem if it were written in celebration of individuality – of the individual's conscious and creative engagement with socio-cultural milieux – and if it were committed to a liberal agenda which sought to cherish and defend that individuality?

Transcendent Individual argues for just such a commitment: a reappraisal of the place of the individual in anthropological theorising and ethnographic writing, and a social-scientific appreciation of the individual as methodological, moral, pragmatic and aesthetic subject. Here is an anthropological account of individual creativity, of the narrativity of individual expression, of the originality of individual becoming, and of the morality of the individual body.

Drawing widely on ethnographic and theoretic materials, and bringing into debate a range of voices – Nietzsche, Wilde and Forster, Bateson and Gerald Edelman, George Steiner, Richard Rorty and John Berger, Edmund Leach and Anthony Cohen – the book approaches individuality in terms of a range of issues: biological integrity, consciousness, agency, democracy, discourse, knowledge, consumerism, globalism and play.

Written in an accessible style, and juxtaposing literary and philosophical against anthropological voices *Transcendent Individual* presents its readers with a social-scientific issue of importance and topical concern.

Nigel Rapport is Professor of Anthropological and Philosophical Studies at the University of St Andrews.

Transcendent Individual

Towards a Literary and Liberal Anthropology

Nigel Rapport

ROUTLEDGE

London and New York

First published 1997
by Routledge
11 New Fetter Lane, London EC4P 4EE

Simultaneously published in the USA and Canada
by Routledge
29 West 35th Street, New York, NY 10001

© 1997 Nigel Rapport

Typeset in Times by Florencetype Limited, Stoodleigh, Devon
Printed and bound in Great Britain by Hartnolls Ltd, Bodmin, Cornwall

British Library Cataloguing in Publication Data
A catalogue record for this book is available from the British Library

Library of Congress Cataloguing in Publication Data

Rapport, Nigel, 1956–
Transcendent Individual : towards a literary and liberal anthropology /
Nigel Rapport.
p.   cm.
Includes bibliographical references (p. 202) and index.
1. Ethnology–Philosophy. 2. Ethnology–Authorship.
3. Individuality. 4. Ethnology in literature. I. Title.

GN33.R36   1997
305.8'001–dc21
97–7414
CIP

ISBN 0–415–16966–6 (hbk)
ISBN 0–415–16967–4 (pbk)

What, however, does it mean that we find an insatiable pleasure in making ourselves into our own possibilities, and cannot
– in spite of knowing what it is – cease to play the game of our
potentials? It is to questions of this kind that literary anthropology has to address itself.

Wolfgang Iser
Towards a Literary Anthropology

To
Elizabeth
and
Callum

Contents

Acknowledgements

In the preparation of these essays, a number of individuals were kind enough to act variously as mentors, interlocutors, critics and confidants. Above all, I benefited from the generous commentary of Vered Amit-Talai, Eduardo Archetti, Aleksander Boskovik, Anthony Cohen, Peter Collins, Andrew Dawson, Roy Dilley, Jeanette Edwards, Anna Grimshaw, Claudia Gross, Ladislav Holy, Allison James, Tamara Kohn, Joanna Overing, David Riches, Anne Rowbottom, Jonathan Skinner, Marilyn Strathern and Deborah Wickering.

Three of the essays appeared in earlier incarnations in *Anthropology Today*, and I owe Jonathan Benthall, the journal's editor, a great deal for the invitations to contribute, as well as for his patience with my efforts.

At Routledge, Heather Gibson has remained a most supportive editor and a stimulating fellow-traveller in the enterprise of literary anthropology.

Finally, I do not forget the support – and all else – of Elizabeth Munro, to whom (along with Callum) the volume is dedicated with love.

NJR
St Andrews 1997

Manifesto
Towards a liberal and literary appreciation of the conscious and creative individual

1 This is a book of essays all of which bear on the theme of *individuality* – on the individual's conscious and creative engagement with certain socio-cultural environments – and the links between individuality and the writing of social science. The essays have an iconoclastic agenda: the writing of social science (in particular socio-cultural anthropology) as imbued with a belief in the *transcendent subject*. Here is a book of essays intent on a social-scientific appreciation of the individual who makes himself or herself *ex nihilo* and in an originary fashion – who comes to be, who achieves a consciousness, outwith and beyond the socio-cultural environment in which he or she was born and has been socialised/enculturated.

2 A number of *keywords* might be stated, for later elaboration: Individual, Individuality, Creativity, Consciousness, Writing, Narrative, Discourse, Form, Meaning, Interpretation, Personalisation, Anthropology, Literature.

3 The individual agenda of these essays is *methodological, ontological, aesthetic* and *moral*.

To paraphrase Oscar Wilde, only by 'intensifying one's own individuality', through precise consciousness of oneself in a socio-cultural environment, can one hope to appreciate the individuality of others and thereby approach an understanding: one must look inward in order to see outward; by looking outward one realises one's inwardness. Here is a necessary and continuous dualism. Far from a narrowly introspective or overly idealistic exercise, then, it is the case that how we conceptually understand ourselves and our lives-in-society, how we validate our claims to self-knowledge, and how we transpose such knowledge into narrative, are all entirely crucial to our project of apprehending otherness, and, indeed, indistinguishable from it (cf. Stanley 1993:50; also Cohen 1994:136). In Wilde's words, personality is "an element of revelation" (1913:156; and cf. Chesterton 1936:170).

Moreover, such an approach is not only methodologically potent but ontologically necessary. For it is in individuality that the roots of the social and cultural lie. Except for the conscious individual, there is no social mover: no possibility of social process or organisation, of structured relations, routinised interactions or institutionalised behaviours. And except for the creative individual, there is no cultural dynamo: no possibility of cultural symbols or norms, of interpretive regimes, classificatory systems or forms of life. In short, to return to Wilde (1913:123), there can be 'no unity without individuals': no commonality without diversity, no socio-cultural sharing or coming together without individual discreteness (cf. Rapport 1993:169ff.).

For Wilde, again, this makes the individual a source of wonder, a thing of beauty. I find so too, and I celebrate such individuality in these essays. I try to bring to social–scientific account an aesthetic appreciation of the work of the individual in creating the forms of life by which societies operate and in construing the meanings by which cultural symbols are animated.

Finally, this imbues the essays with a moral quest. Here is an attempt to write a 'liberal' social science which feels free to champion the individual and feels constrained to criticise that happenstance and circumstance where individuality is threatened or denied. Here, too, is a defence of liberal theorising in the face of conventional social–scientific depreciation which contends that this theorising does little more than articulate the prejudices of a politically naive Anglo-American intellectual class, and that such theorising is anyway impotent in an age dominated by global communitarianism – by resurgent ethnicities, renascent localisms, typifying bureaucracies and militant fundamentalisms.

4 The essays in this book intend to be *wide-ranging in terms of genre*, showing little respect for disciplinary distinctions (between anthropology, literature and literary criticism, culture studies, philosophy, psychology, and sociology) where these would seem to fracture the individual (the liberal–humanist) subject, dividing off one significant aspect from others. Similarly, the essays intend to be *tonally various*, juxtaposing 'ethnography' (my own, from the northern English dale of Wanet, and others') against 'theory' and 'analysis' so as best to convey a sense of experiential fullness and subtlety.

Oscar Wilde's literatured name has already been raised, emblematically, and the book might indeed be dedicated to his writing. For he has written literarily so much of what I should like to write social–scientifically (cf. Kiberd 1994:*passim*). He inveighed against the conventional fetish of his time for hard-and-fast classification, recognising that 'to define was to limit' (1954:217). Against the urge to essentialise, against the practice of monothetic descriptions, he recognised the truth of multiplicity and that multiplicity was truth: "a truth is that whose contradiction is also true" (1913:263), whether that multiplicity referred to the identities which the individual would 'write' for himself or the realities which could be disinterred in a socio-cultural environment. Above all, Wilde repudiated the belief that individual lives were singularly determined or predetermined by their environments, or limited in any hard-and-fast fashion. There was a radical autonomy to the self – like a work of art which may be created and recreated through imagination, conscious knowledge and play. There was a transcendency to the individual by which he was able to invent himself and his traditions (1910:15–16,47–8).

Notwithstanding, I shall also have important recourse to other names. Precisely: the idea of the transcendent individual, the individual who writes herself and, in the process, rewrites the socio-cultural environment around her, is most fully a *Nietzschean* one. It is the essential, objective, inherent nature of the individual self, Nietzsche believed, to be self-caused and free. This is a belief I share. Likewise, I share a belief in the way Nietzsche justified his idea: on aesthetic grounds. One can only use artistic models for understanding the world and for evaluating people and actions, Nietzsche claimed, for like an art-work, a literary text, the world requires reading and interpretation in order to be mastered, understood, made liveable. Furthermore, like an art-work, the world can be interpreted equally well in vastly different and deeply incompatible ways; since the realisation of the death of God (as hero and author, as theorist and analyst), the world can no longer be made subject to a single, overarching interpretation (God's will or intention; language or grammar; social structure; the unconscious). Indeed, perhaps *the* fundamental drive in human life is the tendency for the individual to rearrange that which confronts him in his own way: the will to stamp his own impress on what is and what is to come. And is this very will not a thing of beauty? Is not individuality an art-work in itself? The individual is a work of art that has given birth to itself, and, equally, the world he or she creates is as beautiful, as full of artistry as it is individual. And again I agree; borrowing *E.M.Forster*'s words, the individual "seems to me a divine achievement" (1972:66).

There are two seeming paradoxes here. First, the idea of God and divine transcendentalism is being kept alive after all, merely under a new name: Individual. Second, what began as an argument phrased in terms of Nietzschean existentialism has ended up with phrasings of Forsterian liberalism. As for the first, the transcendentalism, the 'divinity', of the individual is situational, transitory, only, and a matter of action not substance; individuals are 'divine' in their originality, their creativity, their uniqueness, but they are mortal, short-lived actors, and the substance of their creations is perspectival, not factual or complete. Individuals may be 'divine', transcendental, in how they act, but they are merely beautiful in what they do, in the substance of their original creations. As for the second, I have written elsewhere of the convergences between Nietzsche and Forster on a humanistic affirmation of life, on the question of a creative responsibility towards the world and the responsibility to be creative within it (Rapport 1994:65–6). But further than this, I believe a path can be taken between a recognition of one's individuality in a godless world and recognising the individuality of others, and hence the need for mutual respect, for maintaining a civil, humane conversation between others and oneself. One may be an individual actor but inevitably one acts within an environment made up, *inter alia*, of other individual actors. Hence, recognising one's own individual integrity and worth, one's duty to oneself to be oneself, must also give onto a recognition of others', and of the beauty of an environment of infinite variety (cf. Wilde 1968:285). And hence, the path from existentialism to liberalism, from Nietzsche to Forster – or to *John Stuart Mill*. For Mill, individuality must live in a social space which is aimed, as far as possible, at guarding against the individuality of one actor hindering or despoiling the individuality of another.

In short, while the agenda of these essays centres on the transcendental individual subject, on the Nietzschean *ego*, it does so in a liberal–humanist context, in a Forsterian/Millian social milieu. My objective is to account for the individual in a moral way which relates him to his fellows.

5   These essays set out to be wide-ranging in another way too. For it is not only disciplinary distinctions that I would transcend, but also those between the academician and the layman, in particular *between the academic social-scientist and the field informant*. "Every man is a scientist, by disposition as well as by right", George Kelly once famously proposed, in framing a humanistic psychology, and "every subject is an incipient experimenter" (1969:144). Whether scholar or dunce, each individual has the initiative, the consciousness, to devise a personal system or systems of mental constructs, his or her perspectival criteria, in terms of which people and events come to be construed, encountered, plotted and anticipated. Through her personal constructs, each individual actively reaches out to the world (a world made other by her consciousness) and places certain meanings upon it and herself. In the process of her life (in the process that is her life), these meanings of the world will accrue, multiply, develop, change and contradict one another, but the initiative will remain with her. Finally, and paradoxically, in this way, the individual subject becomes the main subject of his own personal constructions; and while in and of the world, his active consciousness gives onto a narrative which he writes of and out of the world.

The individual subject I address in these essays is both the self of the social scientist and the self of his or her informants, then, and I examine the necessary relationship between the two in the origination of anthropological data. Furthermore, I address consciousness in social scientist and informant, and the status of interactional routines which might be said to interrelate the two; I argue for the necessity of a social–scientific approach which is not averse to thinking itself inside the heads of other people. Finally, I address the conscious writer, and the continuing writing of social reality by the individual social scientist as by his or her informants; I examine writing as the expression of consciousness whether the socio-cultural environment be deemed 'academic' or 'lay', 'modern' or 'traditional'.

Commentary on the academic, the modern, the scientific, in short, is juxtaposed here against that of the lay, the traditional, the folk.

6 By *individuality*, I should stress, I do not mean individualism. For while the presence of individualism as a particular historico-cultural conceptualisation of the person – the social actor as ostentatiously and conventionally 'distinct', sovereign and auto-nomous, and as this giving onto his dignity and social value – may be variable, I take individuality to be universally and ubiquitously present.

I do not extend the argumentation, then, concerning the dawning, the provenance and the prevalence of 'the cult of the individual' in contradistinction to the hierarchy of the collectivity (cf. Macfarlane 1978, 1989; Dumont 1986; Morris 1991), nor the comparison concerning the forms of local representation of the person (cf. Carrithers 1985; Marsella *et al.* 1985; Jackson and Karp 1990). Rather, I state the universality of the individual as the fount of agency, consciousness, interpretation and creativity in social and cultural life; this by virtue of his or her sole ownership of discrete, corporeal, sense-making apparatuses. Consciousness bounds the (otherwise permeable) individual human body, and is itself a manifestation of that 'unique embodiment': of the indi-viduality of the being and the becoming of each individual body (Edelman 1992:136–9).

The variability of individualism in no way translates as a contingency of individuality, therefore, whereby one may some-how contemplate people living unself-consciously, "amid various unconscious systems of determining forces" (Rabinow 1977:151). Instead, I conclude that the traditional 'primitive' who is not self-aware and self-critical, who leads an unexamined life, somehow amalgamated with others, incapable of a sophisticated and con-scious elucidation of his cultural practices and social institutions, does not exist (cf. Shweder 1991:14); likewise for the post-struc-turalist 'person' who is simply 'the effect' of a position assigned him or her by historico-cultural discourses (Easthope, in D.S. 1995: *passim*). There are always individuals who, willy-nilly, effect their own meaningful perspectives on and interpretations of the world.

The key insight into individuality concerns *form and meaning*. The well-spring of social life and cultural process lies beyond the formally apparent: beyond the public, collectively and commonly held sets of cultural symbols which classify and label life; beyond the consensual sets of practices, verbal and other, by which social interaction is negotiated, managed and undertaken. For what resides beyond these is individual consciousness. Individual consciousness 'writes' itself in terms of cultural symbols and social practices, and hence is responsible for their continuing presence in a human milieu; individual consciousness animates these forms with meaning and purpose. True, such consciousness is limited by the forms and practices by which it can express itself and hope to communicate itself at any one time, but individual consciousness is none the less responsible for animating those forms and practices with its own individual 'energy' – its agency, intentionality and meaningfulness. Furthermore, it does so in an individual – creative, idiosyncratic, ambiguous, situational, multiple – fashion.

As with individual inwardness and outwardness, in short, form and meaning represent a necessary dualism, in dialectical tension. Meaning is "an internal perception", as Wagner puts it (1991:38–9); it is inside the body that forms are "perceived and known", that the very understanding and archetype of 'perceiving and knowing' is sourced. To privilege the formal and outward, as social science has tended to do (if not collapsing the distinction completely and offering an account of the formal (the structural, the consensual, the institutional, the collective) as all there is, as a thing-in-itself), is to descend to socio-cultural determinism.

7 The individual, liberal–humanist subject that I set out to describe (and celebrate) in this book, therefore – as seat of consciousness, as well-spring of creativity, as guarantor of meaning – is to be contrasted with the *dissolved, decentred, deconstructed* individual actor and author as he or she appears in Durkheimian, Structuralist and Post-Structuralist schools of social science, especially as this 'line of thought' has been developed during this century in France and imported into the British academy in certain predominant forms of sociology and social anthropology. It is against these schools that the argumentation of this book faces up. For I cannot find myself in their descriptions, and, with their anti-humanistic conceptualisations of others (as products and pawns of social structures or social relations, systems of signification, habituated practices or unconscious urges), I cannot see how I can be content to imagine others. These essays have an *autobiographical* inspiration, then. I take my own self as the measure, the precedent, the paradigm case of an individual subject – and argue that any social scientist must do the same. Biographical commentary is only made subtle, made sensitive, through an autobiographical consciousness.

In a recent review, Richard Sieburth remarked on the irony that the number of autobiographical writings now being published in France is some twenty-five times what it was in the late nineteenth-century. Despite the much-vaunted unfashionableness of 'la litterature personelle', despite current post-structuralist pronouncements on the death of the author – celebrations of Pascal's denigration of "le moi haissable" – here is a vital and inventive genre of writing whose quality at least matches that of the French novel, drama or poetry. Indeed, Sieburth (1994:10) would include the recent provocative confessions of two staunch anti-humanists, Derrida and Althusser, as being amongst the most human of these documents.

I would take the irony to indicate the relative ease with which one can anti-humanistically impersonalise (dehumanise) others while wishing yet to personalise (reserve a comparatively humane treatment for) oneself; one creates a marvellously ingenious, elegant and circumscribing model of the lack of individual agency of others (their false consciousness, their unconsciousness, their collective consciousness) while omitting (the possibility of) one's own creativity as model-builder from the model – if one does not omit one's own placement in the model tout court.

Also I would take the irony to indicate the actuality and universality of the individual self, and hence its being expressed, its achieving expression, whatever the fashionableness or institutionality of current (impersonal) expressive genres. However the individual is conventionally, normatively, meant to seem, whatever are the socio-cultural conditions concerning the conceptualisation and appearance of the individual self, still it is the individual who acts and his or her creativity which the process of society and culture evidences.

8 For Michael Sheringham (1993: passim), what can also be seen to characterise current autobiographical (French) writing is its inter-textuality. In the process of writing themselves, in disclosing both the cohesiveness of their lives, and their significant socio-cultural context, their culmination in the present and their continuation into the future, individual authors make clear how they see their writing in terms of a textual and personal heritage. Thus, as Rousseau declared his Confessions would be more accurate and sincere to the self than Montaigne's, and as Stendhal took Rousseau's text as his context, so now Derrida seeks in his *Circonfessions* innovatively to un-write the personal imprint of all the individual others.

Inter-textuality equally characterises this exercise in autobiographical essay-writing, Indeed, my understanding of a broadly 'literary anthropology' is of a social science which deliberately maintains a conversation with whatever ideas and texts appear provocatively to elucidate the subject under review. In terms of the textual heritage which I would claim for this book, the individual authors and writings with which I most frequently converse in these essays, the following names must be admitted: Nietzsche, Forster and Mill as already mentioned, also Gregory Bateson, Edmund Leach, James Fernandez and Anthony Cohen, George Steiner and John Berger. My ideas on the transcendent individual can be understood in terms of (anxious) readings of their influential writings.

Indeed, the inspiration of a wide range of writers and texts should become apparent in the course of these essays. However, if I were to identify one writer and one text at this stage as being especially inspirational, then it would be to flag *Richard Rorty's Contingency, irony, and solidarity* (1992). Rorty's project, his bravura act of writing, is to reconcile the writings of Nietzsche and Mill: to show that the egoistic and aesthetic philosophy of Nietzsche and the public-minded and liberal philosophy of Mill can be made to work together in the life of one person, become that person's life-philosophy, even if the philosophies cannot be made substantively commensurable – even if "the demands of self-creation and of human solidarity [are] equally valid, yet forever incommensurable" (1992:xv). Nietzsche sought to exalt (and to exemplify) private perfection: the self-created, autonomous, individual human life; Mill sought to codify (and to inculcate) civil society: to make public institutions and practices more just and less cruel towards the end of furthering the mutuality of individual liberty. To effect a correspondence between the two would be to say that a just and free society allows its citizens to be as privatistic and aesthetic as they choose so long as they cause no harm and spoil no chances of others. There might be no way theoretically to bring the philosophies of justice and self-creation together, but then, Rorty explains, in terms of individuals' everyday lives there is also no need. Simply, here are two kinds of tools in the toolbox of life-philosophies (as Wittgenstein might have said). One makes us aware of our half-articulate need to become a new person – aware that we need not only speak the language of the tribe, that we may find our own words, that we may have a responsibility to ourselves to find them. While the other reminds us of the failures of our public institutions and that we have a responsibility to others to improve them. All one need do is stop trying to hold all the sides of one's life in a single vision, or describe them with a single metavocabulary.

Quite so. Certainly, the aesthetic and the moral, the existential and the liberal, appear in these essays as experientially related, overlapping, interwoven, but yet distinct themes.

9 Other *thematic overlaps* within and among these essays focus on relations between: movement and individual identity, movement and narrative, narrative and individual identity, individual identity and world-making, world-making and narrative, world-making and play, play and creativity, creativity and social structure, creativity and individual identity, individual identity and morality, morality and liberalism and biology, biology and consciousness, consciousness and movement, consciousness and narrative and discourse . . . and all these and the writing of social science.

10 However, if this book is a collection of essays in which a number of themes interweave themselves, then the themes also represent for me different ways of approaching the same phenomenon: *the individual writing of socio-cultural reality* – which I describe as "individuality". By focusing, in separate essays, on the creativity, the consciousness, the meaningfulness, the acts of 'writing', the transitoriness, the homeliness and the morality, of this individual subject – in social life and in social science – it is such individuality which I hope the essays as a collection illuminate.

Moreover, collected essays can intend to be no more exhaustive, holistic or integrative than their individual subject matter; while they approach 'the same phenomenon' of individuality, they can remain as polythetic and diverse, as eschewing of common denomination, of singular underlying or overarching structuration, as the individual himself (cf. Rapport 1993:*passim*). Both Clifford Geertz (1988:148) and George Marcus (1986:191) – mouthpieces of late modernism *and* of early post-modernism in anthropology – suggest looking beyond the traditional monograph to the likes of the essay for a fitting conveyance of contemporary experience of the world. For here is the perspectival, the partial and the multiple. Here, following Nietzsche, is a collection of compositions of the world, juxtaposed against one another, each of which may complement others but whose creation and number is potentially without limit (cf. Parkin 1987:64–6).

11   The essays may be read in the *sequence* they appear, or, alternatively, as more discrete pieces and in other sequences. Whatever the reader's order, a coherent narrative should emerge, of increasing argumentational density. Each essay read should afford context to the next. Because, as I say, when writing the essays, I felt I was always approaching the subject of individuality, always gaining vantage on individual experience, even though in different terms. The individual in terms of:

liberal democracy
    human rights
        biological integrity
            agency
                self-creation
                    interpretation
                        meta-experience
                        narrative
                    writing social reality
                cultural grammar
            discourse
        social structure
      the impersonalisation of the world
    social-scientific method
creolisation
    movement
        play
            literature
              anthropology

Chapter 1

Writing Individual Knowledge and Personal Relations
Eschewing the paths to impersonalisation

> Generalisations are true or false in proportion as they represent or misrepresent all the individual doings and happenings. ... 'The Book of the Recording Angel' may be regarded as the ideal limit to which [social science] approximates as generalisation tends to zero.
>
> A.M.MacIver

What MacIver claims above idealistically, William Blake ("Jerusalem" (1975)) would claim poetically: 'Art and Science cannot exist but in minutely organised particulars. To generalise is to be an idiot. To particularise is alone distinction of merit'. Kierkegaard (1940), meanwhile, claims it philosophically: '"the public" is an abstraction made up of individuals when they are nothing, when what makes them real people is inoperative', and Aldous Huxley (1964) claims it novelistically: 'the general in any man's conversation must always be converted into the particular and personal if you want to understand him'.

And yet generalisation, 'impersonalisation', the conceiving, knowing and phrasing of the world and its features in terms which deny or devalue the individual, the particular and the personal in favour of the collective, the general, the impersonal, is ubiquitous. Whether the discourse concerns folk constructions of academic, lay or expert, commonsensical or theoretical, everyday or esoteric, profane or sacred kinds, there seems to be a common resort to the impersonalisation of generalisation.

Indeed, in social science it is commonly regarded not merely as a virtue, but as a *sine qua non* of verity. Durkheim's notion of a "social fact", of an objective and institutional phenomenon external to, constitutive and coercive of the individual, encapsulated both the fundamental explicans and explicandum of his discipline of sociology – was basic to *The Rules of Sociological Method* (1966 [1895]). While the notion of an impersonal, formal social reality above and beyond the actions, subjectivities, motives and intentions of individuals lives on in Giddens' *New Rules of Sociological Method* (1976), in the form of a concept and domain of "action" which individuals in interaction unintentionally give onto and which ultimately comes to embody the causal conditions and structuring force of such interaction (1976:155–160). (Thus, it is through an institutional analysis of such macro-structural forms and processes, Giddens can conclude, and not in the "triviata" of everyday individual interaction, that basic socio-cultural truths are to be found (1973:15; also cf. Gellner 1959:263)).

In this essay, I set out to do two things. To enumerate a number of significant ways in which 'the world becomes impersonal': tentatively to specify reasons why we generalise, to isolate impulses toward generalisation, its possible purposes and benefits. Furthermore, to argue that the only real knowledge of the world is individual and particular, and that it is of this that social science should treat.

Reading a recent review of V. Gatrell's book *The Hanging Tree: Execution and the English People, 1770–1868* (1994), and of the 'sleazy insouciance' with which administrative tribunals, councils, home secretaries and prince regents would treat the petitions for mercy compiled and proffered by condemned criminals and their supporters – the absurd randomness and callousness surrounding who would be pardoned and who would hang – I was reminded of a sentence of Camus's which had troubled me for some time: 'One condemns to the death penalty a guilty man, but one always carries out the sentence on an innocent one.' What I found haunting about this characterisation was that I believed it but I could not satisfactorily explain why: some murderers, (say terrorists, Nazis, psychopaths), surely were guilty through and through? In this essay, I should also like to provide myself with a greater understanding of why I sympathise with Camus's sentiment. For I now think it perhaps hinges on a distinction between the impersonal and the personal. Only distance and ignorance (administrative, bureaucratic, social, cultural, emotional) confers a propensity to fix things forever: to posit an absolute, fatal guilt; only on an impersonal level can someone pass an absolute judgement and condemn to death. From close to – as close to someone as to carry out a death penalty – one accrues a knowledge of inevitable relativity and situationality, and hence an appreciation of a certain innocence: the personal ever confers the mitigation of contextualisation. (And maybe Camus would have agreed – if in other terms – with van der Rohe: 'God is in the details.)

FIVE WAYS IN WHICH THE WORLD BECOMES IMPERSONAL

1 The cognitive impulse

We grant the world that we cognitively construct a (false) impersonal ontological status – we 'ontically dump' our conceptualisations onto the world – in order that we can keep thinking new thoughts and freeing ourselves from categorical givens.

"Ontic dumping" is a term of Carol Feldman's (1987:*passim*), describing a cognitive process she says characterises all thinking adult human beings and which babies learn as they acquire language. Every cognitive act, she begins, contains two components: achieving a knowledge of the world – an 'epistemic' component – and forming a conceptualisation, a representation of (this knowledge of) the world – an 'ontic' component. 'Ontics' entail the constructing of states of affairs, the creating and construing of real objects, which can then be taken as given; ontics are concepts and notions and topics, descriptions and forms and images. 'Epistemics' entail the original mental acts we undertake so as to come to knowledge, solve individual problems, *ab initio*; epistemics are definitions, orderings, commentaries, interpretations. Epistemic operation, in short, engages with the new before it becomes the given and the taken-for-granted. Ontic conceptualisation, meanwhile, gradually builds up into an ontological theory: a theory of the nature of the world and its component parts; a cognitive store of how things are and might be, of past objects and possible future ones.

Moreover, while there is no linear or singular relationship between these two cognitive components – 'a situation' (epistemic) can be 'described' (ontic) in any number of different ways – there is an ongoing processual relationship, Feldman continues. For once epistemic processes of knowledge formation have resulted in (issued forth as) ontic objects, we treat the latter as though they were, and always have been and will be, external to us. That is, having constructed a world and its objects, we then treat them as if we had merely discovered them, as if they were 'really real' and not ours at all. As Bruner put the case, our thought may be "in here" but our conclusions we put "out there": epistemic operations and their output are given ontological status; processes turned into products. Here is a situation of 'ontic dumping' which amounts to a universal human practice – and also failing (1990:24).

That ontic dumping is a failing, of social scientists as of anyone else, is the thrust of this essay as a whole, so let me leave Bruner's judgement hanging for the time being and return to Feldman for further explanation of why such dumping takes place. First, ontic dumping occurs, she postulates, so as to make cognitive space for new epistemics (for what Goodman has referred to as the continuous act of new 'worldmaking' (1978:*passim*)). It is in our nature to keep thinking new thoughts, construing different worlds, with the result that new objects and concepts are made up, new conceptualisations. This in turn has the effect of prior, given objects and extant concepts being further externalised and distantiated – made increasingly 'real', 'out there'. And so the process is continuous; ontic dumping is part-and-parcel of our continual freeing of ourselves from the lineaments of the present. We abstract ourselves from present structures and 'go meta', but at the expense of giving those structures a false, impersonal, ontological status.

Also, ontic dumping occurs because of the tool people most usually employ for their worldmaking: language. Here is a more or less shared fund of ready-made verbal forms, concepts and images, existing categories, symbols and representations, which people use to objectify the epistemic – and whose ready-made nature soon gives the lie to the personality and individuality of the original epistemic process. Once a world has been represented in language, it comes to be dumped because language readily appears 'out there', impersonal: a store of collective referents, the crystallisation and epitome of cultural forms and categories, of social norms and practices (Berger and Luckmann 1969:66).

In short, converting our ongoing mental processes into linguistic objects appears to endow them with a collective reality which renders the momentary and processual as precedent and static; also the private as public, and the personal as impersonal. The world is made impersonal because the formal "clothing of our language makes everything alike" (Wittgenstein 1978:224): causes us to forget, in Feldman's words, that there is "a more personal language of thinking than the social language of discourse" (1987:135).

2 The social impulse

When the forms individuals create and adopt to house and carry their meanings come to be more broadly accepted and used, passed between innumerable hands and mouths, so they become ambiguous, featureless, clichéd, impersonal: the common coin of a generality.

The world consists of innumerable contents, Simmel begins (1971:*passim*). These are given determinate structure and identity by marrying them to certain forms. This relationship between form and content (or meaning) is necessary but not determinate, fixed or intrinsic. The same form can house any number of meanings, and the same meaning be housed in innumerable forms.

However, while meanings are innumerable, forms are not. At any one time, there is a finite number of words, images, gestures, signs – symbols (Geertz's 'vehicles of a conception') in common usage in a socio-cultural milieu; there are only so many ways of speaking, dressing, signing, behaving, whatever it is an individual wants to mean. Moreover, these finite forms assume a certain fixity and inflexibility. The individual can feel himself trapped in a world of unresponsive, insensitive, generalised forms, inadequate to his personal needs. This is "the ambiguity at the heart of all social existence" (Jackson 1989:33): the eventfulness, flux and creativity of individual life faced by the seemingly frozen forms of ongoing cultural tradition.

It is not that forms are any less individual creations than meanings. It is that once created, once objectified (made into something others can recognise as an object of exchange, an object for their own potential use), forms begin becoming independent of their individual creators. Indeed, the forms become the very vehicles of sociality, the means by which individuals come together, interact, and 'communicate' with one another; forms become synthesising mechanisms. In the process of this synthesis, however, forms change their nature. No longer intimately tied to personal meanings, expressions and needs (in particular those of their creators), they can serve the expressive needs of many, and may serve the interactive needs of all.

Indeed, as interaction becomes wider still, sociality more inclusive, so the shared forms which make the mutuality and reciprocality of interaction possible become further and further reduced in terms of their complexity, subtlety, idiosyncrasy. The forms become common-denominational and institutionalised; from being the intentioned product, the subjective invention, of the mental activity of an individual, they become the stable but rigid medium of interaction and communication of a group; from being the original outer covering or clothing of personal contents, they become hypostatised, seemingly things-in-themselves, self-sufficient systems, empires functioning according to their own logic and law. And while, in their use, individuals continuously rein-corporate these objective forms into their personal world-views, translate them back into the domain of the subjective, as a cultural set of symbols in a social milieu and beyond, the forms can seem to amount to a detached, stultifying, oppressive array. "The words in my mouth have gone dead", Ionesco could lament, now muddled, cheapened, petrified, made imprecise, through overuse (Steiner 1978:196).

In short, Simmel concludes, the world is made impersonal by sociation: by individuals interacting in terms of mutually shared forms whose very commonality detracts inevitably from those forms' original provenance in and pertinence to an individual and personal world-view.

3 The religious impulse

When the gods and the cosmic order which human beings create (bolstering their nomic constructions of order in the world with other-worldliness) inexorably become independent of their human creators, we find ourselves living in a world which is impersonal inasmuch as it is outwith human causation, choice and control.

Historically, religion has been the most widespread and effective means of maintaining, legitimating and validating the worlds which human beings have individually and collectively constructed, Berger begins (1990:*passim*). Human societies are enterprises in world-making, affording human beings a sense of meaning, order and routine which is not provided by their biological circumstances alone, and thus potentially keeping at bay the anomy of a random, entropic, absurd universe. And yet, there are occasions when the facticity of everyday routine, when the commonsensical expectation of mundane interaction, is not sufficient to deal with life's eventualities. Ignorance and forgetfulness, suffering and misfortune, dreams and daydreams, accidents, insults, fights, fail-ures, above all, deaths, may all call into question the interactional routine and commonsensical knowledge by which life is usually lived, and threaten confusion (cf. Leach 1969:1). These uncalled-for occasions and occurrences bring into stark focus the dividing line between order and disorder and emphasise the precarious-ness of the former, its constant dependence on human activity and consciousness. To alleviate this dependence, to make the order of the world seem more sure, more autonomous, more proper and permanent, 'religion' is called into play: something which substi-tutes human agency and responsibility by the superhuman and which bolsters a frail human order by subsuming it within an ulti-mate, universal, 'cosmic' meaning and order. The human order or 'nomos' becomes a microcosm or reflection or incarnation of an all-encompassing universal order.

Religion serves to "cosmize" the order which humans have created, therefore, projecting it onto the universe as such, endowing the order with 'natural' law, grounding the order in 'sacred' reality: in a nature which is awesome and mysterious, which transcends human beings and yet includes them. Nomos is substituted for a 'cosmos' which is more or less inevitable, inef-fable, infinite, immortal and independent of human will, wish or control. In short, religion, the establishment through human activity of an all-embracing sacred order, is something capable of maintaining itself whatever the disorder which threatens and irre-spective of human weakness.

Another way of defining the sacred, however, Berger continues, is the creation of otherness. Human creation (causation, produc-tion, responsibility) becomes a world apart, and circumscribed; ultimately, human activity becomes 'destined', 'fated', 'the will of God or the gods'. In short, the sacred world becomes one in which human beings lose themselves, their personalities, their personal responsibilities, their frailties.

And another way of talking about this would be a recognition of religion's propensity for alienation. Precisely the same quality which stabilised the human order also dehumanises and imper-sonalises it, transforming human products into alien mystery, into superhuman facts; while it may no longer be frail, precarious and contingent, instead, the order of the world is mystified and made other, its human accountability and immediate accessibility denied.

In conclusion, then, religion is "an immense projection of human meanings ... which comes back as an alien reality to haunt its producers" – even unto death (Berger 1990:100). The world is made impersonal, in short, by a fictitious inexorability serving to negate its human plasticity.

4 The objective impulse

In a desire to know others as we know ourselves, to extend the certainties of a subjective, personal knowledge out into the world beyond ourselves, we imagine objectivity: a mimicry of subjective perception but magically/rationally independent of an individual observer. In the process we misconstrue the phenomenon of knowledge, and invent a world of abstract concreteness, of impersonal and disembodied points of reference.

The perceived world is always the reaction to the world by a self, Wagner begins (1991:*passim*); here is a refracted world, deflected through the prism of the self. Moreover, subjective perceptions can only be elicited in others through iconic means and in iconic forms: by embodying them in verbal or non-verbal imagery. Meaning is a personal, internal perception (both in terms of the things perceived and the means of their being perceived), but in attempting to externalise and communicate this, one inevitably has recourse to the institutionalisation that is language and the mediation that is visible behaviour.

This gives onto a perennial uncertainty and doubt which Wagner calls "the reflex of subjectivity" (1991:40): can intuitively apprehended, subjective experience be objectively described? is an individual ultimately able to communicate his self-perceptions or share those of others? is not symbolic meaning (both that intended and that elicited) always hermetically sealed within "the personal microcosm" (1991:37)? is not others' behaviour only ever construable as a formal (iconic) analogue of one's own? Nothing, Wagner concludes, is more "clear, distinct, concrete, certain, or real than the self's perception of perception, its own sensing of sense", but other selves, other perceptions and senses, remain 'outside bodies' only, whose meanings are invisible (1991:39; cf. Laing 1968:16).

It is from this subjective doubt, this contingency, this despair at doing justice to personal perception, to internal certainty, that the impulse towards objectivity is born. Inspired by subjective knowledge as an archetype, we imagine gaining that knowledge of others: we wish for an objective verity and verifiability. 'Objectivity' is an impersonal idiom or discourse which becomes a magical token promising a manageable "word-world": order, orientation, determinacy and systematisation in regard to others; a self-like knowledge in the disorientating environment of other people (Jackson 1989:3–4).

However, such knowledge remains a pretence, a self-delusion. Moreover, it is a delusion which undercuts the very means and process of our actual (personal) knowledge of and being in the world, which distances us from the realities of phenomenological existence. In particular, we isolate seeing from other modes of knowing, give the visual primacy over other senses as the basis and validation of data, and proceed to use the distance which vision affords to claim a knowledge which is non-interventionist and independent of the thing envisioned (cf. Dias 1994:164–5; Jonas 1954:*passim*). Thus we reduce drastically the complexity of the 'experiential sensorium' (Fernandez 1992:127) which is our actual engagement with the world while claiming thereby to engage with it more reliably. In short, in an attempt to extend our knowledge of the world, we make a world in which we (as observers and actors) are absent, and in which only impersonal (rational) forces hold sway; objectivity, Jackson concludes, translates as "a euphemism for indifference" (1989:4).

The world becomes impersonal in our desire for an Archimedean point of view and reference, a method of understanding which transcends the situatedness of the observer – a situatedness which is ultimately responsible for our very being-in-the-world.

5 The negatory impulse

Through various metaphysical postulates (concerning, for example, power, asceticism, and identity) we seek to deny our complex humanity, in order to achieve a being-in-the-world which is seen as purer, more essential, more knowledgeable, more real. The world becomes impersonal as we deny the existence or the importance of aspects of our own interaction with ourselves, or our interactions with others, and so misconstrue our human social environments.

John Berger describes relative powerlessness in a social milieu as an awareness of being moved hither and thither by events, of being remote from the centres of causation: being aware of 'a tide stronger than one's own volition' in which one's practice is none the less caught up (1975:111); while powerfulness resides in a sense of being a prime mover, a decider, able to affect distant events through a theorisation, an abstraction and a generalisation of the circumstances (prior or current or desired) surrounding them (1967:96–7). What both powerlessness and powerfulness share, however, is an idiomatic mapping of the world as determined or constituted (in certain significant ways) by reifications, by impersonal things: here are 'the more or less distant causes of one's affairs'; here are 'the circumstances of more or less distant others'. In each case, there is a crucial distinction made between what is close, concrete, one's own ... and what is otherwise.

To put this differently, both cases are imbued with notions of denial: a denial, on the one hand, of the complexity, the distinctiveness, the idiosyncrasy, the integrity, of those within one's power, or those for whom one is deciding, or the others about whom one is generalising in one's abstract theories; on the other hand, a denial of the human (particular, situated, contingent, fallible, contrived) nature of the network of (powerful) people and events in which one's life is caught up, a network with which one could, in theory, strategically interact, to greater or lesser extent, for the effecting of practical changes to one's own life and others'. Both cases, *in extremis*, lead to a denial of humanity, one's own and others': the sadistic denial of the powerful in which those within one's power are more or less unlike oneself (in human feeling, potential, need, desert and so on) and so can be treated with (possibly destructive, certainly callous) contempt – slavery, the Spanish Inquisition, the witch hunt, Nazism; and the masochistic denial of the powerless in which the forces that control one's life and those in charge of them are more or less beyond reach (practically, virtually, morally, properly) and so must be left to run one's affairs (possibly fatally, certainly indifferently) without an attempted calling to account – the deferential dialectic, bureaucratic irresponsibility, religious martyrdom, Determinism.

The negatory impulse, (sadistic and masochistic) can also be found in the metaphysics of asceticism in its various forms. From those who practise rigorous self-discipline, austerity and abstinence in order to achieve religious knowledge and virtue, to those who practise the scientific method in order to achieve positivistic knowledge and control, there is what Appleyard calls a common 'radical anti-humanism': a replacement, a denial, of the human elements of complexity, contingency and intimacy in favour of a wished for metaphysical purity (conceptual, physical, agential, social) (1991:*passim*). While Christian asceticism may be founded on an aversion to an original human sinfulness, and a desire to (a belief in) escape from the Satan-riddled world of humanity to the divine heavens, Western science is comparably empowered by a commitment to materialism – technology and unconsciousness – by a zeal to gather non-human knowledge, and a desire to (a belief in) escape from the complications of the human self to a world of mathematical clarity, determinism, systematisation, and logical simplicity. 'To know the mind of God', as Stephen Hawking recently described the aspirations of modern astro-physics, is to describe a project and a distinctive metaphysic which, in both its religious and its scientific guise, is based on a negation of the human: understanding the world as if it were impersonal, as if it could be depersonalised.

Finally, the negatory impulse can be found in the social division of the world into 'insiders' and 'outsiders'. As people map out the social world around them into what Schuetz called 'contour lines of differential relevance' (1944:500) or what Sahlins identified as sectors of differential reciprocity (1968:85), so, in any one situation and at any one moment, the world becomes divided into 'members of my community or group', 'people I know or like', 'people like me' on the one hand, and 'members of an alien community or group', 'people I do not know or like', 'people unlike me' on the other. Indeed, such a setting up of social boundaries has been theorised to be fundamental to the establishment and maintenance of a social group (Barth 1969:*passim*), if not of a social identity *per se* (Boon 1982:*passim*) – groups and identities which are today said to be threatened by the continuing 'massification' of humankind (Riesman 1958:376), the increasing size, density, and structural homogeneity of human society.

Far from the perceived threat to such boundary- and identity-making processes, however, what more concerns me is the negatory threat posed by such processes *per se*: the way in which divisions of the world into insiders and outsiders (whether the divisions are made relative or absolute, dualistic or graduated (cf. Leach 1968:62)) inevitably entail a negation of the integrity of what is seen to lie on one side of the boundary as opposed to the other. That is, setting up an identity of me/not me, us/not us, invariably involves nay-saying: I/we are what it/they are not. Whether such nay-saying entails a negation of more on this side of the boundary or that, or even manages to effect a mutuality of distinct but commensurate denials, there is an integrity which is lost, and an 'indifference' which is born (cf. Herzfeld 1992:*passim*), as the differentiation of social or group identity is gained; not all the possible behaviours, sentiments, expressions, in all their possible complexity and diversity, are to be admitted as one's own. More usually, of course, it is the outsider (the stranger, the foreigner, the alien, the inhuman) whose negation – reduction, generalisation, stereotypification – is more severe. In being other than me/us, it is excluded from personal relations as not worthy, not sensible, not intelligent, not equal, or not necessary.

In short, the world becomes impersonal in our various conceptual plays (of power, purity, theory, identity) which would strategically deny part of our human reality – our complexity; others' integrity – in order to win a world-view which significantly limits human intimacy and belonging.

PERSONAL RELATIONS AND INDIVIDUAL KNOWLEDGE

"I know" E.M. Forster once wrote in ironic fashion "that personal relations are the real life, for ever and ever." (1950:26) – as if any knowledge of reality was 'for ever and ever'. Here, in fairy tale prose, is a fairy tale proposition, which, it seems to me, provides a precise mythic counter-balance and counter-view to the five paths to impersonal knowledge sketched above: the five impulses, rhetorical strategies, intentional and unintentional cognitive and linguistic and interactional and epistemological mechanisms, by which personal relations and individual knowledge become impersonal and general.

To these five paths to impersonalisation, it seems to me, Durkheimian social science (certainly, social anthropology as variously canonised (van Velsen 1967:145–6; Pelto and Pelto 1978:36; Peacock 1986:83)) is a willing accomplice. It reifies – ontically dumps – its epistemological constructs: 'collective conscience', 'collective representations', 'social facts', 'the cult of the individual'. It routinises and generalises the formal creations of its individual exponents: 'joking relations', 'lineage theory', 'dynamic equilibrium'; so that in order to find means of self-expression free from institutionalisation, individual social scientists must engineer paradigm shifts: from Functionalism to Structural-Functionalism, to Structuralism, to Neo-Marxism, to Symbolism. It claims that the Gods it has created, as well as their goods, forces and powers

('Society', 'Culture', 'Kinship', 'Ritual and Religion', 'Political and Economic Relations', 'Language'), are outwith its control, leading autonomous lives of their own determination, orientation and evolution. It claims to gain access to objective sociological data (on 'suicide', on 'mechanisms of solidarity', on 'marital prescriptions and preferences') which are beyond the personal ken of individual participants in a socio-cultural milieu because of their lack of learning or impartiality or self-reflexivity or freedom of thought. Finally, it denies the personal complexity of its own involvement in the lives of others, of the interface between research and its researchers' own lives, of its knowledge practices *per se* (so that research subjects become 'primitives', 'tribesmen', 'role-players'; researchers become 'scientists' who speak impersonally and omnisciently; and 'pure research' takes place in a domain distant from the otherness of advocacy, literature, intimacy, and so on). In short, it is almost as if, for much of its history, actual people have been incidental to the Durkheimian project – irrelevant if not departicularised: generalised into one impersonal (defining, limiting) category or another. What emerges are "synthetic fictions", "fictive matrices of uniformity", which Cohen (for one) concludes to be not merely dull, redundant, unambitious, arrogant, insensitive and intellectually barren, but positively discreditable (1989:10–12, also 1978:7; and cf. Sapir 1956:200–203).

What I would wish to do, in contrast, would be to translate Forster's mythic belief in the personal into an idiom of social-scientific method. This would begin by asserting that social science should set out to analyse the above impulses toward impersonalisation and their working-out in a socio-cultural milieu but not be a party to them, not take their consequences on board as ontological or methodological postulates of human reality. Rather, to recognise that these impulses are, in Jackson's words, 'instrumentalities not finalities' (1989:1). The human world can be and certainly is made to seem 'impersonal' – ontologised, institutionalised, sacralised, objectified, negated – but this is not its necessary or actual nature. Impersonalisation is a strategy, a rhetoric, an instrument to denaturalise the world. Notwithstanding, were one to look beneath the impersonal (categorical, stereotypical, generalised) surface of such a world, one would see the complexity, the multiplicity and diversity, the inconsistency and contradiction of a congeries of personal relations abutting against one another (cf. Rapport 1993:*passim*).

For the actual nature of the human world is of individuals in interaction. This is its causation – the cause of there being human worlds of culture and society – and its manifestation – the practice of human worlds is individuals interacting one with another. Distance, powerlessness and powerfulness, religiosity, ignorance, asceticism and so on, may obscure this fact, may transmogrify the personal into the impersonal, but, to repeat E.M. Forster, 'personal relations are the real life'. There is no ontologisation, institutionalisation, sacralisation, objectivation or negation which does not manifest itself through personal relations, which is not practised in terms of personal relations, and which is not animated, maintained, originated – in a word, caused, by personal relations.

Moreover, knowledge of these personal relations is individual knowledge. There is nothing else for it to be. There are no collective knowing organisms to which human beings are party: cultures and societies, institutions and associations cannot know; only individuals have the minds and memories to know. Which means, finally, that personal relations may be known differently by their different individual participants. While it is certainly true that human life is lived in personal relationships, and while human individuals depend on others (living and dead, real and imagined, particularised and generalised) for all manner of securities, physical, emotional, intellectual – while human individuals contextualise one another – nevertheless, they begin from different points (bodies, brains, consciousnesses) and, ultimately, they end there too. The personal relations in which individuals live may eventuate in sharing and intimacy of a variety of levels and kinds, but not necessarily in a common or even consistent knowledge of the relations which are being practised.

In short, while the true nature of the human world is of individuals in interaction, the ultimate knowledge of the world is individual *per se*, the possession of individual bodies and brains.

WRITING THE WORLD INDIVIDUALLY AND PERSONALLY

The above opinions may be pulled together under the approximate title of 'methodological individualism', a theme much maligned and misconstrued by Durkheimian social science. Briefly to adumbrate its canons, one might set out with MacIver (1961:*passim*).

Since individual human beings are not mere theoretical postulates – they are met in the flesh – their description in social science is never merely for the convenience of supposition (as it is for 'institutions', 'associations', 'nations', 'races', 'traditions' and 'spirits of the age') *[Simmel (1971:27): 'a society may be informed by an extraordinary multiplicity and variety, but this is no reason to hypostatise or autonomise it']*. Moreover, it is the countless individual acts and doings of such individuals taken together which give rise to the 'stuff' of social science *[Weber (in Mommsen 1965:25): 'social science must proceed from the actions of one or more separate individuals and adopt strictly individualistic methods']*. Hence, the ideal social-scientific text would tell the whole story of everything that ever happened to every individual, everything that every individual caused to happen. And while such a 'Book of a Recording Angel' must remain a mythic ideal, the project of the social scientist can still be to précis a greater or lesser part of the Book while misrepresenting its contents, through generalisation or reduction, as little as possible.

Such a précis, Watkins continues (1959:*passim*; 1953:*passim*), must configure a complexity of social situations, institutions and events out of the particular situations, dispositions, beliefs, understandings, inter-relations and resources of particular individuals *[Popper (1965:37): 'sociological models and analyses must be constructed in terms of individuals' attitudes, expectations, actions and relations']*. For since individual human beings are the sole 'moving agents' in history, and since socio-cultural phenomena are nothing but the product, intended and unintended, of the interaction of individual characteristics – individual knowledge and ignorance, individual action, reaction and inertia – it is to the individual latter that the social scientist must turn to gain insight into the collective former *[Mill (1875:469): 'the laws of social phenomena can be nothing but the laws (actions and passions) of individual human nature']*. No social knowledge can be arrived at which is not also individual knowledge. A social system is a collection of people "whose activities disturb and influence each other" (Watkins 1959:511), and no social reality exists which could not be altered by appropriate and sufficient individual knowledge and desire *[Hayek (1969:60): 'in social science, things are what individuals think they are']*.

To talk of individual knowledge and desire is to talk of psychological processes and influences. And just as any general characteristics of a social situation must be derived from piecing together what is known of individual situations, so the social derives from piecing together the psychological; there is no irreducible social domain *sui generis [Simmel (1971:32): 'a description of a social situation is an exercise in psychological knowledge']*. This is not to say that social realities are direct reflections of individual psychological realities, are individual psychological realities writ large, because individual intentions often have unintended repercussions as these intentions are construed and reacted to by other individuals *[Popper (1966:324): 'individualistic analysis takes into account the relations between individuals acting in certain situations, and the unintended consequences of those actions']*. Nor is this saying that individuals always operate with knowledge which is sufficient or appropriate to their desires; the outcome of action and interaction may be very different, opposite, or only vaguely related to the intentions of those involved. And nor is this saying that individuals do not run into obstacles and constraints which can frustrate, even destroy them. What it is saying, to return to where we began, is that, notwithstanding, one must eschew seeing routine collective phenomena as something possessing their own internal dynamic, obeying their own laws and having their own qualities and effects; eschew seeing individuals as the playthings of inhuman, impersonal, historicist, determinist conditions or tendencies; eschew seeing individuals as confronted and constrained socially by other than the desires, intentions, habits, loyalties, inertias, rivalries – also the miscarried plans – of other individuals *[Simmel (1971:27): 'society exists where a number of individuals enter into interaction; society is interaction']*.

As for the genre by which the social world may best be 'individually written' in this way, a literariness would seem to be the key ingredient. In particular, we hear from Kundera how it is the novel which can be celebrated for its 'keeping alive and holding safe a world where the individual, his original thought, his inviolable private life, is respected' (1990:165). Likewise, from Rorty, we hear how the novel can be praised for the way it personalises the world, for the way it brings home to us the 'pain, suffering and humiliation' of others (1986:xvi). Indeed, it was precisely on this account that Forster felt he could differentiate between an earlier generation of literature and social science (1984:*passim*). Literature, the novel especially, was "sogged with humanity", he said (1984:39). And while the social scientist may be equally concerned to record human character, he appeared content to restrict himself to what could be known of its existence from scouring 'the exterior surface' of social life and to what could approximately be deduced from people's actions, words and gestures. Whereas the novelist determined to go into 'the inner hidden life' and its individual 'source' so as to 'know people perfectly'. In the latter at least, Forster opined, we may find a compensation for 'the dimness' [the impersonality] of social life where each of us knows from experience that there is much beyond the 'outer' evidence but where other 'inner' subjectivities may, more often than not, appear to be closed books.

Moreover, it was for this reason that Forster concluded that literature was 'truer' than social science, fiction 'truer' than history: because of the novelist's command of the secret life, the personal life, of the individual, his determining to link up the inner and the outer. However, such a differentiation, it seems to me, need no longer be validated. In eschewing the impersonalising impulses of a Durkheimian social science, we can embrace a mode of writing which marries the literary to the social-scientific, which sees the social as always mediated by the individual, which accepts that 'barbarous writing is bad social science' (Campbell 1989:170–4).

In a passage which Carrithers once described as far removed from Durkheim's collectivism as one could find (1985:244), Schopenhauer placed highest value on a biographical (and auto-biographical) idiom for the way it could give onto 'knowledge of the true nature of humankind' (1969:247):

> In history proper, it is not so much men that act as nations and armies, and the individuals who do appear seem to be so far off, surrounded by such pomp and circumstance, clothed in the stiff robes of state, or in heavy and inflexible armour, that it is really very difficult to discern human movement through it all. On the other hand, the truly depicted life of the individual in a narrow sphere shows the conduct of men with all its nuances and forms. ... It is quite immaterial whether the objects on which the historical action hinges are, relatively speaking, farm-houses or kingdoms. For all these things are without significance in themselves.

And his conclusion is hardly different from Redfield's (1963:59):

> As soon as our attention turns from a community as a body of houses and tools and institutions to the states of mind of

particular people, we are turning to the exploration of something immensely complex and difficult to know. But it is
humanity, in its inner and more private form. . . . While we talk
in terms of productivity, or of roles and statuses, we are . . .
moving among an apparatus already removed, by our own act
of mind, from the complicated thinking and feeling of the men
and women who achieve the productivity, or define and occupy
the roles. But it is the thinking that is the real and ultimate
raw material; it is there that events really happen. And the
choice of a human biographic form for describing the whole
turns us to it.

In prescribing a literariness for social science, then (in intending
for myself a 'literary anthropology'), it is the gap between the
individual and the world which I would hope might be bridged –
might be seen to be there to be bridged. So that the particulari-
ties of individual lived experience are not eclipsed by
generalisation, or otherwise abstracted, reduced, typified by total-
isation. But rather that, in social-scientific writing, the world is
made personal.

Chapter 2

'Going Meta'
Structure and creativity

Why should we not enjoy an original relationship to the universe?

Ralph Waldo Emerson

Be yourself! Be unique! Be original!

Friedrich Nietzsche

God is man's stolen essence.

Ludwig Feuerbach

PROGNOSTIC

In The Anxiety of Influence, *Harold Bloom argued that the history of poetic traditions could be seen to proceed in terms of a continuous misreading of prior poets and existing poetry – through caricature, parody, distortion, misrepresentation and wilful revisionism – by those currently living and writing. He described this misreading as "an act of creative correction", which was necessary for clearing an imaginative space in which one could write oneself, create one's own voice (1975:30).*

For to write with the voice of another, to write variations on extant poems or to accept someone else's description of oneself, was merely to execute a previously written narrative and to take one's place within a previously determined schema. In "strong poets", this instilled the great anxiety that their indebtedness to the past might mean that they would fail to create themselves; and it was to allay these fears that such poets wrestled persistently with the work of their 'strong precursors'. Hence, strong poets spent their lives acknowledging and yet appropriating their own contingency. They might be situated in all manner of social, historical and cultural forms of life but they were nevertheless capable of telling the story of their situatedness in words never used before, thus escaping from inherited descriptions. Their formula was: 'where my precursor's poem is, there let my poem be' (1975:80). Poems arose, in short, out of poets' melancholy at their lack of priority, at their not having begotten themselves, and yet out of a sense of priority being possible. In Blake's words, from Jerusalem *(1975:644):*

> *I must create a system, or be enslaved by another man's; I will not reason & compare; my business is to create.*

And in Wilde's (1913:205):

> *A truly great artist cannot conceive of life being shown or beauty fashioned, under any conditions other than those that he has selected.*

In sum, to imagine was to misinterpret, and all new poems were antithetical to their precursors. The history of poetry, Bloom concluded (1975:5), was a history of the influence of the past and yet of its creative appropriation through the "capable imagination" of 'strong individuals' in the present.

In this essay I should like to create a way for myself by rewriting the writing of mainly anthropological others and in the process suggest the outlines of a developmental relationship between social structure and individual creativity.

"YOU ARE YOUR CREATIVITY"

The above epigraph comes from Edmund Leach (1976a), alluding to the imaginative operations of the human mind and its 'poeticism': its untrammelled and unpredictable and non-rule-bound nature (1976b:5). But let me rather begin the argument of the section with an intriguing comment of Gregory Bateson's (1972:126). Extrapolating from processes of schismogenesis among the New Guinean Iatmul, Bateson concludes that each human individual can be conceived of as an "energy source"; here is something capable of and prone to engagement in its own acts, being fuelled by its own processes (metabolic and other) rather than by external stimuli. Furthermore, this energy is then imposed on the universe in the process of creating order.

Bateson's commentary was, of course, to be taken up by R.D. Laing, and his definition of a person as "an origin of actions", and "a centre of orientation of the objective universe" (1968:20). But I should instead like to extrapolate back in time from Bateson *[and back from Bloom]* to a number of pronouncements of Nietzsche's on the priority of individual action over reaction, on the individual who uses his imagination for the conscious purpose of self-creation.

"We invent for ourselves the major part of our experience", Nietzsche begins in *Beyond Good and Evil* (1979a), and we do so by rearranging that which (socially, culturally, naturally) confronts us in the world, reinventing its language of description and relationship, and so stamping our own impress on what is and what is to come. It is, indeed, the essential and inherent nature of the individual to be self-caused and free, to exhibit self-control and to achieve self-determination. As God is recognisably dead, we can claim to serve no higher purpose, and it is through self-creation, not through contacting or manifesting something bigger than oneself, that we may reach 'redemption'.

Nietzsche described such self-creation in terms of a major human drive which he called "the will to power", and he painted a portrait of the ideal exponent of this drive which he named the "overman" or "superman" (*Uebermensch*): humanity's hero, whose individuality is not contained by the terms of an inherited language-game, who more than all others epitomises a fully developed, mature, autonomous, 'powerful' individual, transcending the arrangements, the controls, the determination of others – creating his own mind by creating his own language – and making himself original.

I would prefer to see self-creation willy-nilly as part of the human condition: not so much a willing of power which some individuals possess to a greater degree than others (and to others' detriment), but rather a willing of meaning, of understanding, which all individuals practise and whose inevitable consequence is overcoming – in the sense of going beyond, failing to become completely commensurate with – precedent meanings and understandings. As Rorty phrased it, we can see in the brazen need of the *Uebermensch* or strong poet to boast that he is not a copy or replica merely a special form of an act and a need which everyone has: "the need to come to terms with the blind impress which chance has given him, to make a self for himself by redescribing that impress in terms which are, if only marginally, his own" (1992:43). Even to track down the causes of one's being, to confront one's contingency, is to create oneself – if one describes oneself in new terms, new metaphors. Now, one's idiosyncrasy is more than a specimen of a type already known, and "the length of one's mind" is not set by the language others have left behind (1992:27).

"THIS ONE FACT THE WORLD HATES; THAT THE SOUL *BECOMES* . . ."

In the *Uebermensch* is born 'existentialism's ego', according to Richard Shweder (1991:41), and it is there that I would now turn, in particular to Sartre, to glean further insights into how the creativity of the Nietzschean self-inventing individual can be expected to manifest and express itself.

'Being precedes essence', Sartre famously begins: each human being makes himself what he is, creates himself and his world. Of course he is born into a certain socio-cultural situation, into certain historical conditions, but he is responsible for the sense he makes out of them, the meaning he grants them, the way he evaluates and acts towards them; between the given and what this becomes in an individual life there is a perennial (and unique) interplay. Moreover, he is always able to remake this sense, meaning, evaluation and action; he can negate the essence of his own creations and create again. In short, he might be surrounded by the 'actual facts' of an objective historico-socio-cultural present, but he can transcend their brutishness, surpass a mere being-in-the-midst-of-things, by attaining the continuous possibility of imagined meanings. His experience cannot be reduced to objective determinants (cf. Kearney 1988:225–241).

Imagination is the key in this portrayal: the key resource in consciousness, the key to human existence. Imagination is an activity in which human individuals are always engaged and it is through his imagination that an individual creates and recreates the essence of his being, makes himself what he was, is and will become. As Sartre put it, imagination has a "surpassing and nullifying power" which enables individuals to escape being "swallowed up in the existent", frees them from given reality, and allows them to be other than what they are made (1972:273). Because of imagination, human life has an emergent quality, characterised by a going-beyond: going-beyond a given situation, a set of circumstances, a status-quo, going-beyond the conditions that produced it. Because of imagination, the human world is possessed of an intrinsically dynamic order which human individuals, possessed of self-consciousness, are continually in the process of forming and designing. Because they can imagine, human beings are transcendentally free; imagination grants human beings that 'margin of freedom outside conformity' which "gives life its savour and its endless possibilities for advance" (Riesman 1954:38).

Imagination issues forth into the world in the form of an ideally 'gratuitous' act, gratuitous inasmuch as it is seemingly uncalled for in terms of existent reality: unjustifiable, 'without reason, ground or proof' (Chambers Dictionary, 1966.); in Woolf's words, "something useless, sudden, violent; something that costs a life; ... free from taint, dependence, soilure of humanity or care for one's kind; something rash, ridiculous" (1980:180). For here is an act which, in its gratuity, surpasses rather than merely conserves the givenness in which it arises, which transcends the apparent realities of convention, which seems to resist the traditional constraints by which life is being lived. The gratuitous act appears to come from nowhere and pertain to nothing; it is more or less meaningless in terms of the sense-making procedures which are currently instituted and legitimated; it is beyond debt and guilt, beyond good and evil.

Finally, then, the gratuitousness of the creative act of human imagination makes it inherently conflictual. The indeterminacy of the relationship between individual experience and objective forms of life – the dialectical irreducibility of socio-cultural conceptualisation on the one side and conscious individual imaginings on the other – means that the becoming of new meanings will always outstrip the present being of socio-cultural conditions. In the process of creating a new world, existing worlds are often appropriated, reshaped and reformed. Thus, between imagination and what is currently and conventionally lived there will be a constant tension ("the world hates ...", as Emerson has it in my epigraph (1950:179; also cf. Wilde 1913:169)). For while what is currently lived is itself the issue of past imaginative acts of world-creation, and dependent on continuing individual practice for its continuing institutionality, inevitably, present imaginative acts will be moving to new possible futures. To turn this around, the continuity of the conventional is an achievement and a conscious decision (not a mindless conformity) which must be consensually worked for, or else forcibly – and superficially – imposed.

Excursus 1

In Acts of Meaning, *Jerome Bruner argued that not only is
there a human 'predisposition' to organise experience into narrative form, to render experience as narrative, but also that there is
a constant human readiness to rewrite such narratives, to write new
narratives, and so render experience (the world) otherwise. Willy-
nilly, existing narratives attract variant readings. Even though
contained in those (possibly widely shared) existing narratives
is a sense of what the world is and how it is properly ordered,
even though we posit in narrative our sense of the normative, still
human narratives – symbolic constructions of the world in collective, institutionalised systems of signification – remain in essence
"open, undetermined, uncertain, subjunctive, vague" (1990:51).
Hence, in the writing and telling of narratives is assured not only
a human knowledge of the normative but also a knowledge of
breach and exception, of alternative ways of being, acting, striving,
which we can envision. Our narrational predisposition, Bruner
concludes, "is a perpetual guarantee that humankind will 'go meta'
on received versions of reality" (1990:55). For while in one sense
we might be creatures of our historical condition, possessing cultural languages and social selves, in another sense we are autonomous agents, with the reflective capacity to escape and reeval-
uate and reformulate what culture has on offer and so be other
than we are.*

Excursus 2

In Migrancy Culture Identity, *Iain Chambers argued that writing
embodied a paradox: the writing project was ambiguous in being
both imperialist and revolutionary. To write was to establish a
dominion of perception, power and knowledge; and to write also
involved a repudiation of dominion: an attempt to reveal an opening
for ourselves in the inhabited world by extending, disrupting and
reworking it. By opening up a cognitive space, writing entailed
permitting a certain distance to develop between ourselves and the
contexts that had erstwhile defined our identities. Hence, while
starting from known materials – a language, a lexicon, a series of
discourses – writing none the less afforded a move, a travelling, a
transition, to something more: "an unforeseen and unknown possibility" (1994a:10).*

Excursus 3

In The Language Myth, *Roy Harris argued that innovation in linguistic usage, the 'renewal of language', was a continuously creative process involving individuals in interaction. Indeterminacy – of what was meant, of what was interpreted, of what will be invented – was the rule not the exception, and underlay all acts of communication. Past linguistic practice did not determine present or future linguistic possibilities because individuals would continually adapt the linguistic fund to their current requirements. Hence, an Archimedean point of linguistic reference outside the continuum of creative activity was a myth; the language being practised at any one time was highly varied and characterised by inconsistency rather than a standard idiom. "If language is a game", Harris concluded, then "it is a game we mostly make up as we go along . . . in which there is no referee, and the only rule that cannot be bent is that players shall improvise as best they can" (1981:186).*

"METANOIA . . . CONNOTES A CHANGE OF MIND ENVISAGING NEW MORALITIES"

The essence of being human, Edmund Leach wrote, is to resent the domination of others and the dominion of present structures (1977:19–20). Hence, all human beings are "criminals by instinct", predisposed to set their creativity against current system, intent on defying and reinterpreting custom. Indeed, it is the rule-breaking of "inspired individuals" which ever leads to new social formations and on which cultural vitality depends. And yet the hostility of creativity to systems as are means that its exponents are likely to be initially categorised and labelled as criminal or insane – even if their ultimate victorious overturning of those systems' conservative morality precipitates a redefining as heroic, prophetic or divine . . . Returning to anthropology from the above excursi, and extrapolating not back in time from Bateson to Nietzsche but forward, as it were, to those who wrote anthropology after Bateson, and trying to pick up the same thread of ideas relating social structure to individual creativity, Leach seems a good point to start.

Victor Turner, of course, would be another (1969:109; 1974:169, 231–8, 268–9). Abstracting from the ritual practices undertaken in the liminal period of Ndembu rites of passage, Turner could understand the entire symbolic creation of human worlds as turning on the relation between the formal fixities of social structure and the fluid creativity of liminoidal 'communitas'. Drawing on Sartre's dialectic between "freedom and inertia" (as Leach drew on Camus's 'essential rebellion'), Turner theo-rised that society be regarded as a process in which the two 'antagonistic principles', 'primordial modalities', of structure and creativity could be seen interacting, alternating, in different fashions and proportions in different places and times. Creativity appeared dangerous – anarchic, anomic, polluting – to those in positions of authority, administration or arbitration within existing structures, and so prescriptions and prohibitions attempted precisely to demarcate proper and possible behavioural expressions. But notwithstanding, ideologies of otherness (as well as spontaneous manifestations of otherness) would erupt from the interstices between structures and usher in opposed and original behavioural proprieties for living outside society (ritually if not normatively) or else refashioning society as such in its image.

However, it is perhaps to Kenelm Burridge, from whom the epigraph to this section comes, that I might best turn. For in *Someone, no one. An essay on individuality*, Burridge elaborates upon a theoretical model which images a processual relationship between social structure and individual creativity. If 'persons' are understood as those who embody categories of thought and behaviour which are prescribed by tradition and so realise a social order, while 'individuals' are those who create anew, Burridge begins, then most people are 'individuals' and 'persons' in different respects and at different times (1979:5–6; cf. Harre and de Waele 1976:212). As persons are products of material (socio-historico-cultural) conditions, and live within the potential of given concepts – feeding on and fattened by them, killing for and being killed by them – so individuals exist in spite of such concepts and conditions, seeking the disorderly and the new and refusing to surrender to things as they are or as traditional intellectualisations and bureaucratisations would wish them to be. For to become an individual is to abandon self-realisation through the fulfilment of normative social relations (to transcend the truth of established moralities, established accounts of what is right and proper), and to concentrate one's individual intuitions, perception and behaviour instead on the dialectical relationship "between what is and what might be" (1979:76).

Each 'spatially bounded organism', moreover, is able (in terms of both opportunity and capacity) to become both; so that "individuality" might be how one identified the practice of moving to the status of being individual. What individuality does, in effect is to transform the person, a social someone, into a social no-one – an "eccentric" at best.

However, if others are willing to accept for themselves – as new intellectualisations, a new morality – the conceptual creations of the 'eccentric' individual, then his move from someone to no-one culminates in him becoming a new social someone, a new 'person'. That is, persons are the endpoint of 'heroic' individuals, individuals who have persuaded (or been mimicked by) others into also realising new social conditions, rules, statuses, roles; for here, individuality dissolves into a new social identity.

Indeed, Burridge concludes, the cycle of: from someone to no-one to someone, is inevitable, and constitutive of our very human being. While its expressions may vary, individuality is a "thematic fact of culture", the universal instrument of the moral variation, the disruption, the renewal and the innovation which are essential to human survival (1979:116). Different material conditions may eventuate in situations which variously allow, encourage or inhibit moves to the individual, moments of creative apperception. But over and above this, individuals' creativity means that they continually create the conditions and situations which afford them their opportunity. From hunters and gatherers to pastoralists to subsistence agriculturalists to peasants to village people to townsfolk to city-dwellers, new intellectualisations are always being offered – whether courtesy of (!Kung) story-tellers, (Aborigine) Men of High Degree, (Cuna) shamans, (Nuer) Leopard-Skin Chiefs, (Hindu) Sanyasi, (American) hippies, or whatever. In short, there are ever individuals who are determined to be 'singletons': to interact with others and with established rationalisations in non-predefined ways, to escape from the burden of given cultural prescriptions and discriminations, and so usher in the unstructured and as yet unknown.

Since Burridge wrote, anthropology has begun filling in the gaps in the ethnographic record of relations between structure and creativity. For instance, defining creativity as "human activities that transform existing cultural practices", activities that, courtesy of a "creative persona", emerge from traditional forms and yet

move beyond them and reshape them, a recent volume, *Creativity/
Anthropology* (dedicated to Victor Turner), brings together cases
of creative 'eruption' from different parts of the world (Rosaldo,
Lavie and Narayan 1993:5–6).

Here we find Marjorie Shostak supplementing the !Kung story
of Nisa with those of Jimmy, the creator of a thumb piano reper-
toire which was subsequently adopted by a large percentage of
the population; N!ukha, a pioneer in a new woman's drum dance
which was to give women an increasingly direct and significant
role in healing; and Hwan//a, whose intricate patterns of bead-
weaving and innovative musical compositions for voice and
instrument express and mourn the might-have-beens of her
personal life. All three individuals evince the creativity that flour-
ishes in !Kung life and the value placed upon it, we hear, and also
the thriving individuation of personality (1993:54–69).

From Barbara Babcock, meanwhile, we learn of Cochiti Pueblo
woman, Helen Cordero, whose "Storyteller" doll pottery rein-
vented a moribund traditional form and engendered a revolution
in Pueblo ceramics, so transforming the life of her pueblo and
innumerable other peoples outside (1993:70–99). Here, Babcock
advises us, we meet one of those whom Ruth Benedict defined as
"gifted individuals who have bent the culture in the direction of
their own capacities" (1932:26). For Cordero's pottery has objectified an individual cast of mind in an accessible material form or
structure, 'materialised a way of experiencing', so as to comment
on and expand the premises of Pueblo cultural existence. Now
women's roles in general (in terms of mobility and economics and
communication) have been reshaped; now they re-present, appropriate and interpret (for outsiders as well) discourses of Pueblo
culture in which they were traditionally displaced.

Similarly, through James Fernandez (1993:11–29), we meet
Ceferino Suarez, a versifier from village Spain (also sculptor and
musician), whose insightful, resourceful, ironic and lively search
for and assertion of a social identity which was adequate to his
individual persona – despite the disinterested, frustrating and
constricting socio-cultural categories surrounding him – evidence
a "play of mind . . . that transcends the materials out of which
it arises" (1993:12). Now, as returned emigrant from Cuba, he
has come to presume the wherewithal to speak for, orate to, and
pass moral judgement on, his Asturian community as a whole
(1993:21):

Attention, noble audience!
If you can be attentive:
This is your servant
And proud to be so,
Finds himself charged
From very distant lands
With the highest authorization,
And by the most sacred document,
To pair up the villages
By means of marriage.

"CREATIVITY/ANTHROPOLOGY"

The new structure to which individual creativity gives rise soon petrifies, however. In Simmel's terms (1971), in gaining independence from their individual creators, structurings of the world congeal into fixed, objectified, generalised, institutionalised cultural forms. And yet, all the while, the creative impulse, the active drive to individuality, goes on. Hence, it is creativity's fate ever to find itself constrained and stultified (at the least threatened) by structure which is inappropriate to its needs – even a structure of its own one-time creation. Notwithstanding, Simmel concludes, this tension between the forms of social life and its creative processes provides the dynamic of cultural history.

For Burridge, the very same dynamic pertains to the world and writing of social science (1979:75). Individual creativity provided the apperceptions which made an anthropological world-view possible, but then routine anthropological analysis has come to fix, objectify, generalise and institutionalise its socio-cultural object: it ever transforms individuals into persons, events into categories, and the continuous vicissitudes of life into a constraining and stultifying, logical and orderly structure. Only a new drive to individuality then challenges the ideological appropriateness of this version of social reality – and so the cycle goes on.

For Simmel, the distress and damage caused by fixed structural forms amounts to a tragedy. Burridge, meanwhile, finds relief in a quasi-spiritual certainty that individuals can none the less be counted on continually to perceive a 'real truth of things', whether in social life or in social science (cf. Jorgensen 1994:*passim*). Likewise, Marilyn Strathern is stoical, if less dogmatic. For her, the writing of social reality (anthropological and other) can remain innovatory, always polemical, while its true cumulative achievement is "constantly to build up the conditions from which the world can be apprehended anew" (1990:19).

In writing a course for myself between Nietzsche, Simmel and Sartre, between Bateson, Leach, Turner, Burridge, and Fernandez *et al.*, it has seemed that individual creativity has remained a submerged strand in anthropological perspective, drowned out by the demands and rigours of social structure. Maybe this is to be expected. The charisma of creativity will ever be routinised and institutionalised, Weber advised – new cultural forms ever congeal (Simmel), communitas ever become normative (Turner) – in the process of it being apperceived and apprehended by others (anthropologists included). Nevertheless, it seems to me that unless we work to keep creativity ever a part of our anthropological world-view, in a dynamic dialectic with structure, then our vision will be not simply impoverished but severely impaired.

What it comes down to is our anthropological attitude towards structure, what it represents, and how it is to be represented. Social structure, especially in its 'deep' French manifestation (Durkheim, Levi-Strauss, Godelier), but also its 'conventional' Anglo-Saxon one (Radcliffe-Brown, Fortes, Gellner), has been seen as a more or less *sui generis* mechanism which determines relations between elements of a society – indeed, to an extent determines those elements (their being and behaviours) as well (cf. Park 1974:*passim*); here are individual elements buried under a vast weight of collectivities (cf. Brittan 1973:171). A Nietzschean/Sartrean (/Simmelian) perspective would correct this through an appreciation of structure as "discursive idiom" (Jackson 1989:20); here is structure understood as a shared language which forms the basis (the form) of individual interpretation, which articulates, mediates and typifies individual experience, but cannot be taken at face value as encompassing, capturing or determining that experience (cf. Parkin 1987:66; Rapport 1990:*passim*).

There are two corollaries of this. First, social structure is not *sui generis* and does not exist through inertia, but depends on the continuing, conscious, concerted activity of different individuals to intend, produce and sustain it ('language', for instance, 'is rooted in individual specificity: in the finally irreducible personal lexicons, meanings, ideolects of individual speaker-users' (Steiner 1975:46; and cf. Holy and Stuchlik 1981:15–16)). Second, social structure does not inexorably give rise to homogeneity, stability, consistency or communication. As a discursive idiom, a fiction, it is always subject to creative interpretation, to individual manipulation and re-rendering, to "alter-cultural action" (Handler and Segal 1990:87).

The latter phrasing comes from Richard Handler and Daniel Segal's illuminating work on the ethnography of the novelist, Jane Austen, and the social-scientific insights underpinning it. For Austen, we hear, social rules (and the norms and institutions with which they accord) can be seen less to regulate conduct or ensure the reproduction of an established order than to give communicative resource, significance and value to the pragmatics of different individuals' world-making, their 'serious play'. Rather than taking the rules of conventional etiquette and propriety literally or normatively, her heroines and their partners treat these structurings as matters for metacommunicative comment and analysis – and thereby displacement – in the construction of an individual and a situational order. In Austen's work, Handler and Segal sum up (1990:3), it is the "fiction of culture" which is celebrated, and the creative potential (the capacity and proclivity) of alter-cultural individual world-making: world-making which is not merely intra-paradigmatic (Geertzian) – which plays constructively with extant forms and makes interpretations within a prior cultural framework – but whose re-interpretations 'go meta'. How much more realistic, they ponder, might not an anthropology be which similarly pointed up the enduring human condition to render all social rules ultimately contingent . . .

And so the last words are due Nietzsche (1979b):

We have not truly got rid of God
if we still believe in grammar.

Chapter 3

Individual Narratives
'Writing' as a mode of thought which gives meaning to experience

The only two things that can satisfy the soul are a person and
a story; and even a story must be about a person.

G.K. Chesterton

[N]arrative is present in every age, in every place, in every
society. . . . All classes, all human groups, have their narratives,
enjoyment of which is often shared by people with different,
even opposing, cultural backgrounds. . . . [N]arrative is international, transhistorical, transcultural: it is simply there, like life
itself.

Roland Barthes

INTRODUCTION

Human beings are narrating animals, Barthes suggested. Carried
variously in articulated language, in image and in gesture, their
narratives are ubiquitous: in myths, legends, fables, tales, novellas,
epics, histories, tragedies, dramas, comedies, mimes, paintings,
films, photographs, stained-glass windows, comics, newspapers and
conversations (1982:251). In this essay I want to begin with
Barthes's suggestion but treat it in a non-Barthesian fashion.
Narratives are universal, I shall say, because individuals are continually and continuously authoring them: individuals are writing the
story (better, stories) of their lives, of their societies and selves;
they create them and they live by them. For the most part, individuals keep these stories or narratives in their heads. Sometimes
they write them down on paper; sometimes they write them into
action – others' as well as their own. But always these stories
represent the orderly, meaningful and multiple visions they hold

of what, how, when and why the world is; the stories which individuals write are their personal world-views. And in the process of writing them – however much their inspiration might be living in a social-cum-natural environment; however much their medium might be a public and collective system of signification (language); however much the narratives might represent 'a tissue of quotations drawn from innumerable cultural discourses' which 'hem in' what may be said (Barthes 1982:293) – individuals create something particular to themselves. Individuals' narratives exhibit an artistry and uniqueness (an individuality) which removes them from the over-determination of the language in which they are written, the collective, public forms which they employ, and which thereby expresses the unique and undetermined nature of the lives lived through them.

ANTHROPOLOGY AND WRITING

Raymond Williams once spoke of the way in which the process of writing had become social-scientifically 'naturalised' in the academic environment of modern industrial society; we ask 'what is the writing about? what knowledge, facts and experience does it contain?' but we treat the process itself as non-problematic, as transparent, and as commonsensical, once the skills of writing have been acquired in childhood (1983:1). Anthropologists, perhaps, has been less prone than others in the academy to this lapse, since they more often treat those who do not and may not seek to acquire the writing technique to which Williams was referring at all. Hence, anthropology has emphasised the historico-cultural specificity of such writing, and the effects which its arrival precipitates. Anthropology has postulated, *inter alia*, that the technique of writing represents an objectification of speech and a proliferation of words and meanings which causes more layering and less indexicality in cultural traditions, so that individual members become palimpsests who participate less fully and more sceptically, less securely and more selectively, in their traditions (Goody and Watt 1968:57–8). Or again, here is a technique for the fixing of discourse, preserving it as a possible archive of later analysis and translation, and creating a quasi-separate world of texts which comes to eclipse the circumstantial world of orality (Ricoeur 1981:145–9); here is a means of keeping present moments at bay and at the same time preserving them, recontextualising them, as ongoing, univocal, unifocal and reconsultable (Clifford 1990: 57–64). Or again, here is a technology which lends itself to the social institutions of its time and place so as to serve a number of possible functions (hierarchical, educational), and thus to structure a particular ideological reality for those who employ (rather, are employed by) it (Street 1984:8). In short, in anthropology, writing comes to be conceived of not so much as a neutral medium of knowledge, facts and experience, a window onto an independent reality, than as a way of knowing in itself.

Nevertheless, there is a way in which writing has still become 'naturalised' in this anthropological treatment which I would wish to question. It is that writing has been treated wholly as a particular technique or technology: the inscription of words or forms on a page or material surface. Whereas it seems to me that writing would more profitably be regarded as the orderly inscription of words or forms *per se* – whatever the precise technique and technology of that inscription. Hence: words in phrases and sentences, but also musical notes in chords and phrases, daubs of paint in shapes and relations, religious icons in mouldings and arrays, physical behaviours in habits and routines, prescribed roles in institutions and hierarchies. Furthermore, inscription takes place on any number of surfaces, as it were: fields, houses, footballs, spaces, bodies and memories as well as pages. Here is writing conceived of as the orderly use of symbolic forms (that is, forms which carry meaning for their user) for the making of orderly worlds: writing understood not as a technique of communication but as a mode of thought giving meaning to experience.

To elaborate, I would define writing as the composition, in symbolic form, of a sequence of thoughts and ideas and senses such that a set of meanings is created and retained from passing experience for further possible retrieval, amendment and elaboration. Writing is the practice of symbolically reflecting on and making sense of experience; as Stock puts it, a separating of experience from the ratiocination about it (1983:531). By 'writing', in short, I would have us understand a meta-experience: the considered ordering of experience in symbolic form, and the conscious production of meaning. It issues forth as novels and poems and songs and plays, but also as shapes of field-systems and patterns of their ploughing, also as ways of shaping, carrying, tattooing and clothing bodies, also as styles of dancing and politicking and orating and marketing and warring. Importantly, the reflexive practice is constant even as the form of its expression varies (cf. Bruner and Weisser 1991:137).

Moreover, in this sense, writing is universal – and always has been. Such 'writing' is the special preserve neither of certain cultures and times (literate versus non-literate), nor of certain social classes and occupations (professionals versus workers) (cf. Berger 1979:6). Indeed, there is even an argument to be made that such writing was fundamental to the evolution of our humanity; that reflecting on and giving meaning to experience in a sequential fashion enabled our forebears better to image, project and hence predict the possible behaviour of peers – based on a sense of their own narrational progression, an appreciation of the meanings behind their own actions (Humphrey 1982:476–7; Lewin 1988:*passim*).

Certainly, both in social environments which practise largely oral techniques of communication and those which have developed 'literate' ones, there will flourish the ubiquitous practice of scrutinising and abstracting from experience so as to produce orderly narratives. Orality and literacy do not necessarily entail different habits of thought; or, as Turner puts it (cited in Ashley 1990:xix):

> there were never any innocent, unconscious savages, living in a time of unreflective and instinctive harmony. We human beings are all and always sophisticated, conscious, capable of laughter at our own institutions. . . .

In this essay, I wish to further explore and elaborate upon these ideas, in particular in the context of individual lives: the individual practice of continually and continuously writing individual narratives of meaningful lives.

NIETZSCHE AND WRITING

There seems widespread social-scientific agreement on the close relationship between narrative and selfhood. The self is a reflexive being, Kerby writes (1991:41), which 'comes to itself' through its own narrational acts. Such acts of self-narration do not merely and innocently describe the self but are basic to its emergence and reality. Narratives articulate acts, events and event-sequences within a significant framing context or history so as to provide "a primary embodiment of our understanding of the world, of experience, and ultimately of ourselves". And if narrative is, "the privileged medium for understanding human experience", then the development of selves in narratives is 'one of the most characteristically human acts' (1991:1,3). There is a human readiness or predisposition to "organise experience into a narrative form", Bruner concurs (1990:45), which dominates much of life in culture. Through such rendering, we construct an orderly world, locate ourselves within it, and make ourselves meaningful and understandable to ourselves and others; our narrations are 'navigational acts' (Bruner and Weisser 1991:133).

What I would wish to have stressed, however, is the continuousness and continuity of this relationship between self and world. Individuals are always and everywhere writing narratives of their selves, amending and elaborating their sense of themselves and their worlds, making of their selves and their worlds what Existentialists have come to describe as 'an unfinished project'. Individuals not only write their stories of social reality, they are also ubiquitously engaged in rewriting them.

It is to Nietzsche that this insight is mostly owed. Writing is perhaps the most important part of thinking – of acting, of living – Nietzsche expostulated (cf. Nehamas 1985), because in an important sense writing gives birth to the human world. The human world is like an art-work: something which can be interpreted – read, written – equally well in innumerable, vastly different and deeply incompatible ways: something with "no meaning behind it, but countless meanings" (1968:no.481). Indeed, like an artwork, the world requires interpretation in order to be understood, made livable, mastered, by its inhabitants. These inhabitants may themselves be part of the world, may be making interpretations from situated, interested and partisan perspectives, but none the less, it is they who create the world, create themselves and their perspectives in their interpretations. They compose the world as they write it; and their compositions add to the complexity and multifariousness and indeterminacy of the art-work that continues to be interpreted – by others, by themselves – in the present and future.

The form these writings take, Nietzsche continued, are various. The books of the philosopher, certainly, but also the various habitual practices and modes of life of others. Amidst the profusion of versions and forms, he averred, there is only one singularity: the continuation of profusion. Interpretations continue to be made because to interpret is to be human; while to make individual interpretations, self-caused and free, and to have these develop and change as one moves through life and changes one's perspectives, is to be an individual human being – likewise self-caused and free.

NIETZSCHE AND ANTHROPOLOGY

If Nietzschean interpretation has inspired Existentialism in this century, not to mention Post-Modernism ('there is no immaculate perception'; 'there are no facts, only interpretations'; 'truth is a mobile army of metaphors') and the philosophy of consciousness (Henri Focillon: "The chief characteristic of the mind is to be constantly describing itself" (cited in Edelman 1992:124)), then anthropology has not wholly missed out either. Malinowski's deep debt to Nietzsche has been acknowledged, how his Functionalism was founded on Nietzschean insights (cf. Thornton 1992: 20; Thornton and Skalnik 1993:16), while Geertz borrows a Nietzschean tag (*froehliche Wissenschaft*) to describe his discipline (1986:105), and Shweder goes so far as to say that the credo of modern anthropology *tout court* – that society and morality derive from the projection of mental representations onto the universe and their imposition as symbolic forms; that socio-cultural reality is not other than the stories told about it, the narratives in which it is represented – derives from Nietzsche (1991:39; also cf. Thornton 1991:2).

However, for illumination over how the Nietzschean insight on the recurrent writing of interpretations of the world can be best taken-up by anthropology, it is to the philosopher Richard Rorty (1992) that I would first turn. "All human beings carry about a set of words which they employ to justify their actions, their beliefs, and their lives", Rorty begins. Compassing projects, hopes, doubts, loves and hates, these are the words "in which we tell, sometimes prospectively and sometimes retrospectively, the story of our lives" (1992:73). The words represent the boundaries and also the limits of an individual's mental ordering of the world; they house his sense of self and of society. Moreover, if they are called into question, doubted or challenged, then their owner has no non-circular argumentative recourse. For beyond these words, an individual has no further linguistic resource. Hence, Rorty would call such verbal sets, 'final vocabularies'.

None the less, what Nietzsche was most keen to emphasise concerns the ironic attitude which an individual may hold toward his final vocabulary. Here is a recognition that the world is as full of final vocabularies as it is full of other people, and that choices can be made between these, including the choice to compose a new vocabulary, *ab initio*, especially for oneself. This recognition is a resource which can always take an individual beyond a final vocabulary, indeed, beyond language as such.

Nietzsche did not only teach this in his philosophical writing, he also sought to demonstrate it in the writing of his own life: to exemplify the "private perfection", as Rorty puts it, of a self-created, autonomous individuality (1992:xiv). This he did by employing a philosophical language and style for the stating of his hopes for himself and humanity which was particular to him, and, at almost the same time, by signalling a recognition of the contingency of that language. Hence, even as he sought to remain faithful to it, to live faithfully by it, Nietzsche only desisted from calling attention to the situatedness of his writing (in time and place) and only desisted from a process of continually redescribing his hopes, self and world (in new languages, employing new metaphors) when his mental powers utterly deserted him (and he went mad).

Nietzsche's purpose in doing this can perhaps be extrapolated as three-fold. He sought to demonstrate that such redescription – the continuous rewriting of the final vocabularies in terms of which one delineates one's self and world – was possible; so that we need not only speak the language of the community, that we may find our own words. Second, to demonstrate that such rewriting was beautiful, was poetic, and was the chief way of relating oneself with dignity to the aesthetic nature of the human condition. And third, that such rewriting was necessary and of supreme importance, and represented both an individual's particular responsibility to himself and the foundation of a general human power. For rewriting was a tool which reminded the individual and reminded humanity as a whole that to change how we talked was to change what we were: to rewrite the language of our self-descriptions was thus to rewrite ourselves. Ontologies were as contingent as epistemologies, and the important dividing line was not between falsehood and truth but between the old and the new 'falsehood/truth', between this and that 'falsehood/truth'. Human history was the history of successive metaphors, and it was the poet, as shaper of new languages and maker of new worlds, who

was the vanguard of the species (cf. Shelley 1954:293). There
was nothing more powerful or important than self-redescription,
then, because it demonstrated that the notion of a single 'true'
world, of access to an essential 'reality', was a fable, and that the
world, our selves, and the most important parts of ourselves, our
minds, were constructs of our languages and our individual use
of them in our acts of writing. In short, the dramatic narrative of
an individual or community life did not turn on seeking one
right description, overcoming the contingent and reaching an
absolute context, but was rather a continuing and continuous
process of self-overcoming: telling the story of one's own production in words not used before; "recreating all 'it was' into 'thus I
willed it'".

"THUS I WILLED IT"

Anthropologically speaking, I find the notion of individuals'
continual and continuous ironic writing of reality to be provocative and enlightening. In Chapter 6, we shall meet Kapauku
headman, Ijaaj Awiitigaaj (via Leopold Pospisil) and hear of his
rewriting of a local incest taboo. In this chapter I should like to
provide a set of individual voices which commensurately and
consciously redescribe their societies and selves in (verbal) terms
which take them beyond existing referents and terms of reference.

The first is that of Arthur Harvey, a small-time hill-farmer from
the Cumbrian dale of Wanet (cf. Rapport 1993). Arthur, now
approaching his sixties, lives with his wife, Mary, in a rather remote
farmhouse high on the fells. The farmhouse has seen better days,
as has the farm generally, and Arthur now supplements his income
from his sheep and his few beef cows with piece-work in a nearby
town. Arthur has lost much interest in the farm and is now really
just serving out his time. (Hopefully, soon he can sell up and retire
on the proceeds; even if the farm is run down, the land should go
for a goodly sum as his neighbours seek to expand). Nowadays,
it is only really in the pub that Arthur comes alive, the Eagle
being his favourite, and the domino table his preferred spot inside
it. Which is where I have met him in the conversation below. In
between rounds of dominoes, he and I are sharing a drink at the
Eagle bar, and Arthur is in a talkative mood, suddenly; content
for me to be a sympathetic listener, adding the odd word of agreement, nodding, grinning, while he continues his exposition:

But then even the community in Wanet is less now than before, Nigel, because there are so few young folks here. See? No work, of course ... But then if there was more work the whole character of the place would be different! Aye, it's a puzzle, lad. And I certainly don't know the solution. If there is one at all. Better minds than mine will have to figure that one out ... But then it's not something I can get that fired up about. Personally speaking, I mean. Because it's animals I love, Nigel. I think I can talk to animals: I do that! And they can talk to me, like. (We grin) Like, they understand y' tone ... To understand animals, you just got to think like them.

You know, I recently rescued a ewe. End of lambing time. I found the lamb, like, but no mother about. Then, when I was helping another birthing, I looked up and I found it caught in the branch of a tree, after the snow had melted and gone down. Caught tight in the 'V' of the branch, it was. It was frothed at the mouth, and very weak, and I was sure it would die. But I fed her at home and cared for her, and now she's at my daughter Lynn's and she should recover. And you know, lad, she'll never leave me (if she does) till she dies. When I'll make sure she get's a good funeral. Ha! I will that. (We laugh) How about another drink, lad? You're looking like a man who could do with another. My round. (Arthur orders and we receive drinks)

Cheers! ... But you know, Nigel, I don't really believe in death. There can't be death. I think you must live lots of different lives, in some form of 'you'. It's like your 'you' continues, eh? ... Like, life is all around us, right Nigel? How many microcosms do you think there are in the air between us now as we're talking? Yes, millions. So, it's like death isn't possible. That's why people can remember other lives they've had. You may come back as a worm or a sheep, like, but you must come back in some form or other. Right? So when I'm buried or burnt, or whatever, I won't be dead for long before I get reincarnated ... I might never meet you again, Nigel, but there's still the chance that I will. It's like we talk of infinity: two parallel lines meet at infinity, and the rest; but we don't really understand infinity at all ...

You know, I can kill a kitten or something without thinking about it. But I always feel something for sheep. People say they're stupid and that, but I feel they know as much as we do, as much as anyone. And they know the lesson of survival. So the species continues to survive. See: it's not possible, something like death ... I'm not a religious man, but there must be some controlling force. Directing things. Call it 'Nature', if you like. So there's a natural law of survival and instinct in everything ...

Well, I've bared my soul to you tonight, Nigel. I have that ...

Arthur stopped his speech at this point and we returned to the domino table for our next round. Before I return to his words, however, to the implications of his 'writing', let me place the words of three more individuals (Lame Deer, Mugo Gatheru, and Nisa) beside his for comparison.

Lame Deer is a Sioux medicine man (alias John Fire) who, in the 1970s, told his story to the Viennese-born artist and writer, Richard Erdoes, in New York. Lame Deer lives in South Dakota: to the white men surrounding him, an ageing rodeo-fool, womaniser and vagabond, eking out an existence amid tumble-down iron shacks and faded ritual amulets. In his own estimation, Lame Deer is a Sioux spiritual organiser and leader, still living according to the great vision he received one lonely night as a young man on a hilltop vigil. It is of this vigil and vision that he first tells Erdoes, also of his medicine, spirit helpers and sacred knowledge, and of general relations between Indians and whites. In the following extract (1980:76–8), Lame Deer gives his account of the relations between Indians and the use of alcohol:

Alcoholism is a problem for us, and as long as all this liquor is lying about here, it won't get better. I have often thought about the special effect liquor has on us Indians. In two hundred years we still haven't learned how to handle it. It was just like the measles and other diseases the white man brought us. The illness was the same for them as for us, but we died from it, while for them it was usually just a few days of discomfort.

I figured out a few reasons for our drinking. They might not be the right ones; I'm just speculating. We call liquor *mni wakan* – holy water. I guess visions were so important and sacred to us that having our minds altered and befuddled by whisky impressed us in the beginning like a religious experience, a dream, a vision. It didn't take much to make us drink; it still doesn't. ...

But you can't blame our drinking nowadays on a desire to have visions, or say that we guzzle the stuff because it is holy – though I want to tell you that even glass-eyed winos often hold up their bottles and spill a little of the precious stuff on the ground for the spirits of the departed, saying, 'Here, my friend who left us, here's something for you,' or 'Here, my old girlfriend who died, share this drink with me.'

So here is the question: Why do Indians drink? They drink to forget, I think, to forget the great days when this land was ours and when it was beautiful, without highways, billboards, fences and factories. They try to forget the pitiful shacks and rusting trailers which are their 'homes'. They try to forget that they are treated like children, not like grown-up people. . . . So we drink because we are minors, not men. We try to forget that even our fenced-in reservations no longer belong to us. We have to lease them to white farmers who fatten their cattle, and themselves, on our land. At Pine Ridge less than one per cent of the land is worked by Indians.

We drink to forget that we are beggars, living on handouts, eight different kinds of handouts: ex-servicemen, the disabled, widows, gold-stars, mothers, old-age support, foster-parent contracts, Social Security, ADC – aid to dependent children. . . .

We drink to forget that there is nothing worthwhile for a man to do, nothing that would bring honour or make him feel good inside. There are only a handful of jobs for a few thousand people. These are all Government jobs, tribal or federal. You have to be a good house Indian, an Uncle Tomahawk, a real apple – red outside, white inside – to get a job like this. You have to behave yourself, and never talk back, to keep it. If you have such a job, you drink to forget what kind of person it has made of you. If you don't have it, you drink because there is nothing to look forward to but a few weeks of spud-picking, if you are lucky. You drink because you don't live; you just exist. That may be enough for some people; it's not enough for us.

R. Mugo Gatheru is a middle-aged Kikuyu man whose education (and desire to dodge racist slurs of his being in various ways 'subversive') took him from Kenya in the 1940s to schools and universities in India, the United States and Britain. In the early 1960s, encouraged by the American social anthropologist, St Clair

Drake, who became his 'brother', he published an autobiography, *Child of Two Worlds*, in which he sketched his personal journey through tribal socialisation to Western urbanisation. He dedicates his book to "a future Kenya nation in which tribalism has become only a historic memory and tribes mere ceremonial units". In the following extract (1965:213–222), Mugo concludes his account by reflecting on some of his experiences in the USA and England, preparatory to going home to Kenya with his Law degree:

One finds black men living throughout the White Man's World. I am one of these but I am a temporary resident completing my education, and I shall soon return to my own country in Africa. There are, however, millions of people of African descent with permanent homes in the United States, Great Britain and elsewhere, and I am of course greatly interested in them and in their fate. . . .

For reasons which must be obvious, all people of African descent are united by a bond of mutual sympathy which is today, with the practical example of the United Nations, assuming a positive force and influence quite unexpected at its birth in humiliation and subjection. I was therefore well-disposed towards 'my brothers' but it was not until I went to America that I realised that sympathy and good will alone do not necessarily make for true understanding. We had some curious ideas about each other. . . .

My own encounter with the alien society of America was difficult, the experience strange but exciting. I have already told of my upbringing in the rural community of a Kikuyu medicine-man's family and of my struggle to adjust to the urban life in Nairobi when I began my laboratory work in 1945. Despite this, and also the greater strangeness of my time in India and England, my stay in America was perhaps the most stimulating and trying of all. I worked hard to understand the Americans, their methods of education, their colourful and kaleidoscopic society. . . . Never at any time did I lose my identity as a Kenyan, but, so conscientious was my effort to learn all I could of this great country, that after a while I even caught myself reacting like an American, at least in circumstances essentially American, and without any conscious desire to do so. . . .

One thing in the White Man's World still remains a mystery to me. From the time I first heard of it at Stoton until now, I must confess I have been unable to accept the concept of

Christianity. I am not an atheist or agnostic. I believe in One God, the Creator, just as my great-great-great-grandparents did, but I regard Christianity as I do history or law, as a source from which I may advance my knowledge and intellectual capacity. However, I was deeply impressed to find that Christianity has been a strong unifying force among American negroes and that it actually serves to give them a 'tribal' cohesion. . . .

On this day, I sit in London, and thousands of miles away, in space if not in spirit, Jomo Kenyatta stands in Nairobi on a platform draped in scarlet . . . as the very first Prime Minister of Kenya. . . . May God indeed help him and all my people to that peace, prosperity, and happiness which alone can make sense of my life and those of others who have laboured so hard for this day. I am happy also because my studies are now ending, and I shall shortly take my final examinations and I shall be home to help in the building of a new Kenya nation. And I am happy. I am happy because I now look upon the face of my son. My first son, Gatheru, Gatheru-son-of-Mugo, for this is one tradition which I shall not be the first to change.

Nisa is a Kalahari !Kung woman of around fifty, who lives by hunting and gathering in the Dobe region, a semi-arid, savannah and desert-fringe environment, of north-western Botswana. In the early 1970s she told a story of her life to American anthropologist Marjorie Shostak: "I'll break open the story and tell you what is there. Then, like the others that have fallen out into the sand, I will finish with it, and the wind will take it away". Through twenty-one interviews which Shostak paid Nisa to take part in over thirty hours, the anthropologist explains that she gained her deepest insights into !Kung life (1983:42). In the following extract (1983:335–8), Nisa is finally bringing the story of her life up to the present, and after the loss of a number of husbands, lovers and children, is recounting the details of her relations with her current husband, Bo:

I still want my husband. . . . But for a while, now, he's hardly slept with me at all. He sleeps with me one night, then not again for a long time and we just live beside one another. . . . Whatever it is, it isn't good; it makes me feel very bad.

Because I still have interest in sex, but when I want to, Bo doesn't help at all. He isn't interested. That's why I have to look for other men, so I can find it for myself. That's also why

I have Debe and why I like him. He is almost like a husband to me, and he is someone who knows about work. If you're with him for the night, he'll have sex with you until dawn breaks.

My other husbands weren't like Bo. When I was with Tashay, one night we would make love and another we wouldn't. Sometimes, we made love twice in one night – first, when we lay down and again, before dawn. And Besa, he was always interested! He was always aroused, always erect. He didn't let you rest. ... I'd think, 'Why is Besa having sex with me so often? Does he want to screw me to death?'

Because that man, he really liked sex. Mother!

When Bo and I were still lovers and hadn't married yet, in one night he would also sleep with me many times. Even after we married, it was like that. ... That's why, what has been happening recently, I don't like, and why I have been asking him, if he can be like that, what has made him change? I don't know what is wrong. It isn't that he's lost his strength or that he is no longer potent, because he is still very strong in that way. Perhaps it is something in his heart. Perhaps his heart has died, because I've never heard about him being with other women. ...

Some days I feel hurt and angry because of all this. That's when he asks, 'What's upsetting you? Why are you so angry?' I say, 'Because you didn't really marry me. If you had, you would be sleeping with me.' He says, 'Why are you always mourning for sex? What are you, a woman, always complaining about wanting sex?' I say, 'What did you think you would give me when you married me? Did you marry me with the idea that you'd have sex with me or that we'd just live together without it? Did we marry just to help each other with our daily chores?'

Because, when you marry, your husband asks you to help him do things and he also has sex with you. But if he doesn't have sex with you, your heart dies! If the two of you aren't sharing that together, it pulls your heart away. Do you understand that? If your husband doesn't have sex with you, you become disturbed; your desire upsets your mind. It's only when you are having sex that everything is really fine.

I take these different accounts to be examples of individuals interpreting their selves and society, their situations in social relations and milieux, in ways and words which are particular to themselves. Here are individual writings of social reality.

To reprise them, in brief, and point up the artistry and individuality of their writing, we first heard of Arthur's bar-room,
homespun philosophy surrounding death. And the main feature
of the narrative is its very homespun-ness. Philosophising about
death has nothing unique about it, of course; indeed, in its universality, its reputed underpinning of every religious metaphysics,
such philosophising might be said to represent the height of
conventionality. Notwithstanding, what comes across in Arthur's
writing is the close tie between his interpretation of death and his
own life: his farming, his working with, understanding and love
of sheep. Amidst the conventional philosophical theme, the
proverbial phrasing ("Better minds than mine"; "talk to animals";
"life is all around us"; "two parallel lines meet at infinity"; "natural
law"), the semi-Biblical imagery ("a ewe caught tight in the
'V' of a tree"; "your 'you' continues"; "bared my soul"), there
emerges a unique narrative. Out of dumb animals, animals indeed
renowned for their stupidity (sheep), Arthur makes an exemplar
of knowledge and a voice of prophecy. They are dumb (while
we humans speak of infinity and all matter else) but Arthur
prefers their company to the human kind, and finds a mutual
exchange of thoughts, feelings, loyalties, ceremonies and bodily
incarnations giving onto true insight: the infinite survival of the
invisible but personal soul. Drawing together and reworking a
symbolic treasury of cultural forms, Arthur writes his own version
of reality.

Lame Deer's narrative is used as an opportunity to display no
little oratorical showmanship. He takes a well-worn theme, Indian
alcoholism, and turns it into a personal act of cataloguing feelings
which are his own, now dressed in the impersonal clothes of
Indians as a generic kind of man. Having established the long-
lived and continuing behavioural and biological distinctiveness
of Indians ('the effects of liquor are like the one-time effects of
measles'), he lists speculative reasons for Indian drinking which
manage to cover – celebrate, challenge – the religion and religiosity, the emotional loyalty, the aestheticism, the pride and
honour, the mistreatment, of Indian society and culture, and the
double-binds in which it is now caught. Furthermore, in slipping
between 'I', 'You', 'We' and 'They' constructions from sentence
to sentence, Lame Deer manages to slip in a number of different
perspectives on the problem of alcoholism. These both encourage
and enable the reader to enter into the writing and empathetically

to adopt a number of perspectives, and also allow Lame Deer to be the occupant of different locations at different moments. He is both part of the culture of alcoholism and not; part of past religious experience and visions and not; part of Indian winos, and Indian minors, and Uncle Tomahawks, and not; part, in fact, of Indian culture and not. In his writing Lame Deer reasons, makes significance and sense, in a number of paradigms but he is not constrained by any. His oratory is an individual bricolage of Indian, white, sociological, psychological and theological languages.

R. Mugo Gatheru's oratory is far more measured and formal, but his writing is no less individual. It is forceful, even forensic – in the light of the author's choice of the Law as his profession – but above all, it is supremely self-knowing. Mugo knows who he is: a black man temporarily resident in the "White Man's World" (a place made special – peculiar – by specific capitalisation), where millions of fellows of African descent live, to whom Mugo is well-disposed but lacking complete understanding, and whom Mugo will soon leave behind when his education is completed and he returns to his African home to build a new Kenyan nation. Mugo also knows his own thoughts and feelings: from his interest in and sympathy for other blacks, to his overriding desire to further his knowledge and intellectual capacities, to his excitement at being in America and his unconscious adjustment to life there, to his appreciation of the UN and his hopes for Jomo Kenyatta. Now, Mugo knows precisely where he stands in his personal life-course; his present in the latter stages of legal studies in London is exactly between his past in the family of a rural Kikuyu medicine-man and his future living as a Kenyan, with his own family, in a new nation he will have laboured long to establish. Finally, through his writing, Mugo knows where he stands in relation to the cultural practices and the social identities in which he has sojourned. Rural and urban, Kikuyu medicine and Nairobi laboratory, India, England and America, Christianity and the Creator, tribal cohesiveness and traditions of naming – Mugo can and has taken measure of them all and found his own place amongst them by which to make sense of his life.

Finally, Nisa's story is very different in form, but commensurate in style. What strikes me is its forceful and single-minded pursuit of one piece of information: why her husband, Bo, no longer sleeps with her on a regular or routine basis. This is important to her not for the conventional upkeep of their marriage, for this merely entails being seen to live together and share chores. Nor is it important so that she be seen to be womanly. Indeed, she pursues the knowledge she seeks even at the risk of Bo finding her insistence unwomanly. It is important to Nisa for her individual emotional well-being – a well-being she expects to be universal and thus comprehensible to her anthropologist interlocutor too, whatever else might divide them: sex 'keeps your heart alive', 'keeps your heart and your husband's together', 'stops desire from upsetting your mind'. This articulation seems to me poetic and individual. Moreover, like the others, Nisa's narrative is deeply embedded in her own experiences. Hence, what is not good in her social relations is what makes her personally feel bad. Moreover, while it may be conventional among the !Kung for women to take illicit lovers as well as husbands, it is indicative of Nisa's individual turn of mind that in seeking to make sense of her husband's behaviour and give meaning to their current relationship, she compares his sexual performance with that of previous men she has known, whatever the circumstances – inside marriage or outside, long-term relations or short-term – as well as Bo's own performance in the past. In other words, she marshals details where she finds them and categorises them simply in terms of the logic and dramatic structure of the narrative she is in the process of weaving.

In sum, here are four interpretations of social reality from four individuals: four narrative accounts, parts of four individual worldviews, concerning what, how, when and why the world is, and their parts within it. And my argument has been that in the process of writing their accounts, these individuals have constructed something particular to themselves: their narratives exhibit an artistry and uniqueness, a personality, which removes them from any overdetermination by the collective language and the public forms which they employ.

GEERTZ AND WRITING

Perhaps the most celebrated Nietzscheanesque title in anthropology, emphasising the interpretations in terms of which human beings make their worlds and make them meaningful, is Clifford Geertz's *The Interpretation of Cultures*. However, belying any seemingly Existentialist form, 'interpretation' is here granted a rather different significance.

Culture, Geertz wishes to be understood as an accumulated totality of symbol-systems (religion, ideology, common sense, economics, sport) in terms of which people both make sense of themselves and their world, and represent themselves to themselves and to others. Members of a culture use its symbols (winks, crucifixes, footballs, cats, collars, foods, photographs, words) as a language through which to read and interpret, to express and share meaning. And since the imposition of meaning on life is the major end and primary condition of human existence, this reading of culture is constant; culture members are ever making interpretations – of the symbol systems they have inherited. Culture is 'an acted symbolic document'.

Hence, while Geertz admits that "becoming human is becoming individual", he postulates that we become individual in the context of 'cultural patterns': under the guidance of historically created systems of meaning "in terms of which we give form, order, point and direction to our lives" (1973:52). For Geertz we always interpret courtesy of systems of significant symbols in a particular cultural context.

Furthermore, Geertz readily extends the context of symbolic systemics to include individual thought. Representing an "intentional manipulation of cultural forms", of systems of symbols of collective possession, public authority and social exchange, thought, he proclaims, is "out in the world" (1983:151). The symbolic logic and the formal conceptual structuring may not be explicit, but they are socially established, sustained and legitimised. Moreover, they are publicly enacted; they are tied to concrete social events and occasions, and expressive of a common social world. In short: giving meaning to behaviour is not something which happens in private, in insular individual heads, but rather something dependent on an exchange of common symbols whose "natural habitat is the house yard, the market place, and the town square" (1973:45). Hence, outdoor activities such as ploughing or peddling are as good examples of 'individual thought' as are closet experiences such as wishing or regretting. While cognition, imagination, emotion, motivation, perception, memory and so on, are themselves directly social affairs.

In Geertz's adumbrating of "an outdoor psychology" (1983:151), then, culture (as systems of historically-transmitted symbols) is constitutive of mind, while individual experience and memory of the social world are both powerfully structured by deeply internalised cultural conceptions, and supported by cultural institutions; life in society entails a public traffic in significant cultural symbols. Thus, while flagging Suzanne Langer's phrase that "we live in a web of ideas, a fabric of our own making" (1964:126), and seeming to adopt a Nietzschean interpretivist-constructivist-perspectivist stance, Geertz concludes that the webs of significance we weave, the meanings we live by, achieve a form and actualisation only in a public and communal way. There can be no private (individual, unique) symbolisations, for mind is transactional: formed and realised only through participation in cultures' symbolic systems of interpretation; while different 'individual' minds within the culture are in fact neither opaque nor impenetrable to one another, for they think in terms of the same shared beliefs and values and operate the same interpretive procedures for adjudicating reality. To construe a system of cultural symbols, in sum, is to accrue its individual members' subjectivities.

An 'outdoor psychology' which is 'out in the world' – for all its apparent expansiveness and openness – I find a confining metaphorisation (for the same reason that Wittgensteinian notions of 'forms of life' which circumscribe thought and action, which delimit meaning, have been so described (cf. Mundle 1970:163)). It seems to deny any inner, private life and language which is not readily accessible to others who employ (are employed by) the same cultural system of formal symbolic signification. At one and the same time, Geertz appears to champion a humanistic appreciation of the human condition and the anthropological project: "man is an animal suspended in webs of significance he himself has spun", whose analysis is "not an experimental science in search of law but an interpretive one in search of meaning" (1973:5); but then he seems to fall foul of a most restrictive determinism: "culture is best seen as ... a set of control mechanisms – plans, recipes, rules, instructions (what computer engineers call 'programs') – for the governing of behaviour", and it is the "agency" of these mechanisms which is responsible for reducing the breadth and indeterminateness of the individual's inherent capacity to live thousands of lives to the specificity and narrowness of his actual accomplishment in living one life (1973:44–5).

In short, the interpreting – imagining, constructing, writing – Geertz does foresee, the leeway he allows for between cultural patternings 'of' and 'for' social practice, is intra-paradigmatic: contained within a certain encompassing, collective, public and shared cultural context. Initially, he appears to follow Langer's lead when she explains that: "at the centre of human experience, then, there is always the activity of imagining reality, conceiving the structure of it through words, images, or other symbols" (1964:128). Imagination, Langer continues, makes our world. It frames, supports and guides our thinking; it is the source of all insight, reason, dream, religion and general observation, the greatest force acting on our feelings, and bigger than the stimuli surrounding us. And she concludes that: "the scope of our imagination gives each of us a separate world, and a separate consciousness" (1964:103). Geertz, however, would ultimately appear to sign up to a Saussurean-Durkheimian thesis wherein the varieties of individual *parole* simply depend and derive from an enabling collective *langue*. Here, particular linguistic performances are prefigured by a structure of rules and possible relations, by a set of *representations collectives*, so that individual expressions within a cultural milieu add up, at any one time, to a total and autonomous synchronic system of related parts, and so that individual consciousness is a manifestation, temporary, episodic and epiphenomenal, of a *conscience collective*.

CONCLUSION

I find Geertz's efforts, his role in the refocusing of anthropological interest from social structure to meaning, in the rereckoning of the anthropological enterprise as 'fictional writing', both liberating and inspiring (cf. Rapport 1994, 1996), and, ultimately, frustrating. Because I would see language – any system of symbols in common usage – as ever possessed of a dual phenomenology: 'a common surface and a private base', in Steiner's phrasing (1975:173); 'a cultural domain and a psychological one', in Chodorow's (1994:2). What the latter depictions imply is that beneath the publicly consensual, linguistically-labelled cultural categories which describe life, there lies the psyche, with its 'concurrent flow of articulate consciousness' (Steiner 1975:46). Here are those pan-human potentialities, capacities and processes, beginning at birth (if not before) and continuing throughout life, by which 'the world' (cultural categories, images, stories and language; people, interactions, selves and things) becomes endowed, invested, infused, with personal emotion, fantasy, and affect, and so is ever made subjectively, personally, individually meaningful. It is these psychological processes of sense-making, of interpretation, which are responsible for shaping and constituting human life and society, for creating and recreating culture as a meaningful phenomenon in the life of each individual. As Chodorow concludes (1994:4):

> People personally animate and tint, emotionally and through fantasy, the cultural, linguistic, interpersonal, cognitive and embodied worlds we experience, creating and interpreting the external world in ways that resonate with their internal world, preoccupations, fantasies and sense of self and other.

Rather than according primacy to cultural or linguistic reality, *à la* Geertz (Durkheim, Saussure, Lacan *et al.*), then, rather than conceiving of the individual being inscribed into, necessarily accommodating to, a pre-given socio-cultural reality, an appreciation of the way individuals ongoingly write their own worlds must give onto a different picture. There are individuals experiencing cultural and linguistic forms, and through this process creating meaning in terms of their unique biographies and personal histories of intrapsychic strategies and practices. To phrase this differently, 'the interpretation of cultures' gives onto individual world-views; individuals consume cultural symbolic forms in the construction of their own systems of meaning. Moreover, the world-views which individuals mentally and bodily inhabit are matters of individual composition and often private practice, while the contexts in which individuals fashion, speak and live their world-views are ontologically internal to themselves. Meanings are psychologically particular, and diverse (cf. Rapport 1993; 1995).

When it comes, finally, to the narratives of their lives that individuals – continuously and continually – write, then, whatever the symbolic form may be, it is the use of it which is crucial (to evoke that other side of Wittgenstein's word-play). In using the various symbol systems which a culture places at their disposal as tools of their writing, individuals personalise them – and hence make of the symbol systems something 'of and for' themselves.

Chapter 4

Movement and Identity
Narrations of 'home' in a world in motion

It becomes ever more urgent to develop a framework of thinking that makes the migrant central, not ancillary, to historical process. . . . An authentically migrant perspective . . . might begin by regarding movement, not as an awkward interval between fixed points of departure and arrival, but as a mode of being in the world.

Paul Carter

Consequently anthropology is only a collection of traveller's tales.

A.R. Louch

INTRODUCTION

To the anthropological ear, the notion that anthropology and narratology might meet under the rubric of an overriding discipline of "iterology" – a science of journeys – as Michel Butor once suggested (1972:7), sounds frivolous at best. In this chapter I wish to sketch (argumentationally rather than ethnographically) what might be seen as the logic, or a logic, for iterology; to take seriously the notion that the study of social life and the study of story-telling might be seen to be bound together by a commensurate interest in the relationship between movement and identity.

MOVEMENT AND PERCEPTION

Quite a long time ago now, Gregory Bateson put it like this: the human brain thinks in terms of relationships. Things and events are secondary, epiphenomena: "all knowledge of external events is derived from the relationship between them": from the relationships which the brain conceives between them (1951:173). To conceive relationships (and so create things) is to move or cause to move things relative to the point of perception (the brain) or relative to other things within the field of perception. Movement is fundamental to the setting up and the changing of relations by which things gain and maintain and continue to accrue thingness. Indeed, since one of the 'things' that thus comes to exist as an identifiable thing is 'oneself' (the perceiving brain as objectified 'out there'), movement is also fundamental to the thingness, the identity, of the self. Not only is it the pen that one comes to perceive more and more accurately as one watches how it moves relative to oneself as someone uses it, or as one touches it, pushes it, picks it up, writes with it, chews it oneself, but also, through such usage, others' and one's own, one comes better to perceive oneself. Subject and object, perceiver and perceived are intrinsically connected.

Another way of saying this is that the mind operates with and upon differences. Relationships are about differences. Indeed, the word 'idea' is synonymous with 'difference'. If the mind 'treats ideas' (is an aggregate of ideas), then the mind is an aggregation of differences: between ego and alter, between objects in the world. If the mind 'gathers information', then this is data about differences which are seen as making a difference at a particular time.

There are a number of corollaries of this thesis. The first is that the things which thus derive from movement, relations and differences are material and immaterial alike. Ponds, pots and poems, to the extent that each figures in the life of a social milieu, are all the outcome of engineering movement relative to a point of perception. As Bateson phrases it, *all* phenomena are 'appearances', for in the world of human behaviour "to be is to be perceived" (1958:96). Constant movement is the essential characteristic of the way an individual mind perceives and so constructs an environment, whether 'natural' or 'cultural' (cf. Bourdieu 1966:233).

A second corollary is precisely that the mind is 'individual' in this regard. The movement which is engineered *is* relative to the individual perceiver. Bateson recognises this by describing the individual mind as "an energy source" (1972:126), responsible for energising the events in the world, the movements, which underlie the perception of difference; it is not that the mind is merely being impacted upon by environmental triggers (cf. Minh-ha 1994:23). More generally, each human individual is an 'energy source' inasmuch as the energy of his acts and responses derives from his own metabolic processes not from external stimuli. It is with this energy, through this movement, and by this construction of relations and objects, that individuals create order and impose it on the universe: human individuals are active participants in their own universe.

A third corollary, then, is that what can be understood by 'order' is a certain relationship, a certain difference, between objects which an individual mind comes to see as normal and normative; it is one of an infinite number of possible permutations, and it is dependent on the eye of the individual perceiver; this may not be what others perceive as orderly. What is random or 'entropic' for one perceiver is orderly, informational, negatively entropic for another. 'Disorder' and 'order' are statements of relations between a purposive perceiving entity and some set of objects and events; they are determined by individuals' states of mind.

What Bateson established (at least: translated into an anthropological environment from an Existentialist one) was the fundamental relationship between movement and perception, between movement and energy, between movement and order, and between movement and individuality.

STATIONARINESS AND IDENTITY

If these ideas have long been known or at least in circulation within anthropology, then the implication usually drawn from them has been, paradoxically, the relationship between identity and fixity: necessarily and universally finding a stationary point in the environment from which to engineer one's moving, perceiving, ordering and constructing. If (following Silverstone, Hirsch and Morley 1994:19) we may use the concept of 'home' to refer to that cognitive environment in which one undertakes the routines of daily life, through which 'space' becomes 'place', through which one's identity is mediated, then (in the construction and promulgation of essential cultures, societies, nations and ethnic groups) the conventional anthropological understanding was that to be at home was tantamount to being environmentally fixed – if not stationary then at least centred.

Thus, the environment comes to be depicted as normatively fanning out around the perceiver in concentric circles of greater and lesser degrees of consociality, all meeting in oneself at the perspectival centre: from house to lineage to village to tribe to other tribes, perhaps (Sahlins 1968:65); or, as the language of the perceiver classified his environment, a continuum of related terms was seen to place him 'reassuringly' at the centre of a social space and fan out from there: from "self" to "sibling" to "cousin" to "neighbour" to "stranger", perhaps; or else from "self" to "pet" to "livestock" to "game" to "wild animal" (Leach 1968:36–7). To be at home in an environment, in short, was to situate the world around oneself at the unmoving centre, with "contour lines of relevance" in the form of symbolic categories emanating from a magisterial point of perception (cf. Schuetz 1944:500–4). To know (oneself, one's society), it was necessary to gain a perspective on an environment from a single, fixed and homogeneous point of view: to know was to see the world as singular, made proportionate and subjected to the individual eye, sight and site of the beholder. In short, knowledge was validated by making the eye (and hence the 'I') the still centre of a visually observed world (cf. Ong 1969:*passim*; Strathern 1992:9–10).

Even if the actors were nomads, their myths were regarded anthropologically as making of the environment through which they passed a known place, an old place, a proper place, not only fixed in memory but to which their belonging was stationary because permanent, cyclical, normative and traditional; cognitively, they never moved. And even if the actors engaged in ritual journeys outside everyday space and time – rites of passage; pilgrimage; vision quests – in search of sacred centres to their lives (Eliade 1954:12–20), these anti-structural events served in fact to fix them even more; as special, extraordinary, aberrant experiences, the rituals merely emphasised and legitimated an everyday identity which derived from fixity in a social environment. Ritual pilgrims used their moments of (imagined) movement to establish routinely fixed orientations to a world around them (cf. Myerhoff 1974; Yamba 1992). Similarly anti-structural and marginal, finally, were the journeys undertaken between status-groups by actors in hierarchically organised societies (between classes, between professions, between age-grades), for here was movement whose experiential purpose, whose successful conclusion, was eventual stasis. Movement was mythologised as enabling fixity (cf. Strathern 1981:*passim*).

In short, as Levi-Strauss concluded, myths should be understood as machines for the suppression of the sense of passing time and space, giving onto a fixed point from which the world took and takes shape (1975:14–30); a conclusion Leach would then extend to ritual acts in general (1976b:44). As cultures were rooted in time and space (embodying genealogies of "blood, property and frontiers" (Carter 1992:7–8)), so cultures rooted societies and their members: organisms which developed, lived and died in particular places. Travel, Auge quipped (with Levi-Strauss in mind), was something mistrusted by this anthropology to the point of hatred (1995:86).

However, of late there has been a conceptual shift in the norms of anthropological commentary – brought about, perhaps, by the communications revolution of the past forty years and the perspective this gives onto (and itself evinces) of the globalisation of culture, of multi-culture replacing national culture: world markets, goods and labour, world polities, world music, taste and fashion, and, not least, world movement; or else brought about by the recent communicative revolution within anthropology *per se*, 'the reflexive turn' which, paradoxically, has seen the discipline look beyond itself, 'globally', to a world of other disciplines (Literature, Psychoanalysis, Biology) in terms of which it can hope to know itself better. As Keith Hart puts it (1990:*passim*), the world can no longer be divided up into framed units, territorial segments and the like, each of which shares a distinctive, exclusive culture, a definite approach to life. Rather: 'everyone is now caught between local origins and a cosmopolitan society in which all humanity increasingly participates'; human society is becoming more singular and inclusive. For a complex movement of people, goods, money and information – 'modernisation', the growing global economy, the induced, often brutally enforced migrations of individuals and whole populations from 'peripheries' towards Euro-American metropolises and Third World cities (Chambers 1994a:16); the migration of information, myths, languages, music, imagery, cuisine, decor, costume, furnishing, above all, persons (Geertz 1986:120–1) – brings even the most isolated areas into a cosmopolitan global framework of socio-cultural interaction. Here, with ways of life 'increasingly influencing, dominating, parodying, translating and subverting one another', there are no traditional, fixed and bounded cultural worlds from which to depart and to which to return: all is situated and all is moving (Clifford 1986:22).

Thus, John Berger argues that movement around the globe represents "the quintessential experience of our time" (1984:55; cf. Minh-ha 1994:13–14). Emigration, banishment, exile, labour migrancy, tourism, urbanisation and counter-urbanisation, are the central motifs of modern culture; being rootless, displaced between worlds, living between a lost past and a fluid present, are perhaps the most fitting metaphors for the journeying, modern consciousness: "typical symptoms of a modern condition at once local and universal" (Nkosi 1994:5).

Moreover, to bring together current forms of movement in this fashion, as Berger does, is not inevitably to essentialise movement: to claim 'it' is somehow always the same, an effect *sui generis*. Movement remains a polythetic category of experience: diverse, and without common denomination in its particular manifestations. Nor is it to underrate either the forces eventuating in large-scale population movement in the past (famine, plague, crusade, imperial conquest, urbanisation, industrialisation), or the forces arrayed against movement in the present (restrictive or repressive state or community institutions, state or community borders *per se*). To talk about the ubiquitous experience of movement is not to deny power and authority, and the differential motivations and gratifications in that experience which hierarchy might give onto. Rather, what Berger draws our attention to is the part movement plays in our modern imagination, and in our imaging of the modern. Movement is the quintessence of how we – migrants and autochthones, tourists and locals, refugees and citizens, urbanites and ruralites – construct contemporary social experience and have it constructed for us. As Iain Chambers concludes, wandering the globe is not now the expression of a unique tradition or history, for the erstwhile particular chronicles of diasporas – those of the black Atlantic, of metropolitan Jewry, of mass rural displacement – have come to constitute the broad ground-swell of modernity; modern culture is practised through, and the work of, wandering (1994a:16). And hence, anthropology has had increasing recourse to such concepts as 'creolisation' and 'compression', 'hybridisation' and 'synchronicity', to comprehend the changes that such movement causes to social and cultural environments – and to apprehend relations between movement and identity.

CREOLISATION AND COMPRESSION

Let me allude explicitly, if briefly, to three of these recent anthropological expositions, those of Lee Drummond, Ulf Hannerz and Robert Paine.

The culmination of 400 years of massive global migration, voluntary and involuntary, in the recent cultural impetus to modernise, urbanise and capitalise, and in movements of people and traffic in cultural items and information which have become continuous, have transformed most societies. However, the result of these transformations, Lee Drummond suggests (1980:*passim*), is neither new integrations of what were once separate societies and features of societies, now fitting neatly together as one, nor pluralities whereby old separate societies simply retain their cultural distinctivenesses side by side. Rather, what results are socio-cultural *continua* or combinations: "creolisations". Societies are no longer discrete social spaces with their own discrete sets of people and cultural norms – if they ever were. They are now basically creole in nature: combinations of ways of life, with no invariant properties or uniform rules. A series of bridges or transformations now lead across social fences and cultural divisions between people from one end of the continuum to the other, bridges which are in constant use as people swop artefacts and norms, following multiple and incompatible ways of life. Here is a "concatenation of images and ideas" (Drummond 1980: 363). And here, ultimately, is a world in which there 'are now no distinct cultures, only intersystemically connected, creolising Culture'.

Hence, Hannerz continues, the traditional picture of human cultures as forming a global mosaic – of cultures as plural, bounded, pure, integrated, cohesive, distinctive, place-rooted and mapped in space – must now be complemented by a picture of "cultural flows in space" (1993:68), and by "a global ecumene" (1992:34): a world system, a single field of persistent interaction and exchange, a continuous spectrum of interacting forms, which combines and synthesises various local cultures and so breaks down cultural plurality. That is, through mass media, objects of mass consumption, and the mass movements of people, culture now flows over vast distances. Indeed, it may be better to conceive of culture *tout court* as a flow. Thus, for Hannerz, the new world system does not result in socio-cultural homogeneity so much as a new diversity of interrelations: many different kaleidoscopes of cultural combinations, amounting to no discrete wholes, only heterogeneous and interpenetrating conglomerations. For people now draw on a wide range of cultural resources in the securing of their social identities, continually turning the erstwhile alien into their own; they select from the rich treasury of behaviours and beliefs which different cultural traditions now hold out to them, ranging between them, electing to have this and not that, to combine this with that, to move from this to this to that: to "listen to reggae, watch a western, eat McDonald's food for lunch and local cuisine for dinner, wear Paris perfume in Tokyo and "retro" clothes in Hong Kong" (Lyotard 1986:76); to make of each 'local' point a 'global' collage, a "Kuwaiti bazaar" (Geertz 1986:121). In short, people make sense to themselves and others by continually moving amongst a global inventory of ideas and modes of expression.

However, such movement is not smooth, Paine insists (1992:*passim*), nor is it singular. With individuals making different cultural selections and combinations – different to other individuals and different to themselves in other times and places; different in terms of particular items and their relative weighting, and different in terms of the willingness, loyalty and intensity of the selection – and combinations of elements not just previously separate but still incommensurable, so this movement amongst cultures can be expected to be volatile, and advocates of different selections to be exclusionary if not hostile. At the same time as there is globalisation, therefore, and movement across the globe, between societies and amongst cultures, as never before – people treating the whole globe as the cognitive space within which they can or must imagine moving and actually do move, the space which they expect to 'know' – there is also "cultural compression": an insistence of socio-cultural difference within the 'same' time and space; a piling up of socio-cultural boundaries, political, ritual, residential, economic, which feel experientially vital, and which people seek to defend and maintain. Here is a dialectic (not to say a Batesonian schismogenesis) between global movement and local compression (cf. Featherstone 1990:*passim*). So that even if travel is ubiquitous, and one is 'at home' on the entire globe, to travel within one's home is to encounter a world of socio-cultural difference; even to stay home is to experience global movement.

MOVEMENT AND HOME

Moving from Drummond to Hannerz to Paine is not to meet perfectly commensurable expositions of the contemporary world, and there is disagreement over the extent to which a globalisation of culture results in the continuing boundedness of social groups, as well as disagreement concerning the extent to which this globalisation is experienced as colonial or post-colonial – as the imposition of a particular cultural way of being-in-the-world or as the opportunity to constitute and reconstitute the set of cultural forms which go to make up one's life-way (cf. Appadurai 1990:*passim*). More significantly, there appears to be divergence concerning whether the thesis linking contemporary movement and identity is an historical one or a representational one. In particular, Drummond is happy to talk in terms of four centuries of change, while Paine's central motif is a comparison of could-be representations between E.M. Forster and Salman Rushdie. The historical argument would seem to be the harder one to make, and would also seem prone to the kinds of grand-historical reductionism which characterised conventional anthropology in its old dispensation (from 'fixity to movement' as from 'mechanical solidarity to organic', from 'community to association', from 'concrete thought to abstract', from 'hierarchy to individualism'). Certainly, Bateson's propositions claim universal pertinence, while the history and archaeology of frequent and global movement make generalisations about the uniqueness of the present foolhardy.

Where Drummond, Paine and Hannerz do meet is in a recognition of the contemporary significance of movement around the globe – its universal apperception, its ubiquitous relationship to socio-cultural identities. Whether or not this pertains to an historical shift, is imposed or opportunistic, there is in the contemporary world a sense in which metaphors and motifs of movement are of the quintessence in the conceptualisation of identity. In folk commentary as in social-scientific, there is a recognition of the fundamental relationship between movement and cultural practice and expression.

More particularly, there is an implicit recognition in the above anthropological expositions of the changing relations between movement and home. Increasingly, one is seen as moving between homes, erstwhile to current; or as moving between multiple homes (from one compressed socio-cultural environment to another); or as being at home in continuous movement (amongst creolised cultural forms); and so one's home as movement *per se*. This is certainly the explicit thesis of John Berger. For Berger, in an age which conceptualises itself in terms of global movement, the idea of 'home' undergoes dramatic change. In place of the conventional conception of home as the stable physical centre of the universe – a safe place to leave and return to – a far more mobile notion comes to be used: a home which can be taken along whenever one decamps. For a world of travellers and journeymen, home comes to be found far more usually in a routine set of practices, in a repetition of habitual social interactions, in the ritual of a regularly used personal name (cf. Rapport 1994:*passim*). It might seem, in Heidegger's words, as if "homelessness is coming to be the destiny of the world", but it is rather that there develops another sense of being-in-the-world. (It is not that in an age of global movement, there cannot be a sense of homelessness – far from it – but that a sense of home or of homelessness is not necessarily related in any simple or direct way with fixity or movement). One dwells in a mobile habitat and not in a singular or fixed, physical structure. Moreover, as home becomes more mobile so it comes to be seen as more individuated and privatised; everyone chooses their own, and one's choice might remain invisible (and irrelevant) to others' (cf. Rapport 1995:*passim*). In short, home is increasingly: "words, jokes, opinions, gestures, actions, even the way one wears a hat"; "no longer a dwelling but the untold story of a life being lived" (Berger 1984:64).

To recap: the emphasis on a relationship between identity and fixity has been at least challenged in anthropology of late by representations of the relationship between identity and movement. Now we have 'creolising' and 'compressing' cultures and 'hybridising' identities in a 'synchronising' global society. Part of this reconceptualisation pertains significantly to notions of home; part-and-parcel of this conceptual shift is a recognition that not only can one be at home in movement, but that movement can be one's very home. One's identity is "formed on the move": a "migrant's tale" of 'stuttering transitions and heterogeneities' (Chambers 1994a:24; 1994b:246–7). And the personal myths and rituals that one carries on one's journey through life (that carry one through a life-course) need not fix one's perspective on any still centre outside one's (moving) self. As Berger concludes, one is at home not in a thing or a place but 'in a life being lived in movement', and in an "untold story" (1984:64).

HOME AND STORY

The link Berger would make between home and story I find very provocative; and his claim that the story remains untold I find highly polemical. Because a story, a narrative, can itself be conceived of as a form of movement; and because stories, narratives, can be approached from two very different directions, the one describing the art of narration as the orderly telling of people, objects and events which did not previously exist, the ultimate creative act, and the other claiming, in contradistinction, that it is narratives which do the telling, which pre-exist their particular narrators, speak through the latters' lives unbeknown to them, and to that extent remain 'untold'. Let me elaborate.

Narrative has been defined as: "the telling (in whatever medium, though especially language) of a series of temporal events so that a meaningful sequence is portrayed – the story or plot of the narrative" (Kerby 1991:39). Also, narrative is the cultural form which is 'capable of expressing coherence through time' (Crites 1971:294). The content of narratives, then, treats a movement between events so as to give onto meaning and coherence in time. Also, the medium of narratives entails a movement from a start to a finish (if not a 'beginning' to an 'ending'), and is "everywhere characterised by movement": the passage of words, the slippage of metaphor, the caravan of thought, the flux of the imaginary, the movement of calligraphy (Chambers 1994a:10); the "consecution" of linguistic signs, the movement of meaning (Arshi *et al.* 1994:226). To recount a narrative, in short, is both to speak of movement and to engage in movement. One tells of people, objects and events as one moves them through time and one moves from the start of one's account to its end. Narrative mediates one's sense of movement through time, so that in the telling one becomes, in Rushdie's (telling) observation (1991:12), an emigre from a past home.

But precisely who or what does the telling, and who or what is told? Two answers are suggested. For Kerby, it is the narrative which tells the self of the narrator, which gives that self identity in the movement of the telling. The self arises out of signifying practices, coming to know itself and the world through enculturated narrational acts. In a particular socio-cultural environment, the self is given content, is delineated and embodied, primarily in narrative constructions or stories. It is these which give rise to the possibilities of subjectivity: "it is in and through various forms of narrative emplotment that our lives – ... our very selves – attain meaning" (1991:3). And being merely an outcome of discursive practice, the subject or self has no ontological or epistemological priority. Rather, 'persons' are to be understood as the result of ascribing subject status or selfhood to those 'sites of narration and expression' which we call human bodies. And the stories they tell of themselves and others are determined by the grammar of their language, by the genres of their culture, by the fund of stories of their society, and by the stories others tell and have told of them. In Crites's words (1971:295–7), consciousness 'awakes' to a culture's "sacred story". It is this story which forms consciousness and in which consciousness lives, rather than being something of which consciousness is directly aware. And it is of culture that this story tells, in the bodies and lives of its members: it is the story that tells, it is not told. In short, we are back with Levi-Strauss: "[M]yths think in men, unbeknownst to them"; not to mention Heidegger: "It is language that speaks, not Man. Man begins speaking but Man only speaks to the extent that he responds to, that he corresponds with language, and only insofar as he hears language addressing, concurring with him"; and Lacan: "Man speaks, then, but it is because the symbol has made him man"; "man is inhabited by the signifier".

But there is another answer to the question of narrative which allows that through narrative, human beings, individual men and women with agency, tell the world, and tell it anew, continuously reorganising their "habitation in reality" (Steiner 1975:23). Thus, for George Steiner, language might be conceived of as having a public and collective face but more significant than this is its individual and private base. At the base of every language-act resides 'a personal lexicon', 'a private thesaurus' constituted by the unique linguistic 'association-net' of personal consciousness: by the fact that each individual's understanding of language and the world is different. Embodied in language, therefore, are the 'minute particulars' of individuals' lives: the singular and specific ensembles of individuals' somatic and psychological identities. All but the most perfunctory of language-acts represent personal narratives in which individual speakers tell of themselves and their world-views.

Furthermore, it is the intensity of this personal association which causes individual users continually to make their language anew. Language, and discursive practice in general, is subject to mutation by its speakers at every moment and at bewildering speed; so that the concept of a normal or standard idiom in a community of speakers is a statistical fiction; and so that what is represented in the narratives which speakers and writers produce is the generation of a personal "language-world" and a new reality (Steiner 1978:155–6). In sum: "the language of a community, however uniform its social contour, is an inexhaustibly multiple aggregate of speech-atoms, of finally irreducible personal meanings" (Steiner 1975:46).

In these two approaches to narrative, it seems to me, we also find encapsulated the two notions of home that this essay has considered: home versus movement, and home as movement; and the two conceptualisations of identity that the essay features: identity through fixity, and identity through movement. That is, although both approaches recognise narrative as a form of movement in itself, recognise that movement is a ubiquitous feature of social life, the relationship each would posit between that movement and members of a social environment (the way each would posit individual narrators relative to that movement) is very different. The first approach, above, had the selves of narrators and recipients of a narrative fixed and stationary within a narrative, as it were. The narrative might move through them, but their identity derived from their maintenance of a position within it; if they were to move beyond the ambit of their culture's narrative constructions or their society's narrational acts, leave home as it were, they would no longer be recognisable 'sites of expression' and they would lose their ability to know, to perceive themselves and the world. This is equivalent to the traditional anthropological approach to the relationship between identity and fixity. Meanwhile, the second approach, above, has members of a sociocultural community continuously moving between different 'habitations of reality' as they tell different stories, remaking their language in the process. They are at home in personal narratives which move away from any notion of fixity within a common idiom, and their identities derive from telling moving stories of themselves and their world-views. And this is equivalent to a contemporary anthropological recognition of the relationship between identity and movement in the world today.

When Berger speaks of notions of home in an age of movement as increasingly to be found in 'untold stories', he seems to me to be sitting on the fence between two opposed positions. For untold stories leave their narrators stationary as the stories unfold, while the experience of the narrators he is describing is 'quintessentially' to be found in global transience.

Of course I am not being fair to Berger. What he means to say (cf. 1975), it is clear, is not (the post-structuralist point) that people in transit across the globe today do not tell stories because their condition is overdetermined by the systems of signification which make stories out of their lives and hence 'tell' them, but rather (the social-democrat point) that people in movement across the globe today do not have the resources (temporal, financial) to sit down and formally record the stories of their lives; and even if they did their stories would remain 'untold' because they would clamour for attention alongside millions of others; while those in a position to make their stories heard are deliberately suppressing them or at least ensuring that it is their own which are instead broadcast, disseminated and recorded.

None the less, the point I would make, the way I would have narratives understood, is somewhat different again. Because it seems to me that the world in motion that anthropology has now woken up to (and begun to address conceptually through 'creolisation', 'compression' and so on) brings to our attention something basic to the human condition, universal in human life, whatever the socio-cultural milieu, and whatever the conventions of representation; something which, over and against its history of conceptualisation, has always been (and will always be) true of human beings; something which Gregory Bateson was fully aware of some forty or fifty years ago, but which has somewhat slumbered in our anthropological consciousness since; something to which our disciplinal theorising, our will to fixed systems, has continued to blinker us. And that is the basic relationship between identity (knowledge, perception) and movement: the universal way in which human beings conceive of their lives in terms of a moving-between – between identities, relations, people, things, groups, societies, cultures, environments – as a dialectic between movement and fixity. It is in and through the continuity of movement that human beings continue to make themselves at home. Finally, they recount their lives to themselves and others as movement: they continually see themselves in stories, and continually tell the stories of their lives.

Needless to say, this is something of which commentators outside anthropology have claimed manifest (and manifold) awareness:

People are always in stories.

John Berger

We live in a narrative from breakfast to bedtime.

Robertson Davies

We all live out narratives in our lives and ... we understand our own lives in terms of the narrative that we live out.

Alasdair MacIntyre

Our lives are ceaselessly intertwined with narrative, with the stories that we tell and hear told, those we dream or imagine or would like to tell, all of which are reworked in that story of our lives that we narrate to ourselves in an episodic, sometimes semi-unconscious, but virtually uninterrupted monologue.

Peter Brooks

We dream in narrative, day-dream in narrative, remember, anticipate, hope, despair, believe, doubt, plan, revise, criticise, construct, gossip, learn, hate and love by narrative.

Barbara Hardy

Man is a sort of novelist of himself who conceives the fanciful figure of a personage with its unreal occupations and then, for the sake of converting it into reality, does all the things he does.

Ortega y Gasset

To be human is to be in a story.

Miles Richardson

Reading the narrative that these extra-anthropological commentaries (on narrative) amount to, cushioned and calmed by the repeating syllables, is surely to find oneself at home in the notion that it is in the motion of narrative that people are at home.

MOVEMENT AND ANTHROPOLOGY

There is one more twist in this tale. When the philosopher A.R. Louch proposed in 1966 that anthropology should be seen as a collection of travellers' tales – and that this was perfectly fine, the tales were "sufficient unto themselves" (1966:160) – few anthropologists would have been satisfied with his description.

This has now changed. Again in conjunction with a description of the ubiquity of movement in the world, with 'our heightened awareness of global interdependence, communication, diffusion, integration, sharing and penetration' and our allowance that anthropologists are no more aware of 'the world cosmopolitan consciousness' and its operation than their transient ethnographic subjects (Marcus and Fischer 1986:viii,38,86), with an appreciation that there is no fixed and stable Archimedean point at which to stand and observe because we are all historico-socio-culturally situated, because all knowledge is in flux (Clifford 1986:22), anthropology now conceives of its enterprise very differently. There is an acceptance that anthropology, in essence, is 'a kind of writing', 'a telling of stories', legitimate to the extent that it convinces its readers of the claim that its author and narrator has 'returned here' after 'being there': journeyed into 'another way of life' so as to inscribe 'what it was like There and Then in the categories and genres of the Here and Now' (Geertz 1988:1–5,140–5); and that cultures, indeed, need to be rethought 'in terms of travel' (Clifford 1992:101). In short, there is now an acceptance that anthropological knowledge derives from movement and represents itself through movement; the identity of the anthropologist is inextricably bound up with his having undertaken a cultural journey – a journey into reflexivity, a journey alongside other cosmopolitan journeymen – and the proper home of the anthropologist is the narrative account of his journeying.

To the travelling of 'the other', the informant (whether exile, migrant, tourist or counter-urbanite), then, must now be added "the increasing nomadism of modern thought", no longer bolstered by sites and sightings of absolutism (Chambers 1994a:18; also cf. Grimshaw 1994b:*passim*), no longer persuaded by fixed, totalising ways of thinking relations (Strathern 1990b:38). So that Louch's statement is now doubly true: anthropology as a study of travellers as well as by travellers.

In conclusion, the notion that the study of social life and the study of story-telling might focus in common on a fundamental feature of the human condition, namely the relationship between movement and identity, and the crucial place of movement in the acquisition and representation of knowledge, seems to me far from frivolous. In Butor's 'iterology', anthropology might find a suitable home (one of many) in which to know itself and its subjects in the contemporary world.

Chapter 5

"Surely Everything Has Already Been Said About Malinowski's Diary!"

In the cover photograph of the latest edition of Malinowski's *A Diary in the Strict Sense of the Term* (1989), Malinowski appears in angelic white (somewhat overexposed) surrounded by three 'fuzzy headed savages'. Malinowski's shirt, trousers and boots look white, his hands, his pate. The only black things about him are his tinted spectacles, as he peers darkly through the glass onto the native world, and the lime pot and spatula he holds between his legs, like his fellow chiefly sitters. But while they earnestly look at the camera or at their spatula, Malinowski stares off into space, his whole body angled askance; it is as if a ghostly image had been superimposed upon a blank in the native scene. Moreover, it less appears as if Malinowski had decided upon his lime pot and his heavier-than-average spatula, and the decorated kula armshell which he (alone) dangles from a forearm, than that he had been adorned with them: he sanctifies the scene like some idol ... "Posed before the *niggers*" (*Diary* 27.1.1918).

On this front, it does not appear as if the canon of translation-via-liminality, of anthropology 'not in a culture or an era but dialectically in between' (Boon 1982:237), is provided with the most compelling of exemplars. But then the *Diary* is not to be judged by its cover, I shall argue in this essay; nor by its title, for Malinowski's diarian writings in the field are as important a professional product as his more generically conventional publications, allowing us an insight into the authorial self of the individual who wrote the social reality of "The Trobriands".

Malinowski frequently iterates how his Melanesian fieldwork location amounted to a 'wretched prison'. Distant from erstwhile friends and mother in Poland, lovers in London, fiancée in Melbourne and conscripted peers in war-torn Europe, estranged from the missionaries and the mass of 'negroes', and in only superficial contact with his own 'boys' and neighbouring white expatriates, Malinowski cuts an extremely marginal figure. Geertz (1967) has pointed out how passionately Malinowski seemed to be living in a European world while working in a Melanesian one, and the diary is indeed peppered by anxious reference to outside relations and states of affairs he is powerless to intercept; his writing is punctuated by the reconstruction and reconsideration of far-off places and people: Z., T., N., Mother, Stas., N.S., E.R.M. It is these and his books, letters and memories which Malinowski primarily uses as yardsticks to judge behaviour and evaluate events, nothing immediate possessing that much reality except as metaphorical comment or reflection (the woman Ineykoya's death and the Death in Europe). There may be Swedish gymnastics to perform here, photography, 'plump blondes', pretty 'neolithic savages' to be 'pawed' (when they are not 'performing some strange ritual') – all of which can be diverting, when not vexing – but it hardly compares to the whirlpool of occurrence (however horrible) back in civilisation and beyond reach. In his prison, that is, Malinowski does not serve what denizens of a criminal under-world would deem 'good time', instead catching himself in a number of hopeless love–hate triangles: civilisation – savages – resident colonialists; Polish culture – Anglo Saxon – German; writing ethnography – reading novels – living lustily.

It is unbearable, and Malinowski is unable to decide from one day to another, where he stands; disgusted by his lack of real character in ever having left Europe, he longs to return. But then how can he return so precipitously without first assuring himself of the wherewithal for achieving notoriety once he lands? Malinowski rarely forgets his mission, in fact scorning his expatriate neighbours who have "such fabulous *opportunities* – the sea, ships, the *jungle*, power over the natives – and can't do a thing!" (27.12.17). True, some days he cannot face ethnology himself, the life of the natives seeming "utterly devoid of interest or importance", "as remote from me as the life of a dog" (27.12.17), and then he escapes into 'trashy novels'. He is always brought back, however, by the remembrance of the mark he will make on the outside world, and by thoughts of his 'external ambitions': Sir, *Who's Who*, FRS, CSI (17–24.6.18). But then what is doubly unbearable for this liminal figure is the fear that the war-torn outside society will not survive long enough for him to be somebody within: indeed, having left it will he ever again regain entry, and on what level? Is it not an unbearable irony that the means selected for achieving fame in his chosen society should take him to its very savage edge! Hence his conundrum: the longer he stays *in situ* the more capital he can potentially store: while the longer he stays away the more likely those ensconced in civilisation will have forgotten his departure or that he was ever there.

But Malinowski does not return, at least not immediately, which is the significant point. The diary (rather like those memorial knots in Dinka grass, of Liendhardt's later, celebrated description) is a cognitive *aide mémoire* which keeps Malinowski's place in the outside world open: keeps the memory quick, and stows it securely until he really can return to it. The outside world might seem like a dream (or conversely, the Trobriand world might seem like a nightmare), but through his diarian writings, Malinowski is able to keep the two in cognitive connection: to make some sense of each in relation to the other (cf. Riches 1995:*passim*).

Not that this is Malinowski's purported logic behind his diary-keeping; at least not in so many words. He professes to seek to 'record events in chronological order so as to morally evaluate them, locate the mainsprings of his life and plan the future' (28.9.17). "The chief defect of the English", he elaborates, is "lack of 'stratification' in their lives": they do not systematise events continuously, just letting one flow after and replace another (22.11.17). By means of the diary, Malinowski would do differently, and achieve a deeper view not only of the history of events (for these are mere subjective constructs anyway (13.11.17)), but also "feelings and instinctual manifestations" (25.11.17). Thus he would 'consolidate his life and avoid fragmenting themes' (6.1.18).

Malinowski describes this procedure as 'conversing with himself', and as "a means of self-analysis" (31.5.18). What is significant here is not just that, as Hoebel pointed out (1967), identifying the essentials of his self and belabouring its defects served Malinowski as 'a device of naive self-therapy' in a situation of intense loneliness and alienation; (where, Forge continues, there is only one person who can start to understand how the fieldworker feels and that is himself (1967; and cf. Stocking 1974)). What is also significant is the form Malinowski's self-knowledge took. Structuring the endless variety of things in his life, isolating, classifying and grasping the deeper currents afforded a means of finally keeping things apart, of keeping a European self pure: "[t]he taming of my lusts, the elimination of lecherousness, concentrating on E.R.M."; such interim sacrifices afforded ultimate happiness and contentment "much greater than just letting go does" (16.1.18). In short, isolating the moral mainsprings of his life entailed remaining true to an external 'Utilitarian hedonist' identity, and eschewing the temptations of a proximate one.

Also of note is the way the diary tends to becomes a capitalized noun for Malinowski and often referred to without a definite article or personal pronoun, as if a cherished place, person or exercise in its own right: "I should take a deeper view of things when writing diary" (25.11.17); "I was pensive; thought about diary and integrating life throughout the day" (6.1.18): one could almost substitute 'Mother' or 'E.R.M.' for 'diary' here. And (vagaries of translation, and of Polish grammatical practices of articling, aside) this makes it pertinent to enquire how we might relate this scriptorial production to others: how is the diary appropriately contextualized in Malinowski's writing practices?

Writing the diary, Leach wanted to emphasise (1967b), is not Malinowski's whole person, not the balanced recorder of his inner personality, but a traumatised fieldworker. Whilst one may want to question Leach's ideal type whereby one text could ever represent the 'balance' of an 'holistic' character, certainly the diary appears partial: it is the 'Mr Hyde' of dreamed of beaches at Folkestone, misspent moments in London, and promenades in Paris, imprisoned in the 'Dr Jekyll' of Mailu, Samarai and Kiriwina. It is in this context, too, that Clifford's comment that Malinowski's diary and *The Argonauts of the Western Pacific* amount to a 'single expanded text' (1986b) makes most sense. For here are the scriptorial representations of two of Malinowski's many part-identities – the exile and the ethnographer – and the dialectical tension between them: each cathartically freed, each embarrassed and delegitimized by the other. Hence, *contra* Malinowski himself, it is not so "remarkable how intercourse with whites ... makes it impossible for me to write the diary" (7.4.18): the diarian self is an expression of a European exiled among Melanesians.

In his introduction to the first edition of the diary, in 1966, Raymond Firth stressed that publication was never intended; (and Malinowski did not live long enough, as Lewis commented (1968), for him to authorise publication and thus cap his career with what would have been a characteristically shocking and disarming *volte face*). Notwithstanding, for the sake of psychological and emotional insights into an outstanding personality (not to mention the royalties) his widow determined otherwise, and so, he, Firth, was keen to introduce the text in such a way as to dampen Malinowski's seeming vitriol and vituperation and draw some of the teeth of the expected criticism. In a second introduction written in 1988, Firth reviews the reception of the publication: from those censorious of all involved in the venture (Powdermaker, Richards, Leach), to those more narrowly disapproving of Malinowski (Hogbin, Geertz 1967) to those more or less approbative (Hoebel, Stocking, Forge, Clifford, Geertz 1988). Where I feel this discussion suffers is in its overriding emphasis on the publish/not-publish dichotomy, and insufficient concentration on the possibly dense and complex, not to say inconsistent, set of relations between one written text and another, between one writerly persona and another. The diary was one piece of work, one set of thoughts, one conversation among many, and the imposition of a public versus private distinction as a definitional frame can be misleading, almost an irrelevancy. For it cuts across the lineaments of Malinowski's own social, not to say intellectual and cognitive environments and greatly impoverishes our appreciation. Let me suppose . . .

> The boy, amazed like the rest of us, raised the light to the man's face. It was black. A surprised hum – a faint hum that sounded like the suppressed mutter of the word 'Nigger' – ran along the deck and escaped out into the night. The nigger seemed not to hear. . . . He held his head up in the glare of the lamp – a head vigorously modelled into deep shadows and shining lights – a head powerful and misshapen with a tormented flattened face – a face pathetic and brutal: the tragic, the mysterious, the repulsive mask of the nigger's soul. . . . '. . . Did you see the eyes of that sick nigger, Mr Baker? I fancy he begged me for something. What? Past all help. One lone black beggar amongst the lot of us, and he seemed to look through me into the very hell.'
>
> Joseph Conrad (Konrad Korzeniowski)
> *The Nigger of the Narcissus* 1897

Nigger . . . brutal . . . soul . . . sick . . . black . . . beggar . . . us . . . hell.

(21.12.17) All that day longing for civilization. I thought about friends in Melbourne. At night in the <u>dinghy</u>, pleasantly ambitious thought: I'll surely be 'an eminent Polish scholar'.

(21.1.18) In the morning, characteristic <u>irritability</u>: the <u>niggers</u> got on my nerves. ... Then I felt a certain relief: began to look at all this – through all this – from outside: <u>Ende gut, alles gut</u>. But if <u>this</u> were to be the end – feeling that I am choking, that the claws of death are strangling me alive ... ; then sat a moment by the sea, content with the stagnation and solitude, when I heard that Ineykoya's condition was worse – she was groaning loudly. I went to see: she had another haemorrhage, groaned horribly, and was apparently dying. I thought of the horrible torment of a haemorrhage and of N.S. and suddenly felt that I was deserting her. I also felt that I wanted to be with her at any cost, to allay her sufferings. Strong reaction. I also thought of E.R.M. and in my nervous disarray I told myself: '<u>the shadow of death is between us and it will separate us</u>'. ... Through all this the cruel <u>customs</u> of the <u>niggers</u> – who were again washing her, preparing her for death.

(25.1.18) During the night Inekoya died. Got up at 3.30 and went there. Deep Impression. <u>I lose my nerve</u>. All my despair, after all those killed in the war, hangs over this miserable Melanesian hut.

(11.2.18) Moments of frightful longing to get out of this rotten hole.

> *[Underlinings indicate foreign words written thus by*
> *Malinowski amid the Polish text].*
> Bronislaw Malinowski
> *A Diary in the Strict Sense of the Term* 1914–18

Civilisation ... eminent ... Polish ... niggers ... outside ... stagnation ... cruel ... death ... war ... hole.

(February 14) Halt at Bouges – French and English soldiers on platform. American camps on the way. Black men in khaki at Cherbourg. Brown landscapes.

The beginning of a new adventure. I am already half way into my campaigning dream life. Funny mixture of reality and crude circumstance with inner 'flame-like' spiritual experience.

(April 23) When I compare the agony of last year with the present, I am glad to find a wider view of things. I am slowly getting outside it all. Getting nearer to the secret places of the heart also, and recognising its piteous limitations. I recognise the futility of war more than ever, and, dimly, I see the human weakness that makes it possible. For I spend all my days with people who, with a very few exceptions, are too indolent-minded to think for themselves. Sometimes I feel as if this slow steady growth of comprehension will be too much to bear. But, if I am not mad, I shall one day be great. And if I am killed this year, I shall be free.

Siegfried Sassoon
Diaries 1915–18

English . . . American . . . Black . . . dream-life . . . futility . . . outside . . . war . . . mad . . . great . . . killed.

Malinowski's diary is one piece in a puzzle. Or rather puzzles, since there are any number for construction: The Intimate Diary Of The Social Commentator puzzle (Stendhal, Malinowski, de Sade), The Diary Of The First World War Gentleman puzzle (Sassoon, Malinowski, Forster), The Writings of European Expatriates In South-East Asia puzzle (Conrad, Malinowski, Kipling), and the Malinowski Trobriand Corpus puzzle (*Argonauts*, *Diary*, *Sexual Life of Savages*), to name four. And in the same way as Stendhal's journey of 'absolutely truthful' daily jottings of 'intimate thoughts, emotions, sensations and events, however trivial and insignificant', allows us to trace a course to his ensuing novelistic style, not to mention moral philosophy, so Malinowski's diary provides clues to the development of his ideas on culture contact and change (17.11.14), on individuality and institutionality (22.12.17/1.6.18), on field methods (6.3.18/21.3.18) and on religion (31.5.18).

More than this, of course, is a diary's presumable importance as an instrument for its maker to journey from one thought, one conversation, one composition, to another. That is, over and above the stated aims of the daily diary – the better to ponder the mysteries of the human heart (Stendhal): the better to add depth to life and reflect on its integration (Malinowski) – we may gain a broader conception of what in his daily mental life, the writer saw fit to transpose. Malinowski may have written his diary by and large in Polish, his fieldnotes in Kiriwinian and English, and his letters to his fiancée in English and lovey-dovey, and he may have written each at different times, thinking through different world-views, but it was all the time written by 'Malinowski', and the connections should be traceable from one text to another, however partial, which more properly contextualize the thoughts in each.

The issue at the centre of much of the discussion about publication, needless to say, is not an invasion of privacy, for all those sorts of intimacies have been diligently excised at the copy-editing stage. Rather it is the light (the shadow) thrown upon Malinowski's racial prejudices. This strikes me as anachronistic. We cannot expect Malinowski to speak outside his social contexts, or in our own. True, Malinowski writes about 'niggers', 'negroes', 'brutes', 'boys', and 'savages', but then we read the same in Conrad in his similarly introspective encounters with primaevality in the South Seas. Again, Malinowski bandies about stereotypical descriptions of Anglo-Saxons, Germans, Poles, Negroes and Australians which gloss individual particulars, but then we find the same in Sassoon, writing similarly from the margins of society, in the shadow of social death, and similarly depicting identities pared down and choked off. Words come to taste of particular 'contextual accents and intentions', Bakhtin advises (1981:293ff.); from Conrad, Malinowski and Sassoon we can identify a certain cognate relationship between words such as: *nigger / brutal / black / death / hell / war / Europe / civilisation / dream / famous*, which Saussure might have isolated as 'an associative set'.

Furthermore, Bakhtin goes on to describe the common practice in complex societies of words being borrowed from contexts of normal usage to effect certain special statements in others: to affect erudition, for example, attempt satire, or social climbing, or savoir-faire. And sometimes the words are so out of place (polluting, dangerous, powerful) that they cannot be said with a straight face: they must be spoken as if in inverted commas, alluding to a quoted source. Or so one would claim. For the inventing of inverted commas ('Surely everything . . . !') both affords the use of polluted words while at the same time a disowning of their standard intentions and implications. Malinowski seems to admit to such verbal borrowing in his diary in two ways. First there is his use of inverted commas to separate off certain phrases: "headache but no feeling of hopeless despair; I felt rotten, but 'not beyond endurance'" (28.10.17) – the ironical quotation marks helping focus and relieve the campness of the hypochondria, the self-love of personal ailments and faults. (Similarly, Sassoon's "'flame-like' spiritual experience" qualifies the simile and helps diffuse its excessive unreality). Second there is Malinowski's polyglot use of English, German, French, Spanish, Greek, Latin and Kiriwinian terms liberally interspersed among the text's basal Polish. Together these borrowings would seem to include much of Malinowski's so-called racist terminology: from the English slang and literary references such as "bloody niggers" or "'Exterminate the brutes'", to the "'pandemonium'" to which his social life among savages amounts. And these borrowings are metacommunicative, I suggest: messages about code as much as content. It is not only that, as translator Norman Guterman footnotes (quoting Webster's New International Dictionary, 2nd edition), 'nigger' was the colloquial term Europeans of the time commonly used to denote natives of the dark-skinned races (Malinowski like Conrad) and, indeed, had been at least since 1857 (OED). More importantly it is that Malinowski used certain terms tongue-in-cheek (like Sassoon): a self mocking reference to Conrad's *Heart of Darkness*, to feeling a "'sahib'" with his "boys". And what is being metacommunicated is that this is not the straight talking of a person at ease with the social milieu, but rather one living in "a continuous ethical conflict" (24.12.17), terribly aware of "the gulf between me and the human beings around me" (11.5.18). Malinowski (unlike Conrad in this) is not observing 'one lone black nigger among the lot of us', but the reverse: one miserable white exile whose estrangement is such that, deprived of a vocabulary of descriptive metonymy to express his feelings of *dépaysement*, he resorts to an exaggerated metaphorisation: "sloshing in the mud", "shadow of death", and so on. Little wonder that Powdermaker and Montagu (1967) find no shadow of such a persona darkening Malinowski's other writings or his later relations with them, his students. The diaries cover an interior conversation and what Winch would call 'internal relations' conducted during nineteen highly stressful months of fieldwork by an unconfident, unhappy, unmarried man who was soon to be left behind.

Besides the proprieties of publication, questions have been raised from the early reviews onwards concerning the fitness of the translation and editing of the diary. Now that a second edition has been issued and a wider, younger audience can already be expected to be engaged, these questions might seem somewhat extraneous. Certainly for this reader, the text flows well enough; I was only brought to a halt by odd occasions where the translator's American spelling radically affected the tenor of the account: Malinowski singing (19.12.17) in time to a Wagner melody the words: "Kiss my Ass" – not 'Arse', as he chases away flying Trobriand witches, sounds to me more like him imitating Clark Gable than Chaliapin. But then what lies behind much of the doubt about the accuracy of the text (e.g. for Leach 1967b) is, no doubt, the selfsame fear of having Malinowski dubbed racist – and the 'absurdity' that this would represent. From this angle, it seems that a new treatment of the text is very much *not* warranted. Even though the acrimonious exchange between Leach and Hsu in the *Royal Anthropological Institute News* (1980:nos 36,39,40) raises doubts about what Valetta Malinowski compliments in her Preface in 1966 as the 'very direct manner' in which Guterman rendered the diary in translation in the early 1960s, on this point I would tend to agree with Hsu. That is, although Guterman is not consistent with his translational symbols, so that not every italicised reference to 'nigger(s)' would seem to signify an English word in the original (as he claims), and at least some are his interpretations of the Polish term *'negr/nigr(ami)'*, I am not convinced by Leach's suggested replacement of today's 'loaded' term with "nothing more contentious than 'blacks'" (1980). For, as Hsu points out and as we have seen, Malinowski does explicitly refer to '<u>bloody niggers</u>', to 'savages', to his "white rage and hatred for bronze-coloured skin" (24.4.18), to his vexation at niggers having the effrontery to aim at him disapproving remarks (11.5.18), and more besides. Translating '<u>negrami</u>' as 'niggers' accords with dictionary convention (e.g. Trzaska, Evert and Michalski 1946 [1927]) and does no injustice to the tenor of the surrounding prose. Nor, again, would an alternative be so easy to find. 'Coloureds', to my mind, has its own highly distinctive connotations which were not Malinowski's, and he always uses 'negro' and 'black' as separate terms. '<u>Negrami</u>' I understand to be a Polish borrowing (distinct from Polish words for 'Blacks' or 'Negroes') to which has been suffixed a standard pluralisation (Jola Glaser: personal communication). It is also described by the dictionary as 'contemptuous' (Kosciuszko 1961). By analogy with such macaronic usage as 'Yids' in English (from the German/Yiddish '<u>Juden/Yidden</u>') in place of the standard 'Jews', not much doubt need remain about the derogation involved, however ironically it is alluded to. In short, I doubt that a re-translation could get us any closer to Malinowski's motivations. What it may do instead is approach more nearly latter-day terminological conventions, and that change in ethos I would take as a cause of regret. Indeed, in the present climate, with our admitted and admissible interests in auto-biography (our recognition that the self of the anthropologist is his or her main ethnographic tool and self-consciousness the major methodology (cf. Cohen 1986)), it would seem an inadmissible tampering. We must beware reconstructing Malinowski as a hero within the frame of our own sensibilities: ancestors who are also contemporaneous are creatures of myth.

Personally, I find the diary more refreshing than offensive. It is also tedious and bitty – but then so is fieldwork – and repetitive and humdrum – but then in no other fashion could it preserve for Malinowski, as if in amber, the routine home life beyond the field, ready to go back to, and thus free him for the flights of fancy necessary for launching into and apprehending an ethnographic situation. What is refreshing is that, as Firth stresses in his 1966 Introduction, here is such a very 'human document': *ecce homo*. Nietzsche once wrote how 'even mould ennobles' and I suppose I had been wandering around with an image of Malinowski, his remote Melanesian locale and the distant date of 1922, as so far removed as to be unreachable: a Founding Father now ascended into ethereal mists, and out of the realms of discourse. But here is revealed no effortless model-builder, no model of saintly com-passion, no selfless philanthropist, no shy backwoodsman, no Europhobe. Here is someone with humour, with cynicism, with idio-syncrasy, who dreams of physical comforts while flippantly musing about his girlfriend: "Too bad that E.R.M. does not dance in my style. *Adage*: 'Those who dance well together, won't live in har-mony'" (15.11.17). It is not, as Firth fears, that here I can find ready ammunition for exploding the myth of Malinowski. It is that the diary makes Malinowski real for me. I do not kid myself, of course, that here is the real or essential Malinowski; I accept, as Leonard Woolf noted in the preface to his wife's posthumous journals, that however seemingly unexpurgated, the portrait offered by a diary is the biased account of a diarist in the habit of writing probably only when in a certain mood; and however seemingly disorganised and non-hierarchical it may be with regard to subject matter, vocabu-lary *et al.*, in comparison with other writings, a diary is nevertheless more consciously stylised than stream of consciousness.

Nevertheless, courtesy of the diary, here is someone with whom I can more easily enter into dialogue. I can sympathise with Malinowski's disliking of fieldwork, his overcoming the chasm of empty days by ticking each one off. I can disagree with his witnessing of an extreme rigidity of native habit "going back to the age of polished stone" (12.11.14). I can share in his appreciative reading of Stevenson, Swinburne, Shaw, Charlotte Bronte, Maupassant, Macchiavelli, Hardy, H.G. Wells, Conrad, Kipling, Conan Doyle and others. Of course, when he injects himself with arsenic, cocaine and morphine, having diagnosed certain obtrusive bodily humours, and then complains about days of lethargy and numbness that follow, he comes to sound more like a Conan Doyle character himself than an admirer of them, and when he talks about meeting 'Baldie', 'Miss H.U.', 'Mrs Henderson', and 'Capt Hope' for supper or 11 o'clock tea, and conversation about natives, planters, missionaries and the latest mail, it is as if he has stepped out of a scene from Somerset Maugham. As with those telling mundanities in Ralph Josselin's seventeenth-century journals (Macfarlane 1976), Malinowski's diary situates him historically and culturally: an individual engaged in practices similar to mine in some respects and largely dissimilar in others.

In sum, as it stands, unfashionably stylistic foibles and all, the diary offers revealing glimpses that link the person who, in 1918, wrote of "the revolution" he wanted to wreak in social anthropology (5.6.18) to what Strathern has described as the revolutionary style of ethnographic reportage of the 1920s for which those efforts have come to stand (1987:258); as such, the diary is an important building block in the intellectual history of the discipline. I should place the diary, as it stands, beside *Argonauts of the Western Pacific* or *Coral Gardens and their Magic* on any pre-fieldwork seminar reading list (while regretting the impossibility of further comparison with his English and Kiriwinian field diaries). Only one with another do we gain a better appreciation not only of what Malinowski intended to say – however his words have been more widely interpreted – but also how he came to say what he did. As a heuristic tool for illustrating fieldwork moods, for uncovering relations between happenstance and hypothesis, for exhibiting the gulf between notebook jottings – "I had a drink with Everett; he spoke about <u>kula</u> and maintained that Misima was not in the <u>kula</u>" (17.11.17) – and classic (or merely completed) monographs, between initial ideas – 'should observe savages on the spot more, should speak their language' (27.9.14) – and the myths they ultimately spawn, and for raising doubts about how those gulfs were and continue to be spanned, the diary is indispensable.

In a most level-headed review, Coy (1980) suggested that 'if Malinowski's diary had not been revealed by a public-spirited second wife, we should almost have had to have invented it'. It is the least we can do now not to disclaim it.

Chapter 6

Writing Fieldnotes
On the conventionalities of note-taking and taking note, local and academic

INTRODUCTION

Fieldnotes. The Makings of Anthropology is a collection of papers, edited by Roger Sanjek (1990a), which concerns itself with a reflexive "unpacking" of the anthropological practice of writing down notes in the field as prologue to writing-up in the academy. In this essay, I review the efforts of Sanjek and his contributors before arguing that the writing of notes in the field may be understood as embodied local practice quite as much as academic abstraction. Fieldnotes possess (at least) a dual conventionality and encapsulate a 'magical' transcendence. More broadly, the practice of 'writing' social reality, of transforming experience into text, into a meaningful narrative, represents a link between the anthropologist and his subjects of study rather than a distinction.

FIELDNOTES

"What does the ethnographer do?" Geertz rhetorises, "He writes" (1973:19). This being the case, it is more than a little significant, Sanjek suggests (1990b:xii-xiii), the sensitive, not to say taboo topic which fieldnotes represent. Even in accounts by anthropologists which aim at the confessional, and despite current deliberation on writing ethnography and ethnographic writing, fieldnotes are passed over. Hence, Sanjek sets out to provide us with a vocabulary for discussion: the variety of fieldnote types, their distinction from letters and diaries; the history of fieldnote usage, the patterns and changes of the past century; the diverse impact of fieldnotes beyond an immediate writer-reader, upon the publications which follow, upon the researches and archives which inherit them.

Sanjek's project can be seen as part of a continuing debate in which many are now fruitfully engaged (and not only in the US (cf. Ellen 1984; Barnard and Good 1984; Paine 1987)): an ideological appreciation of the working conventions of anthropological procedure. His volume was prompted by a charge of James Clifford's that we have yet to address the very first avenue through which anthropology defines and maintains its objects of study. Sanjek agreed, and so invited Clifford first to do so here. Clifford entitles his paper: 'Notes on (Field)notes'.

Ensconced in "the field" – that distant place (Appadurai) and time (Fabian) – anthropologists turn from the momentary encounters of participant-observation to produce an inscribed account which can be reconsulted (Clifford 1990:*passim*). From events which exist only in their moments of occurrence, multivocal and polysemic, they select, translate and narrate 'a day's impressions'. This writing down is composed of three distinct modes which blend and alternate rapidly. There is *inscription* – the writing of notes, keywords and mental impressions; there is *transcription* – the writing of dictated local texts; and there is *description* – the final writing of coherent reflections and analyses, facilitating a later retrieval of overall sense and order. Here, in short, is a prefigured and pre-encoded way of anthropologists discovering and describing things in the field. Writing fieldnotes amounts to a disciplinary institution, Clifford concludes: we abide by a convention whereby 'fieldwork' eventuates in a discrete textual corpus, a raw or partly cooked database from which generalisations, syntheses and theoretical elaborations will thereafter be derived.

Other contributions to Sanjek's volume are then concerned with exposing how fieldnotes are totemic emblems whose idolisation stems from a nineteenth century obsession with the scientist as fact-knapper; how they rather represent knowledge acquisition through pioneering creativity and rebellion; and how they then become our surrogate descendants. It is recognised, moreover, that important questions remain concerning how, precisely, these *aides-mémoire* are to be later read and appreciated. Can anthropologists' fieldnotes be appropriated by others, say their fellow-professionals? Can the qualitative reportage be quantified? In what way should the notes of anthropologists who work in politically touchy environments, without the licence of any special status, be 'protected'? And such questions arise, Rena Lederman contends (1990:72), precisely because we maintain such a suspicious silence about fieldnotes. Little wonder, as Clifford observes (1990:52) that we can reach disciplinary consensus neither about what or how to note in the field nor what or how to write up afterwards.

In fine, the vision which inspires Sanjek's *Fieldnotes* is of universality of information. If the reflexivity of recent years has been built upon "the promise and premise of a world anthropology" (Sanjek 1990c:40), a professional world where "other-fucking in its more vulgar forms is drawing to a close" (1990c:41), then the professionalisation (collective definition, typification and incorporation) of fieldnotes is an inevitable part of the process.

COMMENTARY

Sentiment and American graphic fashion aside, Şanjek's image is an unfortunate one. As is Margery Wolf's, of reflexivity as the exposure of "wounds" to the light: our latest cure for the anthropological "disease" (1990:343). Because anthropology is not a disease and never was. And there is no alternative to 'other-fucking' besides social death.

I do not mean to be glib here. Anthropology cannot proceed without the closest of mutual engagements with the socio-culturally other. In the past such engagements may have eventuated in monologic, skewed reporting, but a dialogic future can only be planned and gained through further engagement. Similarly, in attempting a 'cure' for past anthropological reporting, to focus on the academic conventionality of note-taking alone – and eschew indigenous usage – is to continue a one-sided viewing.

To elaborate, there is the familiar description in *Fieldnotes* of field-research as both an 'ordeal by fire' and a 'promised land' (Jackson 1990:33). Here is a recognition of the homology between an anthropologist's field trip and a neophyte's vision quest; both are formalised (ritualised, stylised) engagements between a community member and what is powerfully (dangerously) marginal to that community. And what Sanjek's volume does well to draw out for the 'tribe' of anthropologists is the point Hoebel and Wallace once persuasively made for the Comanche: on returning from their individual vision quests, the braves-within-the-collectivity habitually interpreted the traumas of their vigil conventionally, as the acquisition of Bear, Buffalo or Eagle power rather than that of lesser supernaturals (Mosquito or Mouse) or new supernaturals (1958:208). What is omitted from *Fieldnotes*, however, is a concomitant appreciation of fieldnotes as *local* documents, which is what I wish to address here.

In brief, I would describe writing fieldnotes not as something which simply abstracts anthropologists from the field and ties them to a self in the academy but as something which simultaneously immerses them deeply in the conventions of a subject community and the self they become there. The fieldwriter deploys *a dual conventionality*, and writing fieldnotes is the formal expression of this duality.

THE DUALITY OF FIELDNOTES

Fieldnotes occupy that abyss between "the brute material of information . . . and the final authoritative presentation of results", Malinowski explained (1961:3–4). Putting it another way (and softening the seeming brute factuality of our 'information' from the field), we might say that fieldnotes are imbued with the conventional reality, the norms of note-taking, of two forms of life; fieldnotes possess and impart to their writer a dual conventionality, local as well as academic.

Moreover, here are conventions which often are very different, contradictory, incomparable. Yet they meet through the strange journey and later the imagination of the fieldworker: the imagination to insist that the persona writing the notes in the field and the persona reading the notes in the academy are both 'his' (or 'hers').

Nevertheless, fieldnotes do not bridge this abyss, or represent a synthesis which provides any simple, linear, repeatable route from field to academy and back. Instead, in the academy the fieldnotes can appear the artefacts of a dream – residues which evidence some perverted reality. In style as well as content fieldnotes bear witness to, amount to, the experiences of another self, that of the fieldwriter. Here is the anthropologist writing according to the conventions of registering information, taking note, of the field. For example:

9.00–11.30 M
  darts – Askrig/Gordon (jokily writ up as God on bd to score) + Phil/Tom (whitewashed > uses excuse of arm – can't raise it – Steven can see that its hurting him – Tom anxiously greases up to Phil who = "friendly" to him) + me/Billy.

> *Doms table Arthur/Jane/Alfred/Kate.*
> *Arrogant, alone Nicholas centre bar avoids the co. as pop grease up eg Steven, Billy, John H. (tries in vain to buy him a 1/2) – Alex M. (tries in vain to tell him about Hayley's comet coming – what's that? Kev doesn't know date either. -Nicholas is it a star → Alex's yes with a tale.*
> *[nb how all try + talk to Nicholas but lose his interest before they finish their sentence.]*
> *Bronwen serving makes my pasty.*

I could 'translate':

> 9 p.m. – 11.30 p.m. I spend at the Mitre pub. Playing darts are Askrig and Gordon (who has written up his name on the scoreboard as 'God', instead of 'Gord', as a joke); also Phil and Tom (who loses badly, and excuses himself on the grounds of an injured arm which he can barely lift: Steven can see it is hurting him. Nevertheless, Tom is anxious to win Phil over; Phil puts on a blatantly friendly face in return). Billy and me play darts too.
>
> With arrogant demeanour, Nicholas sits alone at the centre of the bar counter. He avoids company, even when people such as Steven, Billy and John Hazlitt act ingratiatingly towards him; he refuses the latter's offer of a half-pint of beer too. Alex Moore tries to interest him in the coming of Hayley's Comet, with no success besides Nicholas's asking what that is; Kevin cannot help with the exact date of its arrival. Nicholas then asks if it is a star and Alex tells him it is: a star with a tale.
>
> [Take note of how everybody tries to engage Nicholas in conversation but loses his interest before they complete an opening sentence.]
>
> Bronwen is on barmaid duty and I get her to prepare me another pasty.

But still, such a translation, the expansion of the elliptical style in which I came to take daily note of people and events in the Cumbrian dale of Wanet, does not reveal much besides a somewhat longwinded catalogue of trivia. Outside a paradigm of conventional contextualisation, that is, the words appear unintelligent.

However, knowing I had gleaned enough words to fill a certain number of pages in my diary made each day in the field worthwhile. In part this was because once I had completed a whole notebook I could mail yet another chunk of 'data' out of the dale and know that whatever befell my fieldwork persona henceforward, a fund of past words, at least, would be safe for analysis. In part, that is, I was writing for the academy, a brave ethnographer soon to be interpreting within-the-collectivity. But there was another part to my note-taking, a local part. I was also writing to accrue better relations in the community, and be a better gossiper.

In gossip, John Berger reminds us (1979:8–11), a community has the purpose of painting a living portrait of itself. And Max Gluckman concurs: for a large part of every single day most of a community's members are engaged in gossiping: gossip constitutes a community's very lifeblood (1963:308). For it is through gossip that fellow members manage (and contest) interrelatedness in a common social intercourse: gossip maintains a history, marks out a present and future, which members share and others do not. Indeed, for Gluckman, gossip is not only a hallmark and a privilege but also a duty of community membership; it is good manners to gossip with members about one's fellows, about norms held in common, and bad manners not to (1963:313). However, not to reify (essentialise, equilibrate) the community and its norms, and without functionalising gossip and its effects on the group (cf. Rapport 1995b:*passim*), it is sufficient to say that as a 'narrative' of gossip is continuously worked on, every new episode of every story and every comment on it confirms the existence of a community and its members in a continuous cycle of self-reference: the portrayers are at the same time the portrayed. Hence, gossip provides an individual with a map (maps) of his social environment – its people, norms and events and how he might act towards them; at one and the same time, gossip entails a causal description, an evaluative account, and a means of manipulation (Haviland 1977:10). Finally, its spoken recounting and elaborating is no triviality, for without the continuing narrative, the very relations of community would cease to exist.

Living in Wanet, in effect, meant negotiating interactional routines with a number of significant others; for me as fieldworker, a crash course in what it was pertinent to say, to whom, when. Filling diary pages with words felt worthwhile because they could be seen to evidence increasing local belonging: the notes were the capital accrued from my past encounters, as well as my *aides-mémoire* for the morrow. Perhaps my local neighbours did not need physically to write diaries or annotate scripts: they had the advantage (and the confidence) of many more years residence than I, partnership in far longer-lived talking-relationships. For me, none the less, the more I could memorise of the pertinent details of local information, the more I felt able and appropriate when speaking and acting within local gossip networks. Writing fieldnotes was, to borrow Fardon's phrasing (1990), a 'localizing strategy'.

Far from the stigmata of disciplinary misappropriation, then, fieldnotes were my, albeit amateurish, contribution to the continuing task of social construction. Far from cutting me off from Wanet they were the instruments of my deepening immersion. Indeed, they have served later academic reconstructions of life in Wanet (enabled me to imagine significance within the 'triviata' of recorded wordage) only to the extent that they furthered an immediate, 'indigenous' negotiation of interaction at their time of making. Here is writing, in short, which must be understood as the work of two hands at once.

LOCAL WRITING

Malinowski not only specified the betweenness of fieldnotes. Their aggregation in a field-journal amounted to "a chaotic account in which everything is written down as it is observed or told", he further explained (cited in Wedgwood 1932–34: notebook 18/5/32). It is this sense of the chaotic, I suggest, which fully demonstrates fieldnotes' dual character.

The 'chaos' of notebooks is commonly attributed to a merging of the categorical distinction between the oral and the literary: between "the flow of speech, the spate of words, the flood of argument" in which oral "inconsistency, even contradiction" can prosper, and the 'fixity', 'explicitness' and 'rationality' of writing, where accumulation favours 'critical scrutiny' (Goody 1977:49,37; and cf. Clifford 1990:64). The field diary becomes a chaotic aggregation, in this reading, because its juxtaposition of entries recontextualises and holds up for eternal comparison fleeting moments of interaction: because the conventions of intelligible writing, of sentence manufacture and syntax, cause a radical transformation of the grammar of oral exchange.

My exposition would be rather different. It is not that I deny important distinctions between the conventions of writing and speaking, rather that I find it misleading to treat 'writing and speaking' as metonyms for 'anthropologist and informant', 'academy and field', as we commonly do. That is, even when field-working in locations which can boast longstanding connections with literary traditions (England, India, Israel), we distinguish between the textual and the practical, literary and actual, to the effect that writing notes in the field comes to represent the anthro-pologist wearing his observer's hat which he then doffs before participating once more in the fray. Whereas, writing and speaking, I do not believe it too fanciful to say, are more rewardingly handled as different modes of social exchange both in seemingly pre-literate societies and post (cf. Finnegan 1977:260–1); there is local writing as well as academic writing, even in 'pre-literate' social environments. Hence, what lends fieldnotes a perceived chaoticism is their encompassment of two conventions of writing in one and the same set of phrases and pages.

Local conventions of writing? Let me elaborate. I have described my fieldnotes from Wanet as grounded, in style and content, in practice I learned from settling into that Cumbrian dale and routinising relations there. Fair enough, it might be retorted, in the English countryside there will be indigenous tradi-tions of diary-keeping, letter-writing, corresponding with parochial committees, provincial newspapers and so on for me to draw upon; but still, local conventions of writing among Sioux, Zulu and Kapauku? . . .

Removing to a village of illiterate French peasants, Berger summed up his efforts at creative writing as simultaneously a link and a barrier to his neighbours (1979:6). It barred him to the extent that he wrote for a living, and for a largely urban audience which judged his competence in terms of his ability to transcend the mundane in favour of the theoretical. It linked him because the essence of his writing was a struggle to give meaning to expe-rience: to scrutinise a given moment and connect it to a continuing narrative, and this was something he and his neighbours practised alike. Jack Goody makes a similar observation when he comments on the absence of any communicational hiatus in his stepping across the 'grand divide' into oral communities (1977:8); and, indeed, the crux of his definition of writing approaches what is essential to Berger: a cognitive shift from continuous recollection and rehearsal to considered reflection. The point I am making is that stepping back from the immediate moment, taking note and reflecting, writing up the present into an overarching, meaningful narrative or text, is a convention as indigenous to Kapauku as to Cumbria.

It is in this sense, too, that I understand Bruner and Weisser's claim (1991:130–6), that one comes to know one's life through 'never-ending textualisation': through the formulation and reformulation of a conceptual and narrative account of what that life has been about. The account might be made in speech or writing or simply in thought; it may be implicit or explicit; it is characterised above all by its being actively conceptualised. Hence: "'lives' are texts: texts that are subject to revision, exegesis, reinterpretation, and so on" (1991:133).

Furthermore, in the matter of such textualisation, orality and literacy do not necessarily define differing habits of thought. Both in communities which depend largely on an oral mode of communication and those which prefer a written one there can flourish the practice of scrutinising and abstracting from experience so as to produce a rationalised and objectified text. For "text" here (from its Latin root) implies a 'weaving', Stock reminds us (1990:*passim*), a weaving of language into that patterned composition which I have called narrative and whose exchange amounts to gossip, by which members of a community variously interrelate and define themselves; and "text" here can be written or spoken or both. Thus, every community is a textual community, for 'the separability of experience from ratiocination about it' (Stock 1983:531) is as practicable and conventional in oral as in literary environments.

In a telling conversation, Leopold Pospisil recorded Ijaaj Awitigaaj, a village headman and frequent Kapauku informant, reflecting on his decision to alter the law of incest and create community moieties so that he could marry some especially beautiful women of the same sib and village. When neighbours asked Awitigaaj about this innovation, Pospisil explains first (1971:284), he justified himself as follows:

> "*To marry an Ijaaj (same sib) is all right as long as she is aneepa epee (more remote than a first paternal parallel cousin). In old days the people did not conceive of this advantage, but now it is pio (legal). I have introduced it. She (his first incestuous love) told me, 'Have sexual intercourse with me.' Who could resist? Adii people (who live to the south of the Kamu Valley) have started it (the incest violation) and so I thought we were the same*

as they are and I introduced the change. I married Ijaaj Enaago and Ijaaj Amaadii only after I have become tonowi [headman] so that other people were either afraid to object or they agreed with me. To marry keneka (the girl of the same sib) is not bad, indeed it is nice, in this way one becomes a rich man."

Since it was apparent that the justifications given in the presence of other people were rationalizations rather than a revelation of truth, the writer questioned the headman later when they were alone. Because of their "best friend" relationship, he was required by custom to tell the writer what he really thought. "Why did I marry my relative? Well, I will tell you but do not tell others. I liked her, she was beautiful." To the writer's question about his new incest taboo regulation which prohibits marriage of first cousins, he replied with a sly smile and a friendly punch under the writer's ribs: "Please do not tell others. They would not like me (for what I am going to tell you) and I would lose influence. It would be all right with me if first cousins were to marry. To marry your sister is probably bad, but I am not convinced even of that. I think whoever likes any girl should marry her. I set up the new taboo (law) only to succeed in breaking down the old restrictions. The people are like that, one has to tell them a lie."

Commensurately, alongside the reflection I recorded in my fieldnotes (above) concerning how people would try to ingratiate themselves with an "arrogant" Nicholas, could go the following recorded (and 'translated') ratiocination from Doris, a farmer and close informant of mine. Nicholas, you should know, from being a small sheep farmer, left Wanet and made a fortune in industrial clothing before finally returning with a Rolls-Royce to retire. One afternoon, as Doris and I passed a Jaguar saloon in the dale's narrow roads on our way to checking some livestock, Doris observed:

I wouldn't have one of them big cars even if I could afford one, even if I was a millionaire – and I wouldn't like to be one of them either. We wouldn't be 'Fred and Doris' in Wanet then: it would be 'Frederick' for a start. Rich people aren't popular in Wanet. I mean look at Nicholas and that big yellow car of his. Driving round in it all the time, being nosey, he is. So you can't escape his looking. He's very arrogant, don't you think Nigel? And have you seen him flashing money in the pub? He takes one wad from one pocket and one wad from another when one's more than enough for the bill. I've even seen him put one wad of fivers on the bar so he can get another from his back pocket! He's self-made, mind, like all his family: he came from nowt. But he's still hardly ever around the place, and he's never popular.

What both Doris and Awitigaaj reveal are local actors taking note of everyday practice, and abstracting from it to maintain an overarching text of their community in comparable fashion to the note-taking of the anthropologist. The fieldnotes of participant-observation, we might say, are properly viewed as part of the ethnomethodology of sociation, part of the way individuals in the field come together to create and continue routine relations; certainly, it is of both local and academic conventionalities that fieldnotes can be seen to partake. Putting it another way, here is the 'universality' Sanjek hoped for; here is a world anthropology, albeit not of information but of practice: anthropological field-writing in mutual engagement with conventions of writing of the culturally other.

ACADEMIC WRITING

It is in the academy, perhaps, when the field-journal becomes a wholly read document, that its 'chaotic' nature becomes fully apparent. For here fieldnotes are transformed, made 'whole' and given a place in a 'disciplinary' text. It is within the monolithic-cum-monothetic frame of the monograph that fieldnotes' dual conventionality becomes problematic; as residual dream-images, fieldnotes' other-worldliness appears out of place within the literary genre of waking reality. Hence Richard Schweder's quip (1986:I,38) that "the best way to write a compelling ethnography is to lose your fieldnotes"; for reading fieldnotes, Lederman explains (1990:73), often challenges the 'certainty' of memory and the "sense of the whole" one now carries around in one's head.

What is most significant (and regrettable) here is the notion that the chaotic – or, to designate it more constructively, the dualistic, the neither here nor there – is something which must be eschewed in favour of the singular when it comes to anthropological writing-up. Fieldnotes undoubtedly warrant attention if anthropology is to sustain its reflexive glance, but it seems that in our bringing of "fieldnotes" under analytical focus (*à la* Sanjek *et al.*) we risk eradicating that very ambiguity and duality which is their special life. We alight upon the new noun for deconstruction only to reify it and hence erect a stumbling block to an appreciation of how we 'do anthropology' and might become more self-conscious in our practice in future. For by fractionalising fieldnotes into 'headnotes, scratch notes, records, transcripts, texts, journals, diaries, letters and reports' (as Sanjek suggests (1990d:92–115)) it would seem that we only succeed in distancing ourselves by so many gradations from the practice of our engagement with our subjects of study. Our focus here is static, at best sequential, and aims at a dissection of relations into discrete things-in-themselves. This speaks, in part, of the privileging of fieldwork writing as purely academic convention, which I have discussed, but also, I suggest, of the more general fashion in which Western criticism constructs its objects of study. "The true use of interpretation", Benjamin Jowett commented as early as 1860, "is to get rid of interpretation, and leave us alone with the author". We, instead (to borrow from Oscar Wilde), define in such a way as to limit; we define so as to reduce things to single statements. Here, in short, is critical interpretation of fieldnotes whose fastidious dismemberment kills off their quickness and tension, their innate duality.

It might be argued that such a process is inevitable: that no differentiation is possible between Levi-Strauss's structuralist tenet that 'every effort to understand something destroys that object in favour of another one of a different nature', and Bohr's *Abtotungsprinzip* whereby 'too deep a probing of behaviour kills off the subject of experiment'; criticism inevitably dismembers, dissects and transmutes (e.g. Jackson 1989:194 n.2). But I would disagree. Particularly as regards fieldnotes, whose conventional qualities of ellipsis and minimal contextualisation might be seen to place them in a relationship to monographs comparable to that between poetry and prose. That is, there are deliberate gaps to be filled in between fieldnotes and the sense made of them, for their sense is only partially imparted to the textual statement. In any critical reading of fieldnotes, then, it is surely possible and necessary to preserve the ambiguity of their author's position, to see in the textual gaps a tension between writing for the academy and writing for the field, and (*contra* Levi-Strauss) to refrain from (the destruction of) transfixing the fieldnote text in one single domain of conventional expression or another.

This is not to downplay the pertinence and originality of Sanjek's vision: far from it. Nor is this to advocate a return to the view that we can somehow gain access to the pre-defined, the pre-interpreted: that somewhere exotic we shall come face-to-face in our annotations with facts which are not already parts of theories. Rather it is to call (*après* Sontag (1967:7)) for interpretation which does not 'impoverish': analysis which does not demand singularity of focus, limitation, precision but can accept the subtlety of equivocation. "Fieldnotes" are a magical concept, magical in the dual conventionality of their composition and usage. What they deserve is an analysis "with blurred edges", in Wittgenstein's wording (1978:nos. 69–71), producing a general picture whose lineaments are indistinct and do not prescribe one precise way of viewing or another.

Finally, therefore, to talk as I have about fieldnotes' *dual* conventionality must be seen as an initial strategy only: a first opening of the door to the polythetic. For if to define is to limit then merely to dichotomise (multifocal field encounters/unifocal published reports; fluxional speech/fixed writing) is to collude in simplification. Ultimately, an appreciation of our fieldwriting practice should recognise a juxtaposition of numerous practices of note-taking and taking note, of writing, belonging both within the field and out (and including the convention of a "field"/"academy" abyss *per se*). 'Writing fieldnotes' means operating within a variety of frameworks of sense-making, juggling these in situational usage and personalising them to particular individual purpose.

Chapter 7

Domino Worlds
At home on the dominoes-table in Wanet

> ... someone behind drinks ale,
> And opens mussels, and croaks scraps of songs
> Towards the ham-hung rafters about love.
> Dirk deals the cards. Wet century-wide trees
> Clash in surrounding starlessness above
> This lamplit cave, where Jan turns back and farts,
> Gobs at the grate, and hits the queen of hearts.
>
> Rain, wind and fire! The secret, bestial peace!
> 'The Card-Players' Philip Larkin*

I intend Larkin's poem of Dirk and Jan's drunken revelry ('The Card-Players') to serve as a talisman as well as an epigraph in this essay; I hope to attach the essay to it. So that however pervasive the claims I shall make about the playing of dominoes of an evening (on the dominoes-table in the Eagle pub in the rural, northern, English village of Wanet), and however abstract my analysis, I am always brought back to an appreciation of how dominoes, like card-playing, is a physical activity – part-and-parcel of a physical, bodily communality – and also a recreational activity, deliberately without consequence for the serious, workaday world which proceeds alongside its playing.

For I shall argue that in playing dominoes can be found an inscribing, a writing, of a narrative which concerns home, morality, individual self, and which entails a meaningful commentary on an everyday world thereby transcended. In Larkin's striking poem, likewise, a playing (of cards) is to be understood as something

---

* Taken from the work *High Windows* by Philip Larkin. Copyright © 1974 Philip Larkin. Reproduced by kind permission of Farrar, Straus & Giroux, Inc., and also Faber and Faber Ltd.

which can be both encompassing in its ramifications – connecting with the very natural elements of the world: fire, water, food, love, shelter and bestiality – and encompassed by a whole other world of time and space – by the century-wide trees and starless heavens which put the play cave of hams, farts and spit into perspective.

CARD-PLAYING

Let me begin with two vignettes concerning card-playing, the first from Salman Rushdie, the second from John Berger.

In a hill-park in Karachi, Rushdie recounts (1990:1239), as the heat of the day turns to the cool of evening, men gather, sit cross-legged on the grass, and play cards in happy groups. Indeed, even at the height of the religious puritanism of President Zia's dictatorship, when the moral guardians of the regime closed down nightclubs and cinemas, this card-playing was exempt from censure. "The soft slap of cards being played in triumph or resignation" continued to fill the night air, testament to the card-players' "obdurate mania" and the cards' "enduring vitality" of expression. For in 'the language of the pack', Rushdie continues, is fashioned a supple discourse at once literal, symbolic and allegoric; in its use, chance, skill, drama, intrigue, deception, crime, violence, fortune and wealth can be found conjoined. Little wonder that partaking of this discourse of card-playing is as absorbing as any, and that, spilling over into others, it ramifies into all areas of life. For it is through the discourse that one can come to a real knowledge of participants' character and world-view, one's own as well as others', such as is not possible elsewhere.

In a bar on the outskirts of an Italian city (by the level-crossing, the railway station, the truck route), Berger comes upon a group of card-players (1988:20–21). The bar is rough-and-ready, homely but unkempt, and yet the concentration with which players imbue the card game is vital; while the town may be anonymous and nondescript, yet the card game is convivial and exclusive. The faces of the card-players reveal nothing; their conversation, moreover, is only about the cards played (thumped down onto the table with an authoritative swing of the arm), while cards unplayed are the knowledge of no-one else in the world besides their owner. In this way, each player rules the interest and concern of the others in turn – a dependency only ended by the sequential playing of the cards, at which point the next player for a time becomes ruler:

an unbroken cycle from dependency to independency. Indeed, Berger describes the interdependency of the card-players as giving rise to community: a community deriving from an equity which is more just than any existing outside the game, an equity which compensates for the inequity and the anonymity of the world outside. The suppleness of the language of card-playing is such that through the discourse of the game's action and procedures, rules and techniques, renowned victories and deceptions, (as, similarly, with the playful language of car mechanics, football, beer and D-I-Y of working-class Englishmen (cf. Berger 1967:93)), players are brought close: to a shared intimacy through a shared expertise. While through the code of the cards – absolute, final, extreme – players are brought deep: to an opportunity for pure introspection into themselves and their social lives which a routine, rushed, *macho* and materialistic world otherwise denies. Hence, the card-players become equal partners in a conspiracy which undermines the everyday authority of the outside world. And as they jointly peer into the guts of their game, and their heads metaphorically touch, so they also espy their own individual souls.

What Rushdie and Berger have to say accords nicely with Huizinga's sense of the relationship between what he calls 'ludic' activity (Turner's 'ludic genres') and the creative impulse in culture, in particular the creation of order in the world. For Huizinga has argued (1980:*passim*) that culture is rooted in, based in, develops from, pure forms of play. And 'play' would seem to be a primary category of all animal life, whose essence is fun: voluntary, free and yet intoxicating activity. Paradoxically, what would seem to make it 'fun', Huizinga suggests, is the order it gives onto. Play creates order, (at least) a limited perfection, in the world. Play makes the world a thing of the imagination: of control, gamesmanship, beauty, evil, hierarchy, logic and illogic, multiplicity, and so on. Hence, play can create a number of (limited) worlds at once; here are 'games', rule-bound social activities, of more and less seriousness, import and breadth. Also, play makes worlds appropriately sized, framed, and centred on its players: makes its players central to the world. Finally, play makes worlds whose rhythms and harmony captivate its participants so that they wish to return to the game again and replay it and make it conventional. In short, through play, an orderly world (or worlds) comes to be conceptualised: play gives onto culture. And the process is continuous; so that amid the routinisation, the institutionalisation of play that is culture, space is left for further 'pure', 'sacred' play periodically to reassert itself. Play amounts to a stepping out of 'real life', temporarily but regularly, into a discrete domain with a distinctive disposition and meaningfulness – a meaningfulness often at odds with the order of the world, the institutionality, as it presently stands. Differentiated, framed apart from ordinary life – outside everyday morals, beyond good and bad – here are periods of 'free activity' (however limited and hedged in with rules) to which human beings (like other animals) return to rekindle their creative energies.

In this way, the relationship between extant culture and the purer forms of play is often characterised by tension. At the least, the movement into play space is often accompanied by a change of perspective on the world, by the procuring of a vantage-point from which any present cultural order can be called into question and replaced. One may or may not choose, may or may not be able, to act upon the new worldly orders which play throws up, Turner continues (1983:187–191) (and it is plain how Huizinga's work feeds into Turner's ideas on the creativity of the more spontaneous forms of *communitas* as opposed to the fixity and mundanity of 'social structure'), but what remains important is the "fecundity for thought" that these ludic moments give onto. Furthermore, the ambiguity of the language in which ludic genres (forms of play) often express themselves – at least, ambiguous in terms of the ordinary language of everyday life – means that whether the commentary on the everyday which the play has produced is, finally, one of cathartic acceptance or revolutionary denial is a judgement that non-participants in the practice of the play might find it hard to make. (The language of the card-game, for instance, does not translate easily or directly into the more instrumental, coercive, monolithic and institutionalised language of the workaday world).

What Rushdie and Berger and Huizinga and Turner have to say also accords with Wittgensteinian notions of the relations between worldly order, games and language which led to the neologism of a "language-game" (1978:*passim*). Encapsulated here is an appreciation of the way language (the way we speak about the world) affects the way we live in it. More specifically, Wittgenstein hereby identified some four salient aspects of the play of language in everyday life. One: the way we speak about the world and the way we act within it and towards it regularly add up to a unity, to a "form of life"; our lives come to be formally composed of routine behavioural situations in which words and actions are interwoven. Two: we speak (and act) about the world in a diversity and fluidity of ways at different moments (in different situations), each logical and consistent in itself, but each potentially at odds with every other in terms of the world it gives onto. Three: these diverse ways of speaking about and in the world will themselves be of a diversity of kinds: intricate, subtle, common, new-fangled, expanded, primitive, pragmatic, ritualised, dogmatic, equalitarian, and so on. Four: it is in childhood that we learn a diverse range of ways of speaking, and here that we first encounter the fun of speaking, of conjuring with words, of meeting others through verbal agreement. We learn of the necessary sharing with others which speech involves – sharing knowledge of the rules, sharing agreement on turn-taking and other politenesses – we also learn of the possible exclusivity of speaking, the interestedness involved, the cheating and spoiling tactics which can go on. We learn of the power involved in making speech – in calling speech-acts into existence and then calling the play to a halt – we learn of the possibility of inventing of new rules, and the partiality of such invention, and also, finally, we learn how ways of speaking about the world have an internal structure, a beginning and an ending, which must be abided by if their use is to be meaningful. In short, Wittgenstein described language as amounting to a tool-box into which its speakers continually but sequentially dip, retrieving a particular tool (a particular language-game) in order to serve a particular purpose at hand. There might be no common denominator linking one tool, one language-game, to the others besides the fact that, as Steiner put it (1967:30), we "live inside" the acts of speaking each. (To live inside the act of playing cards, to use the language-game of card-playing, then, is to enter a world of words and behaviours which is distinct, entire, purposive, social (communitarian, exclusionary etc), and irreducible to any other).

Finally, what Rushdie and Berger and Huizinga and Turner and Wittgenstein and Steiner have to say resonates with much of my own experience of domino-playing in the English village of Wanet. Here too is a language-game in which people regularly and routinely live, ludic activity which is fecund for reflecting on, punctuating, making sense of, retreating from, recreating, the world. Domino-playing in Wanet I would also describe as a ludic genre for writing the world's order.

DOMINO-PLAYING

Dominoes may be introduced as a game popular with people of all ages in Britain (particularly with children, but also in certain situations of adult recreation such as pubs, working men's clubs, and Women's Institute socials). The game is thought to have made its way into Britain from France or Italy in the eighteenth century (the earliest mention in the OED is dated 1801) via returning prisoners of war – perhaps since it was a game they had found easy to play with others who did not (otherwise) share a common language.

The game is played usually by two or four people at a time (the foursome possibly representing two teams of two) with 28 rectangular counters (made from wood, bone or ivory). The counters are blank on one side and divided into two parts on the other, each part inscribed with a variable number of spots from zero to six. Thus the 28 dominoes have the following combinations of spots:

0|0	0|1	0|2	0|3	0|4	0|5	0|6
1|1	1|2	1|3	1|4	1|5	1|6	
2|2	2|3	2|4	2|5	2|6		
3|3	3|4	3|5	3|6			
4|4	4|5	4|6				
5|5	5|6					
6|6						

The game begins with the dominoes being placed face down on a flat surface. If two people are playing, then each picks up an agreed number of dominoes, which is sometimes ten and sometimes fourteen, without showing their value to their opponent. If four people are playing, each usually picks up six dominoes, hiding their value from their team-mates (if they are playing in teams) as well as their opponents; (the word 'domino' is the same as that used to describe the cloak and half-mask popular in certain French masquerade dances of the eighteenth-century and before). Since it is usual for not all 28 dominoes to be picked up, this leaves a number face down on the table of whose value no-one is cognisant.

The game proceeds by one domino being placed face upwards on the table (usually the highest double domino in any player's possession: six\six, or five\five, or four\four etc.) and the others following in turn (usually clockwise around the table) setting down one domino each, end-to-end, so that the dominoes come to form *a long row on the table. Each player must dispose of a domino if he can, and the dominoes set down in turn must, in each case, match in one of their inscribed sections, one of the sections of one of the dominoes on one end of the row made up of the dominoes which have been placed on the table previously. If a player cannot match one of the end sections open to him on the table, then he either misses his chance to dispose of a domino, or, in other variants of the game, must pick up one or more dominoes from the pool of those dominoes not selected at the beginning until he can match one. The winning person or team is the player or players who first manage to dispose of all the dominoes they have picked up. Or, if the game reaches stalemate before this point (with no-one being able to carry on matching dominoes), then the winning player or players are those with the lowest total when the numbers on their remaining dominoes are added up.*

The skill of the game is for players first to estimate as nearly as possible what dominoes are in the possession of their opponents (and their team-mates) by judging why they play the dominoes they do when they do, and second to guess at what dominoes might be still lying face down on the table, and by way of these judgements to hinder his opponent(s) disposing of dominoes, (assist his team-mate(s)) and end up being the first with no remaining dominoes in his hand – or at least as few as possible before no-one can match together any more dominoes and the game ends.

PLAYING DOMINOES IN WANET

0\0

ARTHUR: [standing at the bar, finds Robbie sauntering up for a refill] Now, here's my mate! Game of bones, Robbie? Fancy a draw-in? June and I, and Doris, were thinking of having a draw.

ROBBIE: [receiving his pint of bitter from Maggie, the barmaid] Aye, Arthur. Don't mind if I do, don't mind if I do.

ARTHUR: The 'bones' please, Maggie! [Maggie smiles and hands Arthur one of the boxes of dominoes kept behind the bar]. Nigel, Sid? What about you? Up for a game? [Arthur turns around to face Sid and me, leaning on the bar, chatting occasionally, on the other side of him. He raises his eyebrows quizzically, to which Sid nods and I grin, before turning back to Robbie, slapping him on the back and walking with him over to the dominoes-table in the corner. June is already seated there, chatting to Doris, and Walter is perched on the end wallseat].

WALTER: God, I'm in the dominoes' place! [Walter looks about him in pretended shock as Arthur, Robbie, Sid and Nigel descend on him, and he realises that June and Doris are obviously seated there by prior assignation].

SID: Aye! So why don't you bugger off out of it, Walter Brownlea? This is the domino table, not the darts table. Go and sit somewhere else!

JUNE: Draw-in if you like, Walter?

ARTHUR: Aye! Do you want to draw in, Walter? You'll have to get a partner, mind, cos there are about six of us already. [Arthur looks about him]

CHARLES: [walking over from the back room] Can I draw in for a game? Oh, looks like there's enough of you already. Never mind: carry on without me. I had a game of darts lined up anyway.

ARTHUR: Why don't you draw in with Walter, Charles, and that makes eight?

WALTER: No. Thanks, but I think I'll go over to darts . . . You've some courage, Nigel, playing dominoes with these sharks! I admire you. [he grins]

SID: Yeah: 'Bite yer legs off'! Nay, be off with you, Brownlea!

DORIS: Sorry, I'm facing the wrong way now we're starting. I like to watch everything that's happening. Like: who's chatting to who; who's twined! [Doris laughs and pushes her way round the table to sit facing into the pub with her back to the wall]

0\1

The 'dominoes-table' in the Eagle pub in Wanet (informally designated thus, but known by all the regulars) is a large rectangular table with a slight lip situated adjacent to the main door. On the benches and wallseat circling it, ten people can be accommodated with ease. Moreover, the table commands a fine view of most of the rest of the pub – not just whoever enters by the main door (who can be 'vetted' by the occupants of the table as they squeeze past into the rest of the room and say 'Hello') – but who is playing darts, who is getting served at the bar, who is warming themselves by the open fire, who has gone out the back to the toilet, and who has entered by the back door. The table represents something of a focus of interaction in the pub, then, and also a point from which to focus on the pub as such. It mediates people's entry, departure and residence within the walls of the Eagle.

0\2

More often than not of an evening, Arthur and June, old friends in their late-fifties, can be found seated at the table chatting, whether before, during or after a game of dominoes, both by themselves and with others who have played with them or watched their game.

0\3

The most popular game in the Eagle is where four people play at once, in two teams of two, each person picking up six dominoes at the start of the game and so leaving four face-down in the middle of the table, "sleeping". Besides the two teams playing at a time, there are sometimes other teams of two people also involved. They play the winning team after each round, and when not in a round (having lost a previous one) they either watch, chat to and encourage those playing, or else wander around the pub chatting to and drinking with others present until their turn comes again.

0\4

Playing dominoes is thus a way to be in the pub for an evening with a schedule, as it were, a routine, which punctuates whatever else (chatting, drinking) one may be doing, while also giving one a legitimate attachment to the place, both spatial and temporal, as the evening passes and one moves in and out of conversation with others; (there is a weekly dominoes knock-out competition throughout the winter in the nearby Mitre pub, where individuals compete one against another, but there the social interaction given onto is very different: staccato, more reserved and formal, and sooner finished). Dominoes in the Eagle provides something of a foundation for sociality. Certainly (like the prisoners of war domiciled on the European continent of yore), dominoes provided

me with a route into relations in the Eagle and in Wanet generally when, as a stranger, I first arrived in the place. As Arthur
would invite me to join a game, I found a way to socialise when
I was otherwise not well versed in a language of topical local
conversation; it felt like a welcome basis of belonging, also a haven
of peace in a storm. Moreover, I found that being socialised into
the dominoes game contained wider social lessons:

ARTHUR: I'll play doms with anyone, won't I June, and let
anyone join in the draw? Not like some people who'll just
play with old friends and refuse to play with anyone new. No:
I'll play with anyone – except on Sunday nights when a friend
of mine comes down from Leyton, and it's widely known that
on that night we play together on the little table over there!
. . . I don't know why we do it, but we always have done, and
now its just for old times' sake. It's tradition, eh June? Yes:
tradition.

ALF: You gotta play more for your partner, Nigel. Help him, be
less self-centred in the dominoes you play. Like: always get
rid of double-six or -five or -four at the start, play them bare,
even if you haven't got more in that set. Cos that's what your
partner will be expecting. That's how dominoes is played in
Wanet.

0\5

Needless to say, the foundation of sociality that dominoes
provides, the work it does to structure time, space and occasion
in the pub, is so routine to regular players and spectators as to
go largely unspoken in Wanet. Instead, dominoes is often an
unremarked activity which accompanies talk of other matters.
What I intend here, however, is a disinterring of that foundation,
a making plain of the language of dominoes in Wanet, a describing
of the world it creates – bounded, small-scale, tranquil, unpredictable, well-mannered, cordial – as well as the perspective on
the worlds around it which it secures – the opportunity to comment
on and subtly rewrite what (and who) lies outside. The game of
dominoes ushers in a milieu, a space, with an ethos of its own,
safe from the flux, noise and entropy of other worlds, without
direct consequence upon those worlds and yet with a view
on them. Moreover, while often unremarked, people in Wanet
did not necessarily refrain from giving a commentary on their

feelings and thoughts towards the game, towards the world and the perspective it provided:

ARTHUR: I like 'doms', Charles, because you can sit and talk and be sociable at the same time.

ARTHUR: Enjoy the evening, lad? . . . I like just sitting quiet and I often need a sit-down after standing working all day, eh? And it's the playing not the winning which is the important part of an enjoyable darts evening.

ROBBIE: Dominoes is an old man's game, lad. A sign of a misspent youth!

ARTHUR: When was that night we were playing here? with Charles and all? That was a super night! I really enjoyed myself. More than ever . . . Just a quiet night and no-one in the pub . . . You know, Nigel, I thought later that was one of the best nights of my life! Really! One of the best nights of my life . . . A quiet evening of dominoes. Just great, right?

0\6

A further description of the world of dominoes which I found in Wanet might be conveniently tied to an elaboration of the interaction I have recounted above, in particular between: **Arthur** (a small farmer and part-time builder, married, in his late-fifties), **June** (a part-time cook, married, in her early-sixties), **Robbie** (a farmer, married, in his early-forties), **Sid** (a farm-labourer, in his mid-thirties, and married), **Doris** (a farmer, married, in her mid-thirties) and **Nigel** (a part-time farm-labourer and student of anthropology, a newcomer to Wanet, in his mid-twenties and unmarried). The interaction might also be conveniently divided into the sequential: Starting, During, and Ending The Game.

STARTING THE GAME

1\1

With the dominoes spread out flat on the table, face down, and shuffled, each person picks up one domino and counts its spots. The persons with the two highest totals will form a team for the contest to come, as will the two lowest totals and the two middle. On this occasion, Arthur and June, with the two highest totals, end up in one team, Sid and Robbie in another, and Doris and Nigel in a third. Because Doris and Nigel scored the least, they sit out the first round of the contest and must wait to meet the winners in the next round. As they slide up the wall seat and out of the way, Sid, Robbie, Arthur and June rearrange themselves so that team-mates are not sitting next to each other and, as turn-taking takes place in a clockwise fashion, play will alternate from one team to another. This ends up with Arthur and Sid sitting beside one another on one side of the table (with their backs to the rest of the pub), and Robbie and June on the other. Once they have decided who will drop the first domino, the play will therefore circulate from Arthur to Sid to June to Robbie and back to Arthur. Having seated themselves, each picks up six dominoes from the shuffled array which lies face-down before them. This is done in a leisurely and polite fashion, since one unseen domino must be seen to be like any other. Having chosen six, each player turns over and examines his or her selection, while ensuring that no-one else can. This is usually done in the Eagle by picking the six dominoes up in one's hands. By placing the dominoes side-by-side it is possible (for the men, certainly) to pick up all six in one fist, thereby shielding them from the others and making them readily viewable as a set. Then, one of the dominoes can be picked out of the fist for play each round with the hand not holding the set, with the remaining dominoes then returned, face-down, to the table to be squashed close together again and again picked up in the fist. (If a woman cannot at first fit all six dominoes in her fist, then she is likely to fit three in each or four and two, until she has disposed of enough to pick the remainder up in one hand.) Thus there is a characteristic stance at the table with each player studying his or her own fist, and frequently removing or rearranging the dominoes in it with the other hand. (If one is right-handed, then it is the left hand which does the holding and the right hand the manoeuvring; the stance resembles somewhat the act of writing periodic messages in a notebook held in one's palm). There is also a characteristic sound at the table as the wooden dominoes make an appreciable click when they are placed down on the wooden table. Thus there are clicks when the dominoes are played, clicks as they are periodically returned to the table for rearrangement in the fist, and clicks as one domino in the right hand or the whole fist of dominoes in the left hand is knocked against the table top to signify that even though it is his turn, a player cannot 'go' because he has not got a domino which matches the numbers he must follow. This is called 'knocking', and can

*either be done by clicking one or more dominoes in the above
fashion, or by saying 'I'm knocking', or by speaking and clicking
at the same time.*

1\2

ARTHUR: Robbie and Sid together! I thought it might be: "The
Colonel" and "The Chief"! [he chuckles] Now these two will
be hard to shift, June.

SID: You better believe it, Arthur. I reckon Robbie and me have
got the drinks sown up for the evening!

ARTHUR: Well, on second thoughts, not *that* hard to shift,
happen! [he chuckles]

DORIS: I thought you said you'd only play dominoes if you were
playing with me, June? Then we get parted, and you leave
me with young Nigel here!

JUNE: I tried, Doris, I tried!

ARTHUR: Don't you underestimate Nigel, Doris. He's become
quite a player since I started teaching him what's what!

ROBBIE: Aye. I can just imagine what you been teaching him,
Arthur Harvey! Don't you listen to a word he says, Nigel.
And anyway, you can't chose your partner, Doris. That's the
whole point of the game. It's like Peggy always complaining
to me when we're out, that we end up playing dominoes apart
and never know what the other's up to from the start of the
evening to the end. But you don't wanna come out and play
dominoes with your wife, do you?!

SID: Nay! Be buggered.

ROBBIE: I mean, you see enough of each other at home, like.
[he laughs]

ARTHUR: I see enough of you after half-an-hour, Robbie!

SID: Nay! You can't play dominoes with y' wife, it's bad luck.

JUNE: Aye. That's what they say. And I can't quite see why
Peggy would want to neither! For myself, like! [she laughs]

SID: So that's what you think about Robbie and his dominoes,
eh June? Well, Robbie and me'll have to see about that, eh?
So: whose drop? Us or you? Who drops?

ARTHUR: Well, they say 'ladies first', don't they? So, we'd have
to give it to you and Robbie, by rights. [he laughs] Nay, June's
total was the highest so its her to drop.

ROBBIE: Aye. Here we go then . . .

1\3

The arranging of partners is the most significant feature in starting the game. If dominoes ushers in a new world, a new frame of interaction – a focus of pub interest, as well as a focus on the rest of the pub and the workaday world and workaday relations beyond it – then the arrangement of partners and opponents is the setting up of determinate relations in this world. One will hope to reveal oneself as openly as possible to one's partner and close oneself off from one's opponents. As Arthur jokes about 'The Colonel' and 'The Chief', then, he marks the new characters whom Sid and Robbie have become, he demonstrates his prior knowledge of their abilities, and he rallies June to the cause of their own partnership; finally, he also frames and signals the ludic nature of the interaction about to ensue.

1\4

The ludic frame is also the occasion for Sid's open boast and challenge that the drink will keep flowing in his and Robbie's direction. Normally, such overt and ostentatious claiming of superiority would be avoided. Now, Sid congratulates himself and Robbie for finding each other. In the same way, Doris openly bemoans ending up with Nigel and not with June, with whom she had been in friendly conversation before the dominoes' draw. This is both a recognition, then, that the draw has drawn a line under previous talking-relations that evening in the pub, and that in ordinary circumstances Doris might have taken this as a sign of disloyalty on June's part. The ludic frame, however, means that she must make a joke of her being 'left out', and that, equally, Nigel must not take umbrage at being regarded as a second-best in this way.

1\5

The distinct frame of interaction which dominoes ushers in is perhaps most clearly flagged in the way that married couples are firmly separated and not allowed to act as domino team-mates. Within the domino frame, relations are begun afresh; certainly there is no great continuation of 'external' relations such as the maintenance of a marriage partnership would represent. (Significantly, at the end of the end, when a pot of money is being set up for the winner of the final round, married couples who are on the table together might be expected to pay for one another's contribution: with the domino partnerships about to break up, the relations of the outside world are once again begun to be recognised).

1\6

Nor does gender really matter within the dominoes frame. There is no convention calling for teams to be made up of one gender or two. At the start of the game, all enter as individuals, equal and separate, and, to some extent at least, their success in the game will depend on what sort of communicative relationship they set up with their partner – and incommunicative relationship with their opponents.

2\2

Finally, the teasing concerning Nigel's apprenticeship to Arthur's domino skills and concerning Robbie and Sid's effeminacy are again demonstrations of the ludic nature of the interaction – open aspersions at which open umbrage may not be taken – and emphasisings of the differentiation between the world of dominoes and that outside. Here, 'ladies first' does not apply; and here, Nigel, the university student and urban 'sophisticate', is being educated by the 'parochial' and 'unlettered' farmer.

DURING THE GAME

2\3

Play proceeds quite rapidly, with people being aware (from long practice) of the significance of certain people playing certain dominoes at certain times for calculating who is likely to be holding what, and what four dominoes are probably lying 'sleeping' in the middle of the table. The best of three games makes up a round, and this takes some fifteen or twenty minutes. It is not too long, therefore, before June and Arthur beat Robbie and Sid in the first round, and Doris and Nigel take the latters' place. Doris and Nigel then beat June and Arthur, and so go on to play Robbie and Sid, who return from where they have been leaning on the bar chatting. The end of each round occasions a chance to go to the toilet or

otherwise stretch one's legs for a moment and 'relax' from the game,
compare notes and judge certain plays, comment on the luck or
otherwise of different hands of dominoes. Meanwhile a member of
the losing team buys the two members of the winning team the prize
of a half-pint of beer each, placing it on the domino table as a
visible trophy. And so the evening proceeds with a regular change-
over of personnel at the domino table and a regular moving by the
domino-players among the other members of the pub, who drink
at the bar and at the other tables, play darts, and come over to the
dominoes-table themselves to watch the games, see how people play
their hands, and chat.

2\4

ARTHUR: Nigel and Doris win again . . . Why did we ever teach
Nigel?

NIGEL: It's a rum do.

ROBBIE: What's that! A 'rum do'? [he chuckles] You picking up
the local talk, Nigel! . . . Nay, [laughing] what a Sadducee and
a Pharisee you are Nigel, for sure! A Sadducee and a Pharisee.

SID: 'Parasite', you mean!

ARTHUR: "Stupid boy", Nigel! [grinning, he mimics the catch-
phrase of the actor, Arthur Lowe, in the TV comedy serial,
"Dad's Army": a term of affectionate contempt by the head
of a platoon of old men in the British Home Guard during
the Second World War for the one sickly and underage recruit
under his command; in the show, the phrase is seen humor-
ously to point up the pomposity of the speaker]

DAVE: [wandering over from the darts board] Don't wear Nigel
out with dominoes. He's got a hard day again tomorrow on
the farm!

ROBBIE: What? You can't get tired from dominoes; it's mental
work.

DAVE: Well, I certainly get tired! . . . God! Arthur and June and
Robbie and Sid – that's a dominoes super-league you're
playing with, Nigel! Watch out!

SID: So you'll have had a hard day today on the farm, Nigel?

NIGEL: Not too bad.

ARTHUR: You know, Nigel isn't asked often enough to draw in
for a game. People forget too often to ask you, Nigel. But
you should just come and barge in if you want a game, eh?

Like old Mick Blythe did last night. Just come over and say you want a game. OK? [Nigel nods and grins appreciatively]

ROBBIE: God! What about Micky Blythe last night? He barges in and demands Alf Hibblethwaite be his partner – and no-one else! So he waits till old Alf comes – and then they only win once! [he shakes his head]

JUNE: You did alright though, Robbie!

ROBBIE: I'm winning nothing tonight! 'Knocking'.

JUNE: But last night you were winning everything.

ROBBIE: Well: that's the way of the bones. We're certainly having no luck tonight against Nigel and Doris, eh Sid? No comment on you, of course, Sid, like. Dominoes aren't like darts when it comes to your partner being at fault, eh? It all depends on the dominoes you pick up.

ARTHUR: That's what they say, anyhow . . . [he winks at Nigel]

SID: God, you're so slow, Robbie. It's lucky you're not a funeral director! . . . And your tie's knotted, you know: I wonder what else is? . . .

ROBBIE: Well I bet I'm the only one in the pub who could knot it!

SID: . . . I could've said something nasty there!

ARTHUR: Yeah, like how it must be hard to get a knotted prick to screw! [he laughs at his joke, and the other men join in]

JUNE: God! You men are so coarse! [she turns and straightens Robbie's tie] What would you do without Peggy?

SID: He'd probably go to work naked.

DORIS: OK: What did the elephant say to the naked man? "How on earth do you feed yourself with that!" [she laughs shyly, and the others smile] 'Pass'. Sorry, I keep saying that! I mean 'Knocking'. I must have been watching too much "Mastermind" lately!

SID: I see they're all in tonight [looking across the bar-room]. Reggie Whistle's 'secretary', and 'Milk Marketing Board' [the others laugh at his characterisations] . . . And Nigel's eyeballs are popping out at all these tourist women about the place. How about 'Doris Day' over there on the bar-stool, Nigel. Fancy her?

JUNE: [laughing] Don't lead him on, Sid.

DORIS: [laughing, with mock embarrassment] Isn't he terrible, June!

SID: And there's the parson's daughter, too. What about her, Nigel? She'd pray over you, for sure!

ROBBIE: My God! Is that the parson's daughter? Hell, but she's developed since I last saw her! Quite a beauty now. Twenty years ago and I'd have been after her myself. [the others laugh] Don't you fancy her, then, Nigel? My Godfathers: I would!

DORIS: I thought you were married, Nigel! So Wendy said.

NIGEL: No. There's just me.

SID: See: that's the advantage of Wanet. You can come here, like Nigel did, and you can say anything about yourself, and no-one knows any better. No-one knows about your past; nobody knows you from Adam! I s'pose it would be the same me being in Manchester . . .

MAGGIE: [coming over from behind the bar with a half-pint of lager] Just so you don't fall too far behind in your drinks tonight, Nigel. [she grins] This is the one Arthur put in for you from the last round.

NIGEL: Cheers! [he smiles and places the new half-pint beside the other one he has just started, and looks somewhat resigned]

DORIS: You're backwatering, Nigel. Get drinking!

ROBBIE: 'Knocking'.

CHARLES: [following Maggie over from behind the bar] You do need a lot of looking after, don't you, Nigel! [he chuckles and leans on Nigel's back, looking over his shoulder at his fist of dominoes]

MAGGIE: And lager's going up to 62 pence a pint soon, Nigel! [Nigel looks up at her, taken-aback] Sorry Nigel! I just wanted to see the shock on your face! No, its not going to be that bad. Lager will be 58p, beer 50p, and Guinness 62p.

ARTHUR: Bad enough! It used to take me a while to drink £1's worth, but not any more.

SID: We'll soon have to play doms for 10p's.

ARTHUR: I said so all along.

SID: Or, if you're on lager, Nigel, you'll have to pay the difference . . . Uh, what dominoes are up? What am I meant to be following? Yan-Yan . . .

DORIS: Aye! Nigel one'ed it up. Well done, Nigel.

SID: Aye, he would. One-Yan: 'knocking'. Bugger it.

ROBBIE: You still not on bitter yet then, Nigel?! You need a six pints' initiation! [the others laugh] Nay, but how can you drink that lager stuff? Look at the colour compared with dark beer!
. . .

JUNE: Aren't they awful stirrers, Nigel! [she chuckles] Never keep their minds on their dominoes for all their talking, eh?

SID: Joanna's always saying I should go get a job at the chapel cos of my great gob. And if I do, Nigel's gonna come and do the collection plate! Aren't you lad? [Nigel smiles warily]

ARTHUR: No, but seriously: If you lose all night at doms or darts now, you can be losing £2 or £3. And it's only going to get worse.

CHARLES: God, you're ruining a gorgeous hand here, Nigel! [he still looks over Nigel's shoulder] You should never have played that double-four. Terrible thing, temptation! Eh, Nigel? [he laughs]

SID: You keep to your own game, Smith!

ARTHUR: Nigel can play as he likes.

JUNE: Aye. And he was quite right to play that there.

SID: Fuck off back behind the bar where you belong, why don't you, Smith!

ARTHUR: Remember how the Eagle used to be? When the land-lords had to fetch the beer from the cellar all the time . . . [he chuckles] That used to keep them busy alright . . .

ROBBIE: And fit!

DORIS: Aye. There was that hatch, there, wasn't there, before there was a bar at all.

CHARLES: OK! I get the message! I'm going. Company's better over there anyway! [the others laugh as he goes, grinning]

DORIS: Ooh! Look at Lynn sitting on the stool over there! That's not been known in the history of the world: her leaving her spot at the bar! . . . And look! It's all because Wendy has moved over there to chat to Molly and Mary.

JUNE: You should've heard what Lynn was saying about Wendy before.

DORIS: What?! . . . Oh tell me later. Isn't it awful, gossiping like this? [she laughs, embarrassed]

ROBBIE: Nay! All these bad habits you'll be picking up here, Nigel. Gossiping, and darts, and boozing, and practising domi-noes . . . It's a rum do alright. [he grins]

NIGEL: 'Knocking'.

ARTHUR: You were playing for yourself not your partner there, Doris! You three'ed it up when Nigel had no threes – and you knew it.

DORIS: [laughing embarrassedly] Oh, sorry, Nigel. I'm hopeless sometimes ... They've even dropped me from the Eagle doms' team, you know, cos I was only ever good at playing with my dad as partner, and I'm not even that now. I can't play doms with my dad these days ... Mind you, I did come back from the dead, 0–2, to win in the knock-out at the Mitre on Sunday.

NIGEL: Oh, did the Mitre win Monday's dominoes' match at Leyton?

JUNE: Against New Inn? Second leg of the second-round match?

NIGEL: Yeah.

JUNE: Yes they did. They got some good young players over the Mitre now, you know. Ben, Dennis, Harry Andrews ...

ARTHUR: Remember what a good doms player Harry's dad was, Joe Andrews?

ROBBIE: Great! And draughts – chequers – too. I've not seen a better player at that than Joe.

SID: Well, I don't mind telling you, I'm getting a bit distraught at all the dominoes I'm losing recently. I've tried different partners and it's no help; look at Robbie here! A real dead loss! ... So I'm starting to think it's me!

ARTHUR: Nay. It's just that so much in dominoes is the luck of the hand. It's like you can't say you're really getting any better or worse, because so much in a game depends on your hand and your partner's, right?

ROBBIE: Nay, its you alright, Askrig! your fault we're losing tonight.

SID: Why don't you fuck off, Milden. [Robbie laughs]

ARTHUR: Well, you *can* have too much of doms at a sitting, you know Sid ...

SID: [stretching his back] Excuse me, Doris! I'm not looking at your dominoes. I'm just trying to straighten my bad back. God! It's bad just now.

ROBBIE: Is that your excuse then, Askrig? ... 'Knocking' again.

DORIS: And me: 'knocking'.

SID: Me too. That's it then. And it's not even worth a count. They've obviously won again ... Beginner's luck, eh Nigel!

ROBBIE: Nay! It must be that I'm too soft-hearted for this ...
I win a few one night, and then I can't keep on concentrating
and winning after that. It's the same in darts: I always end
up easing up and making the scores more equal.

DORIS: You! Soft-hearted, Robbie? That'll be the day.

ARTHUR: Soft in the head more like! [he laughs, and Robbie
pushes him away]

DORIS: Anyway, let's have a count. I'm no cheat: I don't want
to win if I haven't. Eh Nigel?

NIGEL: Right.

2\5

*Counting up the domino scores each still has in his or her hands,
they find that Doris and Nigel have fewer dominoes still to play
and a lower combined total than Robbie and Sid. Hence it is Doris
and Nigel's turn again to remain seated at the table while Sid and
Robbie go off to buy them another beer each, as prizes, and vacate
their seats for Arthur and June and the start of the next round.*

2\6

As a focus of the pub, and a means to focus on the rest of the
pub, playing dominoes on the dominoes-table often eventuates in
a distillation in a 'purer' form of a number of characteristics of
life and interaction in Wanet worlds beyond. For example, talking
with a 'Wanet accent' has a special place at the table, a special
value. Here, players celebrate their own favourite catchphrases –
'its a rum do'; 'what a Sadducee and a Pharisee'; "stupid boy";
swear words – with more regularity and seeming pleasure than
elsewhere; saying them here is more significant and can be
expected to be more effective, more understood, more appreciated than elsewhere. Likewise, they celebrate the distinctive (Old
Norse and Old English) aspects of the dialect of the Wanet area
– 'Yan-Yan' – in a way rarely heard elsewhere (where 'One-One'
would be the ubiquitous phrasing). At the table, people are most
themselves, and their village heritage is most itself. Moreover,
it is here that usurpation of local accenting by outsiders is most
ruthlessly castigated and ridiculed; Nigel is not allowed to get
away with mimicking Robbie's 'rum do' without some concerted
ribbing.

3\3

The distillation of the dominoes-table also means that behaviour
here is often meant to be the best; here, norms of propriety are
most expected and claimed. Hence the warning and indignation
in Doris's voice when she accuses Nigel of 'backwatering', and not
keeping in line with the consensual drinking rate; as well as
Maggie's efforts in politely carrying over his beer to him from
behind the bar. And hence, Doris's (otherwise redundant) statement on never cheating. Meanwhile, Arthur and June are
particularly polite in making Nigel feel at home and wanted at
the table, pointedly telling him, for example, how to 'read' the
local talk aright ('Aren't they awful stirrers'); while Arthur repeat-
edly pooh-poohs the significance of winning and explains away
Sid and Robbie's defeat as bad luck. Robbie himself assures Sid
that unlike a darts-partner, he does not hold Sid at all responsible
for their team's fortunes.

3\4

This purity and moral propriety also feeds into the comments
players make on seemingly extraneous details in the lives of those
playing the game (including themselves) as well as the wider lives
of those not playing. When Sid teases Robbie for his slowness,
when Robbie agrees boastfully about the size of his sexual organs,
when June mentions Peggy's long-suffering care for Robbie, and
when Robbie admits to his own soft-heartedness, what is being
demonstrated is not only a full and shared knowledge of one
another and themselves, and their ease and openness in the
conveyance of information between one another, but also the way
that their knowledge reaches into the essential core of a person
or a relationship. There is no place here for ignorance or for
disguise. It is in this sense too that Sid's caricaturing of fellow-
locals and visitors in the pub – 'Whistle's secretary', 'Milk
Marketing Board' – can be understood. In the caricatures is an
exaggerating of their essential features. Here is the insight which
goes behind workaday formalities and also the license to speak
those insights out loud. For this reason too, interrogating Nigel,
the recent and relatively unknown newcomer in Wanet, so as to
ascertain information which has not been forthcoming off the
dominoes-table, is also legitimate. Thus: what sort of a sexual

threat does he represent? is he married? which women does he fancy? are they local or offcomer or tourist? and how truthful will he be, allaying local fears and rumours? Even Maggie and Charles, the bar-staff, take the opportunity to approach the table and adjudge Nigel's reactions to the dominoes being played and the beer being consumed alongside them.

3\5

The distillation also makes for a rather particular relationship between the world of the dominoes-table (and those partaking of it at a particular time) and the rest of the pub. The boundary is never a hard-and-fast one, for domino-players are always leaving the table for the bar and the toilet, while those in the rest of the pub will frequently saunter over to chat to the domino-players and comment on particular players and plays. Nevertheless, domino-players are accorded a certain respect for the 'purity' of their pursuit, adding to the fact that regular domino-players – the 'super-leaguers', as Dave refers to them – tend to be of an older generation than those who, say, play darts regularly; (hence, Robbie's comment that dominoes is 'an old man's game'). Similarly, domino-players are accorded respect because they are local pub-regulars who have frequented the Eagle (borne witness to its carryings-on) before many of its present drinkers were born – even before the present structure of the building was as it was. When Walter makes a joke, then, about mistakenly sitting 'in the dominoes' place', Sid rebukes him peremptorily ('So why don't you bugger off out of it'), while Arthur and June extend their *noblesse oblige* and offer him a part in the game. For the same reason, Arthur's sitting down to play with Nigel – indeed, extending to his 'apprentice' a place at the table whenever he wishes – occasions raised eyebrows from non-players (such as young Walter and young Dave) and an aggrieved sense of a diluted interaction from other adult players (such as Doris and Sid).

3\6

The boundary of the domino world and the respect it should translate as also means that the domino-players do not appreciate Dave's reminder that Nigel has more work to do on the farm. For in dominoes, the routines and constraints of the outside world no longer hold sway; in dominoes, talk of the overpowering influence of work is out of place, is disrespectful. While to suggest the ludic genre of dominoes might in some way give onto the tiring world of work is a category mistake. Likewise, players do not appreciate Charles's criticism of Nigel's playing, for Charles is properly in the position of a (grateful) spectator. It might be proper for players to criticise one another – as Arthur does Doris minutes after Charles has been sent back to the bar (indeed, back down into the pub cellar of yore) to mind his own business of landlording – but it is certainly inappropriate coming from those outside the 'magic circle'. Finally, it is with some indignation that talk at the dominoes-table turns to the question of the future price of beer and the effects this might have on the norms of domino-playing and its structuring of reward. Domino-players might have foreseen the changes before they arrived, and might have already planned necessary counter measures before they are forced upon them by the outside commercial world ('We'll soon have to play doms for 10p's.', 'I said so all along.'), but still, the disrespect evidenced by the change borders on the sacrilegious; it is not right for the norms of domino-playing to be dictated by the world outside. For there is something of the dominoes-table which properly partakes of the timeless: a game where fate consistently holds sway, and where (as Arthur is remindful) even such workaday characteristics as maturity and skill which develop over time have no impact. This is why talk on the dominoes-table can bear absolute witness to the changes wrought by time on the world beyond the table. Changes in the structure of the Eagle can be charted, Doris's changing relations with her father can be recorded, and the life-cycle of local generations can be celebrated: from parson to parson's daughter, from old game-playing skill in the Andrews family to new. From outside time, the dominoes-table temporally fixes and frames the outside world.

4\4

Different people may be differently at home with the rarefied world of the dominoes-table, none the less. For many of the young, it is a focus of light-hearted teasing and bantering, as we have heard. For some in middle generations (such as Robbie, Sid and Doris), there is the insecurity of not knowing whether they yet properly belong, properly measure up, and the ambivalence of whether they yet wish to. Hence, Doris's distantiating comment that even in the middle of a game she has the TV quiz show, "Mastermind", more on her mind than dominoes's proper wordage; also, Robbie's admission that he cannot play well consistently, and Sid's admission that he certainly has not been playing well recently. In this way too can be understood the various comments which would distance (young) Nigel from the rarefied atmosphere of dominoes-table: Robbie's rebuff that whatever Arthur might feel about Nigel barging into a game, he certainly intends to slander Micky Blythe for exhibiting precisely that impoliteness; Sid's threat that when the beer prices go up, Nigel will have to pay the difference between lager and bitter: local domino-players cannot be expected to be disadvantaged by his foreign ways; and finally, Robbie's judgement that the habits Nigel will be picking up via the dominoes-table – gossiping, boozing, domino-playing itself – will corrupt his sensibilities because he is out of place in this atmosphere. Even Arthur has occasion to distance himself from the responsibility that participation at the domino table represents through his assertions that 'so much in dominoes is the luck of the hand', and so it is impossible to judge one's improvement or otherwise over the years. At the same time, this is an attempt to relax the younger members of the party Arthur has invited to the table, and make them feel at home. Meanwhile, Arthur and June have a sense of the passing generations and look forward with some local pride to the possible graduation to the dominoes-table (and the more mature Eagle) of some good young players currently serving their apprenticeship in the Mitre pub team.

ENDING THE GAME

4\5

When one or more people have to leave the pub and go home or there is a common feeling that they have played enough, the game will be drawn to a close. But there is no set point or period when this must or does happen. Sometimes play on the table will last an hour, sometimes three, and at eleven-o'clock on a weekday evening, the domino-players are often the last to leave the pub. Sometimes, Arthur and June play a succession of people through the evening; and sometimes, a game with pairs, as tonight, evolves into a game

*of singles as some people go and some stay. Now, as 'last orders'
is called for the first time at 10.25, and the Eagle begins to thin out,
Robbie's wife Peggy comes over from her conversations in the other
room of the pub and reminds him that they should be getting back
to the farm, and Doris says that she must go and extricate Fred
from his darts match and get home to their farm and babysitter
too. It is agreed, then, that now is probably the time to 'put the
dominoes to bed' by having a final game of 'Fives and Threes'.
This means that after the current round is played (with Doris and
Nigel opposing Arthur and June at this point), the dominoes are
again placed face-down on the table and shuffled, as at the start of
a new round, and all the players (including Robbie and Sid) place
10 pence on the table to make a prize fund or 'pot'; (June has run
out of money and has to go in search of her husband, Tom, to
make up her contribution). Each player then selects four dominoes,
turns them over for all to see, and counting up the total spots on
each individual domino, calculates which totals divide by five and
which divide by three. The player whose totals divide most often
wins the game, takes the pot of money – the 60 pence, in this case,
going to Robbie – and then has the job of putting the dominoes 'to
bed', back in their wooden case. The case is then returned to Charles
behind the bar for another evening. Robbie and Peggy make their
farewells, and Doris stands up to go too, but Arthur, June and
Nigel are in less of a hurry and remain sitting chatting at the table,
sipping their beers, content to reconsider the evening's game, the
evening's crowd in the pub, while bidding farewell to the people
who pass by the table on their way to the front door and out.*

4\6

DORIS: [standing by the table] That makes us two-time
   conquerors, Nigel, because you and me also beat Arthur and
   June last time we played together, a few months back,
   remember? Even after their twenty years' experience! [Nigel
   grins but Arthur and June say nothing]. Right, then. Good
   night all.

NIGEL, ARTHUR, JUNE: 'Night. [Doris walks off in the direction of the darts board and her husband, Fred]

SID: Nay, I'm not a big dominoes' player. It must be about a
   month ago I last played – with old Billy from Howth-le-dale.
   Remember when he came down here?

JUNE: Billy Wether. Oh God! Noisy old man, wasn't he?

ARTHUR: Aye! [laughing] He came in first a few months back and he took £1 at dominoes off Alf. And he must've liked it, somehow, cos he was back a few times after that, taking money off folks . . . I reckon it was that last time he was here, when you played him, that he took £3 off Stewart. Old Billy was too good for him, Stewart said! I told him to watch him closely cos he could be cheating . . . But then we haven't seen Billy since.

SID: I heard he's been banned from most pubs in Hogart.

ARTHUR: Well he is so noisy. And I hear he gets well-riled when he's had a few. I mean he's alright in small doses. But he shouldn't spoil other folks' enjoyment by being so noisy and that.

JUNE: Five minutes of his company is enough for me!

SID: Aye! . . . But you like 'the bones', do you Nigel?

NIGEL: Yeah, it's great. I feel like I'm getting the hang of it, working out what people might have, and how they play. Most people, anyway. Someone like Stewart I find hard to follow.

ARTHUR: [laughing] Aye lad! Stewart is hard to follow for everyone, cos there's no system to his play; like, he's got no method at all. So you can't make him out.

SID: Aye. Stewart's a rum bugger. He can't add up, so how does he cope?

ARTHUR: But he wins many a time . . . Stewart and I have had good wins and then immediately bad losses. It's just luck, I suppose.

SID: I last tried to play dominoes with Stewart when there were these two gorgeous women wandering about the place in white dresses! Some offcomer party or something. And I just couldn't keep on playing after a while, but Stewart couldn't see what the difficulty was. [he laughs]

ARTHUR: No, well that's one thing Stewart isn't worried by!

JUNE: Poor thing! . . . Nay, happen it's a blessing! [she laughs]

SID: 'Least there were quite a few locals in tonight. Some nights it's full of the weirdest types, full of offcomers. Eh, Nigel? . . . So, do you see any hired assassins or IRA terrorists left among this lot, tonight, then Nigel? . . . I mean, that bloke must be! Over there walking past Charles. Look at his lapels. And his tie. He's just come in again after planting grenades out the back . . . [Arthur, June and Nigel laugh] I reckon he was following *me* around the bar before. And there's another rum fellow, Nigel. Look! [he points] Just off to send secret messages over the phone. I call him a suspicious guy. And there's another one: Ronald Reagan's brother, for sure! [he points again and they laugh again] It's lucky Peggy whisked Robbie away gay sharpish before; these assassins would have shot him on sight. [he gets up from the table] I think I better go over and chat to that 'lapel assassin', by the bar, before it's too late ... Look! His eyes are gone! He's drunk! He's a teddy boy who's not grown up, that's it, not an assassin. [he walks off, leaving Arthur and June and Nigel still laughing]

ARTHUR: Aye! There goes "The Chief" to sort things out. Quite a character is The Chief, eh Nigel? ...

NIGEL: Uh-huh.

ARTHUR: So did you win more than you lost tonight, Nigel?

NIGEL: Just about, I think. Or I came out about even.

ARTHUR: I was the opposite ... Aye, they say dominoes is a strange game. But what I love in it is its unpredictability. [Nigel nods] For example, on my four or five days' holiday each year, I like to go horse-racing. Last time, on the way home from the races, at Catterick, me and Alf beat Robbie and Fred by a total of 13–2, in two pubs ... The next night, here in the Eagle, we had a repeat contest and it was the opposite: 14–2 or something to them! And that, for me, is the wonder of the game. [Nigel grins] Like: me and June are hopeless as partners, eh June? [she nods] though separately, we're both experienced players. But as partners we get beaten by any young lads. Cos it all depends on how the dominoes come up.

NIGEL: Not completely, though Arthur. There's still the skill of working out what's likely to have gone or to come. That's why you said Stewart was so difficult to play against.

ARTHUR: Well, there's no one way of playing, lad, so you can't just tell people how to do it. There's not just one way of giving advice. Like: a good singles hand – five different suits, say – is not necessarily a good doubles hand – where you and your partner want to complement each other ... Or, like: my son-in-law, Jonty, and me have long arguments cos he says he'd not drop double-6 bare, and I say I would: I'd always try to tell my partner what I had before trying to deceive an opponent ... But anyway, I think I know what you mean. And you're right, lad. There *are* conventions of the game and you can beat opponents if you diverge from them. Or if you bluff them. And I was playing straight with you tonight, Nigel, cos I could see you were following my leads – proof of my strong suits, like – so I played straight. But there are lots of ways of bluffing ... Like I remember once, Wilbur Hackett and me thought we'd take on two good players in a pub in Kendal, and, you know, we beat them hollow because we ignored all the conventions and played quite randomly.

TOM: [walking over from the back room and sitting down on the wallseat] I don't know! I come out to the Eagle to play dominoes, I wait for a game, and then I find I been left out of the draw. And then the wife comes over to me, finally, to pay up for her Fives-and-Threes and putting the doms to bed! Is that what you call friendly!?

ARTHUR: It's your own fault, Ryecroft, for wanting to play with your wife! [they laugh]

TOM: That's true. Nay, I had a good evening. I've just been speaking to our new neighbour – that Wilsden fellow – and he's OK! A nice enough bloke.

JUNE: Aye. I said he was. And his wife too, Emma. They're both teachers at that Kendal college.

NIGEL: Well, that's it for me. I'm off home. Thanks a lot for the game. It was great.

ARTHUR: Aye, well. We'll do it again soon, lad. Like I said. Just come over and ask for a draw-in when you want one.

NIGEL: Thanks, I will. 'Night. [Nigel gets up from the table, waves to Maggie and Charles washing glasses behind the bar, and starts making his way out of the pub]

ARTHUR: 'Night, lad.

JUNE, TOM: 'Night.

MAGGIE, CHARLES: 'Night, Nigel.

5\5

As the game ends, and the world beyond the dominoes-table is set to reassert itself, players negotiate their exits – their returns to workaday identities and relations. They make their parting, ludic comments on the worlds they are returning to, and their already nostalgic comments on a world of dominoes free from outside predictability, consequence and constraint. As Doris leaves the table, then, she reasserts herself as the competitive, adult farmer, pleased to win, and pleased to have shown how the reins of adult responsibility and success have been wrested from the likes of Arthur and June. While, as Sid prepares to leave the table, the character of the rough, gruff "Chief" returns, the self-appointed gate-keeper and guardian to Wanet, ready to save the dale and the day from all manner of offcomer intrusion and terrorism. Here is already a (liminal) parodying of the ludic capability granted by the dominoes-table to see into the essential core of people and things, to turn around the serious fears of the workaday world and caricature them. Finally, Arthur seems keen to celebrate the luxury which dominoes represents of risk-taking without consequence. If unpredictability is the bane of his daily existence, trying to make a meagre living off a small farm and various piece-work cash-jobs, then the very same unpredictability is something he can celebrate and thus triumph over in the world of dominoes. Here (as with betting on horse races on holiday), losing and winning are not serious; here, success or failure at predicting the future do not correlate with the state of one's relations with one's friends, neighbours, families; here, success and failure tend to come in more or less even amounts whatever one's skill, luck, diligence, character, learning, and so on. Playing dominoes, Arthur is able to maintain close and steady relations with people, such as June, no matter the outcome of the activity in which they would appear to be primarily engaged. Furthermore, in dominoes Arthur seems to find a perfect foil to the everyday uncertainties of communication between people. For in dominoes it is possible to play in such a way that, with learning and practice, one is able to discover (and to convey), more or less, what a fellow-player (or oneself) has hidden in his hand or what no player has hidden. This is the skill which Arthur has taught Nigel. It is as if dominoes offers a medium through which to overcome the uncertainties of verbal and other communication in the everyday world: there, the possibilities and parameters of exchange are so broad that it is impossible to be sure that one knows what is hidden behind someone else's words and gestures – however often one interacts with them. On the other hand, Arthur is also able to play with the conventions of dominoes strategy so that by bluffing, a fellow-player is put off one's trail.

In short, Arthur celebrates how in dominoes he gains mastery over both the effects of chance on his present and future life, and the effects of being misunderstood.

5\6

At the same time as players negotiate their leaving of the world of dominoes, they also reprise notions concerning the moral milieu and community which it represents; (even Tom Ryecroft, who has not played dominoes this evening at all, will liaise with the table and its present occupants before departing from the pub, and recount incidents of his evening significant to the domino community – such as the sociality of his, and June's, new offcomer neighbour). Hence, there might be no one way of playing, Arthur admits, but there is, more or less, a conventional, polite, Wanet way. Coming from another dale, Arthur's son-in-law, Jonty, is not fully apprised of the wisdom of this way (and would not drop double-six bare – if it was the only six he possessed). While Tom can expect no sympathy if he seeks to overturn it (and play with June, his wife). It is only Stewart, the local adult who had learning difficulties as a child, whose play cannot be expected to exemplify this local accent. But his lack of method, system or consistency only serves to point up, in its absence, the conventionalism of the rest of Wanet players. Meanwhile, players from outside, such as Billy from Howth-le-dale, demonstrate the boundaries of community equally strongly in their play: they take money off their fellows without self-restraint, they are overweening in their play, they are noisy, rowdy and possible cheats; in a word, they do not partake in an equal distribution of enjoyment around the table of players. Significantly, then, when Arthur *is* outside the community of Wanet dominoes, such as in a pub in Kendal, he can imagine playing impolitely (randomly, unconventionally) so as to beat a pair of good outsiders. And he is proud to come home to the Eagle and own up to the incident later.

6\6

In short, for all, there is something in the dominoes-table and the domino games which routinely take place there with which many in the Eagle pub in Wanet feel at home. Here is something fixed and dependable, something timeless and transcendent, something pure and moral, something ludic and exciting, something conventional and shared, something individual and fateful.

PLAY-WRITING

To write, Virginia Woolf once asserted, is to 'bring order into the world from chaos'; the greater the writing, the clearer and more persuasive the order (1944:41). Playing dominoes in Wanet would seem to exemplify such writing, in the same way as does card-playing (in Karachi and on the edge of a Mediterranean city) as suggested by Rushdie and Berger. As games, they at least share this family resemblance.

In ending, however, let me say a little about what kind of order this play-writing gives onto. And I begin with a point concisely phrased by Nelson Goodman. The order of our humanly experienced worlds does not "lie there ready-made to be discovered". Nor is it determined by passive observation. Rather, it is reached by painstaking fabrication: "imposed by world-versions we contrive – in the sciences, the arts, perception, and everyday practice" (1984:21); contrived in terms of 'words, numerals, pictures sounds or any other kind of symbol in any medium' (1978:94). Human order (as Wittgenstein might have agreed) is a form of life as embodied in a language-game. Playing dominoes in Wanet provides, then, a symbol-system in whose regular and routine usage a version of the world (or versions, rather) is contrived, partaken of, exchanged. Here is both a language in whose terms to read a world order, a world outside the game, and also a means by which to refashion a whole world, to rewrite the world *per se*.

This explains, Goodman continues, the vast variety of versions and visions of the world which human beings create (concerning both the stuff which the world is made of and the things it contains), many of which are irreducible or can be transformed into other versions only with great difficulty and corruption. Also, this explains why there can be no 'immaculate perception' (Nietzsche). Because there is nothing that can be perceived except in terms of one or other system of conceptualisation, of symbolisation; and because there is no one symbol-system or language in whose terms the universe demands or prefers to be described aright. Each system gives onto its different world (at the least, its different aspect).

This is to say that the truth (of the universe and its worlds) is a docile and obedient servant. 'Truth' does not derive from correspondence between perception and a finished, ready-made universe; rather, 'truth' derives from a correspondence between perception and a humanly made system of conception. Hence: perceiving is producing, recognising is imposing, discovering is drafting – is finding a fit; 'truth' becomes the name for the perfect fit: the perfect tailoring and fabricating of the universe, the perfect designing of its laws and patterns. The perceiver's way of looking effects what he finds, so that, as Goodman concludes, "comprehension and creation go on together" in the human mind (1978:22).

With Goodman and Wittgenstein I feel Gregory Bateson would also have here concurred. As he put it (1972:8), the truth about the universe is mediated by the questions we ask of the universe, by the way we participate in it. Thus, "order" is always relative to our recognition; we create the order we perceive by limiting what we agree to classify, to conceptualise, as such. We determine that a particular set of relations between things (out of an infinite number of possible permutations) will be regarded as 'orderly', while all others we define as 'disorderly' or muddled. To conceptualise an orderly world, then, is to simplify, unify, stabilise, and negate much of the manifoldness and fluidity, the entropy, of the universe: to exclude an infinitude of other possible configurational organisings. (Mannheim once described concepts as amounting to "a sort of taboo against other possible sources of meaning" (1952:20) – shades of Mary Douglas 1966). In short, the propositions about the universe by which we live – in terms of which we create orderly worlds – are true to the extent that we believe them to be true and act as if they were true. "Their validity", Bateson concluded, "is a function of our belief" (1951:217).

Moreover, if order is consequent upon belief in specific symbol-systems in terms of which the universe is perceived, then order is synonymous with "knowledge": knowledge about how to look, what to see, and how to classify, how to interpret what is seen; order is information about an ordering (cf. Wiener 1949:18). The more information in one's possession, the more one has already ordered and organised, certainly prefigured, the universe into worlds, objects and relations. Bateson even used a pack of playing cards as his analogy here. Imposing order upon the universe and creating an orderly world in which to live, he wrote, is like knowing the order of the cards in a pack, and believing and acting upon that knowledge in the course of a game (1951:178,250).

To return once more to playing dominoes in Wanet, then, and the kind of orderly world it gives onto, I would say this. To partake of the form of life surrounding the dominoes-table in the Eagle pub is to share a language in whose terms the world can be ordered, indeed recreated. The order is of a very particular and limited kind: essentialised, distilled, purified; and the order derives from a knowledge of a specific (accented) way of playing dominoes: of knowing what permutations are possible and which are proper. But here is also the knowledge by which to account for permutations which are not wished-for or proper – the behaviour, improper or merely interested, of others, and the ignorance or indulgences of oneself. Hence, while to be true to the Wanet game is to try to achieve a certain fit between an ideal arrangement of dominoes and how they actually fall, since one's information is always less than complete, the order which one manages to achieve is usually less than perfect.

Finally, it is always a matter of belief as to just how real and effective this order is. Those beyond the dominoes-table do not necessarily recognise it; since they are not fully immersed in the exchange of domino-signs, if at all, one cannot expect them to have anything but partial access to (and, hence, respect for) domino knowledge, if that. And as for those sharing the table with one, team-mates as well as opponents, with no mutual access to one another's hands and no definite knowledge of how each is playing them, with no complete knowledge concerning what permutations of dominoes each regards as orderly, and with, finally, no agreement between oneself and one's opponents concerning what fit between dominoes in the hand and on the table is to be aimed at, order is relative to the point of perception – to say the least.

In sum, to play the language-game of dominoes in Wanet is to call the world to order in a rather particular (delineated, encompassable, communal, habitual, inconsequential) way. However, even when played among fellow Wanet adepts, precisely the same doubts, uncertainties, disorders creep into the system of conceptualisation as in other symbol-languages. One is led to ask: Is the order I see in the dominoes (the meaningful pattern I read there or should like to read) relative to myself alone? If others do recognise it as possibly orderly, as meaningful, will they nevertheless contest it? And even if they do not contest it, given that no way of knowing is ever perfectly foolproof, perfectly isolated, perfectly safe from disruption (since not all the dominoes are in play in people's hands), will it come about?

But if part of the essential knowledge of the universe that dominoes in Wanet gives onto concerns a lack of knowledge – a doubt that the worlds one humanly creates are ever wholly orderable – part also concerns the possibility of perfect order to which the skilful deployment of knowledge gives rise.

Chapter 8

Hard-sell or Mumbling "Right" Rudely
The hold of conversation: the power of discursive surfaces

It began with the arrival of a postcard in the morning mail, personally addressed (not merely to 'The Householder' but) to "N Rapport, 5 Stratford Av, Manchester, M20 8LZ". "SCRATCH AND WIN", it said. "Simply scratch off the coating from the box overleaf to reveal your noughts and crosses. Three crosses in a row and you have won: **either** a new Austin Metro, **or** a wide-screen colour television set, **or** a karaoke set. Three noughts in a row and you have won: **either** a VW Dormobile, **or** a personal computer, **or** £500 in cash".

I scratched off the plastic coating while I was making my breakfast: I had a row of three crosses . . . That meant I had won a new Metro or television set or karaoke set! I read the rules again to make sure, but it seemed certain: I had won!

I wasn't too excited by the idea of a karaoke set, but a new car or TV sounded great. There must be strings attached but, reading the Conditions of Eligibility for Receiving Prizes on the back of the postcard, the strings did not seem too onerous. And the fact that there were conditions cited, and that I seemed to pass them, convinced me further that I might have won something. The Conditions read that I had to be over 25 years of age, earning more than £12,000 a year, not connected personally or through my family with the "giveaway program", and that if I was married or part of a couple, then my partner should accompany me to the prize-giving ceremony because I had to be able to make a financial decision there and then.

The prize-giving ceremony would take place, I read next, at the (plush-sounding) offices of Infostar, on Oxford Street, in the centre of Manchester. In order to receive my prize, I had to telephone the offices and book an appointment one afternoon that week.

It was asked that children under six did not accompany me to the prize-giving because before the presentation, Infostar kindly requested two hours of my time to show me some products of theirs in which they were sure I would be interested. However, there would be no obligation to buy, rent or join anything, and I should merely bring along my postcard with its computerised number-identification as proof of my identity and the key to which prize I had won . . .

I read the card over a few times as I ate breakfast. Because I couldn't see the catch. There were always "Scratch and Win" freebies coming through the mail – from Reader's Digest or product manufacturers – and more to be picked up at supermarket checkouts. But there it always seemed that winners were merely eligible to enter the next round of a prize-giving draw (if they took the time to communicate with the sponsors), or were winners if they could now think up a good reason for favouring the particular product over its competitors. But all I seemed to need to do in this case was give up a couple of hours of my time. Even for a karaoke set that seemed worthwhile (a bit of a lark) – and it might turn out to be a car I had won!

I saw that the postcard had been mailed in Malaysia; no stamp, just a "Postage Paid" sticker, a code-number, and a P.O.Box number for returned mail. How did anyone in Kuala Lumpur know my name and address? Why choose me as a possible winner? I knew that Reader's Digest and others sent out random mailshots through computerised lists of people who had bought items through the mail in the past, and I knew that banks checked potential customers' credit ratings through some computerised database of names. Maybe I was on one of those? Maybe it was a list of reasonably well-off, upwardly mobile professionals (young and old) who, it was felt, might have some money to put down on the table or invest in some new product or venture? I realised I would feel quite chuffed to be regarded as one of those. I did now earn more than £12,000 a year, but it had not been long ago that I did not. The people who sent me the postcard must have known or at least suspected that I now fell into a certain money-earning category – and that, I admitted, felt pretty good. It was known in the anonymous circles of economic power in the country that Nigel Rapport was now amongst the comfortably off; it had been leaked to a company of foreign investors trying to win friends or secure a toe-hold for their product or name in Britain that Nigel Rapport might be amongst those they could influence and would be well worth influencing – even at the cost of a new Austin Metro.

"Call Now To Confirm A Win: 061–8397000", the postcard said, and when I had finished my breakfast, I did. "I think I have won something", I excitedly told the woman who answered the phone. "I have a cross in the top left-hand box, a cross in the top middle box and a cross in the top right-hand box of the grid. Doesn't that sound like a winning row?" She said that it did. But she didn't sound surprised; more perfunctory. 'When could I come down to the offices to collect the prize? Thursday afternoon? Fine.'

It was Monday then, and I looked forward to Thursday with some anticipation. I told friends and family of my good fortune and was only partially and temporarily dampened by their warnings and pooh-poohings. 'More than likely it would be a time-share sale and it would be a scam; they had been to similar things in the past.' 'I would be put under great pressure to buy (a share in a condominium block or holiday complex abroad), but under no circumstances was I to sign my name to anything.' 'It would be a waste of time, and all in aid of some rubbishy give-away at the end.' 'If I insisted on going, I should just tell them as soon as possible that I was not interested in what they were pushing and that I just wanted my gift and to go.'

These warnings and detractions made me wary, not least because of the force with which some of them were made. 'Get someone to go with you, at least', a Manchester cousin had concluded. But then I felt more sure of myself than she seemed to of herself. And I still thought the case cut-and-dried. I had a row of three crosses on my postcard which translated (without any subjunctive clauses) into a car, a TV or a music-system – or at least, in small print, 'prizes of equal or greater value should stocks run low'. And there was mention of a prize-giving presentation: I foresaw handshakes, photographs and flashcubes; items in the local newspaper and trade journals: good publicity, for them, as an aspiring foreign company; for me, a new car. At the very worst, it would be an interesting experience. Once before, when I was living in Newfoundland (feeling my way into a new field-work site), I had had a vacuum-cleaner salesman come round to my apartment to demonstrate his wares. That had been an interesting hour or so, it had been easy to get him talking (while buying nothing), and I had been left with a free silver (-coated) platter at the end for my time and trouble. At the worst, I could treat this as another fieldwork experience. But really I still thought I had struck it lucky . . .

Thursday afternoon came and I cycled into town from the university; parking a car was such a hassle that I decided that going by bike was the best bet. But then how would I transport my prize home – if it was not a car, that is! I decided I would cross that bridge when I came to it; I could always get a taxi.

Walking out of the sun into the cool, carpeted and seemingly marbelled foyer of the Infostar office block, I was surprised to find myself looking for the lift to the second floor in the company of a couple who were also clutching a postcard. "It looks like they'll be giving away a few cars this afternoon, then!" I joked as we went up in the lift together. They didn't answer, simply gave me an unfriendly and somewhat derisory look. I suddenly felt in competition with them; maybe the cars were going to be in short supply.

I made sure I was out of the lift and at the entrance to Infostar before them. There was a buzzer to push and the glass door was opened by a security guard – which slightly took me aback; the more so because he appeared to be armed. I must have looked worried by the time I had passed through the guard's ante-room into a secretarial office and reached one of the women sitting behind desks in a uniform blue suit, because after she had taken my postcard from me, ascertained my identity, checked I was not married and had no live-in girlfriend, and could decide a financial matter today, she told me to "Smile!" I smiled weakly but I was feeling uncertain.

I was then ushered into a room next to the secretaries' office and was again surprised to find other people waiting: some twenty to thirty people seated on plastic chairs in four or five rows, facing a partition wall with doors like the one I had just entered by. The people turned to stare as I came in and I quickly found an empty chair on the front row. We seemed a motley crew and an anxious audience, waiting for . . . I did not know what. Here was a mixture of economic classes, dress-styles and ethnicities. What did it mean that I had been selected for a prize alongside this group of people?

There was not long to wait, however, before one of the doors in the wall opened and a man entered holding a clipboard. "Mr and Mrs Singh?" he read out from it; a Pakistani couple got up from their seats. "Would you like to come with me please." It all appeared so organised and knowledgeable, and I felt so

off-balance, so much a cog in a larger process which somehow expected me to be there, that I was pleased that before
Mr and Mrs Singh had reached their man-with-a-clipboard (official? bureaucrat? manager? administrator? overseer? controller?),
another man had come through the same door and called out,
looking up from his pad of paper, "Mr Rapport?" He had trouble
pronouncing my name, he had a foreign accent, he was tall and
spare, and I liked him less than the first man who had called the
Singhs; (I wished I could have gone with him). But then the postcard had arrived from Malaysia and maybe the (white) security
guard and secretaries were merely fronting an organisation of
foreign businessmen . . .

I followed my guide through the door he had entered by and
found myself in a large, long room with a cavernous feel to it. At
the far end there appeared to be doors and a corridor leading on
still further. In the wall to my left there were large windows, while
photographs framed the doors in the far wall, and more
photographs, noticeboards and what appeared to be a ship's bell
hung beneath high windows on the wall to my right. The room
was abustle with activity. Men and women dressed in suits and
ties, like my guide, walking around the room, seated singly on
small tables in deep conversation with a couple or a family seated
opposite them, and other besuited men and women in seeming
conference with one another standing around the noticeboards or
huddled over their own tables. They all seemed busy and they all
smiled: they were happy to be busy, they were knowledgeable,
and they seemed to be trafficking profitable secrets between themselves around the room. Above it all was the music, loud and with
a disco beat: it added to the sensation of suddenly entering a happy
club, eagerly engaged in the business of getting on, doing and
becoming.

My guide led me a circuitous route across the floor of small
tables, smiles and talkers to his own empty table near the far end.
He offered me a seat. In my tenseness I could feel my bladder
getting uncomfortably full by now, and I could see that one of the
doors at the end of the room was labelled 'Toilet'. But it didn't
seem right to excuse myself – to ask a favour; to mention my
bodily needs – before we had even begun whatever it was he
wanted us to do together at the table, so I sat down; I decided
that under the circumstances (with the prize-giving to come) I
could hold out for a little while yet.

"My name is Fahwaz Mahmoud", my guide said as we faced each other across the small table. "But whenever I tell people that they say 'What!? Fah-who?? Sounds like Fuzzy-Wuzzy or something! Come again?!'" He smiled. "So why not just call me 'F.M.'? OK? And I'll call you 'Nigel'. Alright?" My tension increased. His introduction came out too pat. It was a patter he had practised many times before and he was too unskilled or too bored already with our exchange to make it quite sound new or authentic. I could feel sympathy for what I could imagine to be the circumstances that had led him to introduce himself like this – hadn't I recoiled from his tripping over my own surname? – but I resented him not giving me a chance to get his name right and set our exchange off on an individual course. I was already being categorised by him as part of a stereotypical group of people whose characteristics I found demeaning: parochial, racist, stupid. I bristled, and gave him a somewhat supercilious glare. I wanted to break free, right from the outset, of any stereotypes he might hold about me and about how our exchange was to proceed: I wanted to be treated – and to treat him – on a personal and personable basis. So I waited slightly before replying, and said in a quiet and slightly bored voice which I hoped would convey my tiredness with his tired categorising: "Hello Fahwaz."

"Did you park OK?" Fahwaz carried on regardless. "Oh, you came by bike!" he seemed a little surprised. "And where do you live, Nigel?" "West Didsbury", I said, but it made no impression on Fahwaz who again carried on: "And what job do you do?" ... But why did my answers make no impression on him? Because this was all just part of a dull, routine, introductory patter? Leading into something else? What else? Or because Fahwaz knew it all anyway. His organisation had sent me a postcard to my home in the first place: knew my name, knew my likely income bracket. If this exchange was a boring charade then were members of his organisation even now burgling my home? (They knew I was not at home, and they knew I was not married or living with someone.) Or was Fahwaz setting me up for something more sinister again. I felt at his mercy. What was going on here? What did they want from me? What would I have to do over the next couple of hours to end up with my prize at the end? I didn't want to jeopardise my chances of winning a car, but what would I have to do to get it? Fahwaz must know that that was why I was here. I didn't mind being taken on a 'tour' around his organisation's product before

then, but when would the tour start and what was the significance
of this fake friendliness?

"Oh, you work at the university – so, are you self-employed?"
"I'm employed by the university ..." Before I could say more, a
bell rang in the room and Fahwaz stopped talking. The whole
room went quiet as all the other officials stopped talking and their
table companions likewise. I looked round to see what was going
on, and there was a woman official standing by the side wall
with the ship's bell-rope in her hand. When she had the room's
attention and it was silent, she said: "Operators. Please be advised
that Week 7 has already gone to Mr and Mrs Chandler! Congratu-
lations." Fahwaz started clapping and all the other officials around
the room did too – even more excitedly. Some of them 'whooped'
and punched the air. There were a few cries of "Yeah!" and
"Alright!" I watched a few of the officials and followed their gaze
to one of the tables in the middle of the room where an 'operator' sat with a broad smile on his face and the couple facing him
wore sheepish grins, accepting the accolades of the room. Did they
know why, I wondered, because I certainly didn't. What had gone
in Week 7? What had they got? Was it something I might have
got? Was I in line for getting what they had just got, or was I not
working well enough or fast enough with Fahwaz? I looked around
at the other members of the public for some inkling of knowledge
or support. Were we in competition?

I did not know whether to laugh at what I had just heard
and seen as being something ridiculous, or to feel embarrassed
for the officials and their display, embarrassed for myself for
feeling so removed from it, or embarrassed for the couple who
had just 'got Week 7' for being so deeply and gullibly immersed
in it.

Before I could reflect further, Fahwaz got back to work
again on our conversation (his interrogation), now with a new
impatience and determination, although with some reticence
(embarrassment?) at meeting my eye after the recent episode.
"So: do you own your house, Nigel?" I nodded. "Yes you do. And
why do you own your own house and not rent it? Because it makes
economic sense; you're right to. If you can afford it, it's more
sensible to own than to rent. Anyone will tell you. Well I'm going
to tell you about something that makes equal sense, that anybody
can see makes sense. And you'll be kicking yourself at the end,
when I've finished telling you, because you didn't know about it

sooner and you haven't saved already all the money you might have. It was the idea of a Scottish man, who sold all his family and relations on the idea, and then he sold the idea on to the Americans who developed it into what it is today: a global organisation. So creative, the Americans are; so many ideas."

Fahwaz shifted in his seat and geared himself up, finally, for the beginning of something. "What sort of holidays do you like, Nigel?" I wondered what to say. 'Holidays' were not a category of experience that I had considered as such for a number of years; not since 'family holidays' as a child: swimming pool, beach and sun in the summer; skiing in the winter. But these days it was a matter of tagging on a few days somewhere at the end of a conference abroad, or driving round Britain visiting friends, or dropping into a travel agent to book a last minute weekend city-break or week away in the sun wherever was still available. In other words, 'holiday' types and destinations had become afterthoughts. But I knew what sort of answer Fahwaz was fishing for: package tours to beachy locations, Club Med, adventure tours, safaris, etc. Notwithstanding, I still wanted to distance myself from his stereotypical and conventional assumptions about me. "No particular sort," I replied, "all sorts." "OK, where did you last go on holiday, Nigel?" "Uh . . . Budapest." (that was the last exotic anthropology conference location). Fahwaz looked a bit wary, but tried not to seem nonplussed. "OK, and how much did that cost you?" "Uh, about £250 for five days." Despite himself, Fahwaz was taken-aback. "That's pretty cheap! What did the hotel cost?" "About £80. It was at the end of a conference I went to there, and the hotel price was part of an arrangement with the conference organisation I went with."

Fahwaz took a deep breath. "OK, Nigel, but how much did your last proper holiday cost?" Again I was silenced, as I tried to think back to the last time I had been on something which Fahwaz would recognise as a proper holiday. "Oh I don't know, Fahwaz," I eventually countered, "I went to Paris for four nights for £135." "Flight included?" Fahwaz asked clutching at a faint hope. "Yes, flight included. It was a special deal with Airtours, from Manchester via Beauvais . . . But anyway, Fahwaz, I get your drift. So these are cheap holidays I go on. But tell me what you want to say," I concluded, seeing that I needed to concede something to Fahwaz for him to move along with the next part of his patter. He was looking at me quizzically enough as it was, trying to picture just what sort of holidays I was satisfied to go on! Some kind of latter-day hippy, it seemed.

"OK, Nigel. Well, let's say that normally a holiday is going to cost you £1,000. Just to quote a round figure. Maybe a bit more, maybe a bit less. But let's say £1,000 as a ballpark figure." The figure seemed astonishing to me, but Fahwaz seemed back on track. I was not sure of the consequences of allowing myself to go further down the road of being categorised as someone who might normally spend £1,000 on a holiday, but it seemed better than stalling matters still further and making Fahwaz more uncomfortable. So I nodded, in a way which I hoped was recognisably 'semi-non-committally', 'just-for-argument's-sake'. "OK," Fahwaz steamed on, "now I'm going to tell you how to get a week's holiday, anywhere in the world, every year, for just £155 . . ." Fahwaz sat back to let the figure sink in – and looked quite pleased with himself. He leaned forward on the table again. "That's right. £155. Now, it's not a time-share, and it's better than the cost of a package holiday. It is actually buying a property abroad for a week per year. It's not buying time in a property, it's actually buying the property for that week. And unlike time-shares, you can sell if you want to. Also unlike time-shares, for a mere £48 you can exchange your week for a week anywhere else in the world! Now how does that sound, Nigel! Good? You buy a week – say in Lanzarote – and you need never go there at all. That week is like your key to a week's holiday anywhere in the world." Fahwaz brought out a pen and began sketching on the pad of paper between us: a house shape, subdivided into numerous little boxes. "Look, here are 52 squares for 52 weeks in the year. And you are buying a 52nd part of the property. We divide up the cost of the property – to build and maintain – by 52 . . ."

I knew by now that although it might not exactly be a time-share sale, it was the next worst thing. This was what I had been warned about, and I didn't want it; I just wanted the spiel to be over and for me to collect my prize and leave. So I tried to sound uncommitted and unimpressed while still 'uh-huh'-ing in the affirmative as Fahwaz went into the details of the operation: how I could rent 4 weeks per year in total because I could 'borrow' on the weeks I owned in upcoming years up to a total of 3 years ahead; and how, anticipating this demand, they only in fact sold 80 per cent of the space in any development – say, in Lanzarote – so that 20 per cent was always left over for extra-rentals; and how each year some 15 per cent of owners would decide not to take up their weeks' ownership and were pleased to rent them out to other owners. How once I owned my week, then it was mine in perpetuity, like any other possession; and I could sell it, rent it, gift it, exchange it, will it, exactly as I saw fit. How the company published five brochures per year, one big and four small, with all the holiday choices and destinations in for me to choose from – including some free holidays for members in places that were underselling that year. How the company owned 7,000 units in thirty countries spread all round the world in every holiday destination I could imagine. And how they built in places where property was cheap – such as Lanzarote ('Had I been there? Beautiful!') – and how once they had finished their unit in a place they made sure no more planning permissions would be forth-coming for anyone else. How I would be met at the airport by a company coach, fully air-conditioned, and taken directly to the holiday resort and the apartment, fully-furnished and cleaned by daily maids, which would be mine to own for the week.

In the middle of his stream of explanation, the bell sounded again, the woman again announced to the silent room that Mr & Mrs So-and-So had bought week such-and-such, and there was more applause, whooping and back-slapping. When it had finished, Fahwaz returned to his exposition at the precise point he had left off without overtly even recognising the interruption. Obviously we were to treat it simply as an intermittent punctuation of our exchange: too noisy actually to speak through, but still not to be 'noticed'. I hoped this was because Fahwaz was now treating me as more of an 'adult' – able to see through the charade, even if not to talk through it. But then was it my imagination that as more bells sounded, Fahwaz's anxiety and his speed of delivery gradually increased? Maybe the bells were to be regarded as timed 'rounds' of our conversation, and something had to be won by him before the final one.

The problem was that as I repeated my 'uh-huhs' to the deep-ening details, trying to sound *au fait* but also non-committal – not wholly convinced or impressed – Fahwaz took my distance to be a lack of understanding. And so he would repeat the elucidation of the details. Only when I then sounded convinced by the logic, and admitted that here was 'a great idea', would he then pass on to the next part of the explanation. "Name somewhere, anywhere, you would like to go for a holiday, Nigel", he suggested at one point. "Russia", I answered, trying once more to steer the conversation into more individual and idiosyncratic waters: if Fahwaz insisted on using up all of the two hours of my time (as the postcard stipulated), exposing me to all the bitty details, then, I reasoned to myself, at least I would attempt to speak with him person-to-person: to escape the bureau-speak, and tell him something of what I actually wished. "Russia!" Fahwaz actually grinned. "Naughty boy, Nigel! But ask me again, next year about there and I might just say 'Yes'. Because we are working on accessing a unit there right now, so it won't be long before you really can use your key there too." 'Naughty boy'! I didn't quite know what to make of that. Fahwaz was playing with me again, playfully castigating me for not properly playing my part in our conversation and giving 'reasonable' answers – and I was put back on my guard. If he was admitting that the whole conversation was a game we were playing together, and he expected me to be recognising the parts we were playing – then what was the real purpose of my being here, and what did he really know of me? ... Quickly I added, "France." "OK, Nigel. We have units on the Riviera, in the Alps, in Paris, in many places that you could exchange your key for ..."

"But look," he finally concluded, "I've been talking enough. It's boring if I just do the talking all the time" – so it was some kind of game of repartee we were engaged in? – "I've explained the set-up to you, you say you understand it, and you agree it's a good idea – is there anything else about it you wish to ask me? Ask me some questions." Suddenly it was like being at an interview, where having nothing to say shows a distinct lack of motivation, not to say creativity. And I really did want to find out more about Fahwaz – whom I kept feeling I could quite like if I could get to talk to him on a more personal tack – and more about what I had come to feel was the large organisation behind him. I asked him about the latter first; he explained, readily enough (if a bit bored), that 'there were seven centres around the country doing the same as this Manchester one this afternoon, and he had come up from Guildford for this. They operated three sessions a day,' he continued, 'and six days a week. But really, the organisation was international. They operated by fax so that they knew at any one time which weeks in the year were being bought by which people, where in the world. In fact, the postcard I received was sent from Malaysia. Did I know why? Because a special price had been arranged by The Company with the Malaysian government which made it cheaper to post all the cards from there, even by airmail, than use the British Post Office!' So even the Malaysia connection was not some piece of information that was really secret and that my perceptiveness caused me to have an advantage over Fahwaz! Even this bit of his company's 'game' Fahwaz was prepared to reveal to me – like the 'play' of proper question and answer – so confident must he be and so powerful his organisation. He tapped the side of his nose and looked down it at me conspiratorially. And I understood: his company knew all the canny business tricks; they were no fools. Would it not be good to be on the same team as them! Was I really going to miss this investment opportunity?

Fahwaz's revelations continued, and so my confidence in 'reading' him and our exchange decreased proportionally. 'Every recipient of a postcard was a winner', he admitted next, 'while the gifts cost his company nothing because they were all promotions.' But how, I wondered, was Fahwaz able to tell me all this? What was his relationship to his patter? And what should mine be? In some desperation, I asked him about himself. He again looked bored, as if the question and his answering were irrelevant and beneath him, but he humoured me. He was married and lived in Burnley; he had two brothers living in Canada. He had been a solicitor, originally, with his own company, but he gave it up to take on this job. And now he earned far more and was very happy. He owned a Holiday Week of his own in Puerto Rico, but through it he'd had holidays all over the world . . .

Eventually I ran out of questions, and Fahwaz ran out of patience. At one point Fahwaz had exclaimed "Good question, Nigel!" which pleased me because of how animated and entertained Fahwaz had suddenly (and temporarily) seemed, and worried me because of what it implied about me becoming part of Fahwaz's category of 'conventional members of the public and their mindset', which I wanted to avoid. I still didn't know if our conversation was going to plan, going as he wished and expected, or not. Was it an interview I was passing? If so, how would my performance affect my prize? Fahwaz kept asking if there was anything that he had said that I did not understand and that I wished him to go over again. While I had thought up all the rejoinders I could without wishing either to seem a fool who could not grasp a complicated concept, or to extend the duration of the exchange for any longer. 'Well', Fahwaz concluded, 'if there was absolutely nothing else he could explain to me about the workings of the Holiday Concept, that was the end of his part of the afternoon'. And he repeated one last time: "So you understand everything I've told you, and you agree it's a very good idea? Good." And he looked around him. "I'll bring my boss over to talk to you now about the financial side of things. I don't do that. That's not my job. My job is just to explain the workings to you and then I hand you over to him for a chat." He seemed pleased to be able to distance himself from the talk over financial matters, and I was pleased that our conversation would apparently end on a convivial note, and that it would not be Fahwaz I would be turning down when I ultimately said that I wanted none of what they were selling and could I now be presented with my prize and leave.

As it happened, his boss was busy at another table and so, as a time-filler, Fahwaz led me first to view the photographs dotting the side and far walls of the room. They all showed happy smiling faces, and tanned bodies in swim suits, enjoying holidays in the sun by a beach or pool; and then more formally dressed smiling faces around a bar or restaurant later that night. Also there were framed endorsements from happy customers: "Never had it so good", "Best decision I ever made." Fahwaz escorted me past the photos as if he were showing off his family: I should feel not a little privileged to see these photographed people feeling so relaxed and at home. So, as we toured the walls, I tried to make impressed and grateful sounds. In fact, at one point I was sure that a prominent smiling face was that of the one-time star of Welsh rugby, J.P.R. Williams, and I was impressed – and also sad that he had signed up to this outfit: I thought I knew him better, and I was uncertain that I would want to go on holiday with him.

All the time of my exchange with Fahwaz to date I had been nursing my increasingly full bladder. There simply had not seemed an apposite moment in our conversation to break off and 'ask to be excused'. It would have felt too much like seeking a favour from Fahwaz, giving him the upper hand and demeaning myself by revealing my lack of control over bodily demands, not to mention lengthening the exchange still more. Finally, after the tour of the photographs, I spotted an arrow pointing to a toilet and broached the subject with my guide. Fahwaz said fine and instructed me afterwards to go and watch a short slide-show they had prepared which would be awaiting me in the film gallery near the toilet, and which would explain their Holiday Operation again.

It was an enormous relief to be alone – after some one-and-three-quarter hours of verbal sparring. I went to the toilet, took advantage of the comparative privacy to say aloud 'Hells Fucking Bells' and 'Thank God' a few times, exorcising the sense of being unable to say what I wanted, to fill the public air with verbalisations I actually felt, and then went to watch the slide-show. I was alone in the auditorium and I began to wonder how it was that even though it had taken Fahwaz and me all this time to reach this point in the proceedings, in my 'inculcation', it was taking those who had entered the room at roughly the same time even longer ... The slide-show was upbeat and jollifying: more photos of happy faces and brown bodies by the sea, accompanied by an unctuous advertising voice-over which told me: "There's never been a better time to buy the holiday home of a lifetime, and the time is Now!" I decided there was no reason why I should subject myself to much of this (there was no-one watching me), so I stood up and turned my back on the screen and walked round the small room in the semi-darkness and felt more like myself again. The little rebellion against the conventions of slide-watching – albeit invisible – helped me regain at least a little composure and self-esteem. After some fifteen minutes of this, the slide-show finished going over what Fahwaz had gone over and I felt sufficiently steeled up to face Fahwaz's boss. I returned to Fahwaz's table, pleased to be tracing my own route through the array of little tables and conversationalists, and not in thrall for once to Fahwaz's guidance.

Fahwaz was sitting waiting for me. 'Would I like some tea? The boss was almost ready for me.' I said 'Yes', but before Fahwaz could call for the polystyrene cup and the plate of biscuits to be brought over (by one of the women operatives), the room was once again called to silence by the chiming ship's bell and we were told that yet another precious week in the year had been snapped up by a lucky family joining the Holiday Club. Shortly after that, the boss arrived at our table. Fahwaz stood up for him and moved his own chair around the table slightly; so that when they sat down they were both facing me. Fahwaz introduced me, and his boss extended his hand.

The boss seemed busy – just off a plane, on a tight schedule, able to fit in a few meetings, settle a few deals, extend a few bene-

fits, before jetting off again. He wore a shirt and tie, but, unlike
Fahwaz, he had had to remove his jacket because of his concerted
rushing around. He was a short man, younger and spottier than
Fahwaz, with an unattractively severe haircut, but Fahwaz seemed
in some awe of him. He spoke in an Irish accent and got straight
down to business: "So Fahwaz has explained the workings to you,
Mr Rapport, Nigel, and there is nothing you do not understand:
you agree it's a great idea?" I nodded, still hopefully non-commit-
tally. The boss and Fahwaz looked at each other. "Good." I wished
that Fahwaz was not there. It was not just that the two of them
at the table with me seemed unfair odds. It was also that it seemed
I would in the end be reneging on an arrangement with Fahwaz
if I did not sign up with the boss – and I wished Fahwaz were not
present to witness that. But I did not see how I could do otherwise. Because I was telling the truth: I did understand what Fahwaz
had told me, I did think that for some people, in some circumstances, it might be a good idea, but no-one had then asked me
if I thought it was a good idea for me. It was as if there was only
one logic – the logic of a good idea, the logic of financial sense,
the logic of what people conventionally, stereotypically, wished to
get out of a holiday – and that since this logic had been explained
to me and I had claimed to have understood it, that therefore
there was no way out of my taking the next step of signing up to
The Idea myself.

Now the boss got out his pad of paper and began scribbling
figures onto it, talking professionally as he did so: "One week's
apartment ownership in Lanzarote: that's £8,200 at cost; less this
month's special reduction of £1,200; less £1,850 deposit payable
today; which would leave you owing £5,000 odd; and with interest-
free credit, I could get that for you, Nigel, at just £26 per week."
He finished writing and handed the pad over for me to see. "Now,
how does that look, Mr Rapport? Doesn't that look a good deal?"
I pretended to study the page in front of me and wondered what
to do. So that was why Lanzarote kept on being mentioned as
example, because that was in fact all that was being sold! I read
the scribbled figures studiously over again (knowing I was
blushing) before deciding there was nothing to do but admit that:
'Yes, it did seem like a good deal.' "Welcome to the club, Nigel!"
The boss's hand shot out towards mine and he beamed a smile
. . . So this was the moment of truth. And somehow because it
was a matter of a physical not verbal exchange which was now

being demanded of me, I felt more able to take a stand against it. There was no way I was going to shake the hand extended towards me, and there was no way that this spare, white-shirt-and-tied, young and pushy operator could make me. I was confident in my bodily capabilities, and they would easily enable me to refuse to be further led on, to stop being bamboozled by the farcical rigamarole of this afternoon's interaction. I sat and glowered at the hand extended towards me, my face feeling flushed, adamantly refusing the gesture until the hand was withdrawn. The boss looked at Fahwaz and then back at me:

"I don't understand, Nigel. I thought you said the deal was a good one?"

"I did. But it's not for me. I'm not going to join anything. It's a good deal but I don't want it. Certainly not in Lanzarote. I thought I could buy my week's Holiday Key in a property almost anywhere in the world?"

"I don't understand. Fahwaz told me you understood what he told you, and you agreed it was a good idea, but now you say you don't want to sign up for it. Why not?"

"I'm sorry. Fahwaz did explain it all very well, but I just don't want it. I'm not a joiner. I don't want that sort of holiday."

"Well, I don't understand. Do you, Fahwaz?"

"No. I don't understand. Nigel told me he understood and he said it was a good idea. That was why I brought you over, boss. I wouldn't have bothered you if I knew Nigel thought this."

"Look, it's not Fahwaz's fault. It's just that I don't go in for this sort of thing. The deal seems a good one, and I can think about it – but I don't think it's for me."

"Is it the money, Nigel? Look. If you buy it this year and you decide not to use it, I could get £500 rent for you straight away. That's the best I can do for you. But you have to sign now. For financial reasons – inflation etc. This price is today's price only."

The boss wrote more figures down on his pad, and showed them to me:

"And the price of the apartment is freehold remember; none of your English leasehold properties."

"Look. It's not the money – although it's not exactly cheap. It's just that it's not for me and I'm not signing. I'm certainly not signing anything here and now. OK?"

The boss and Fahwaz looked at each other again, quizzically. Finally, the boss said:

"Well, there's nothing more I can say. Maybe I should go and leave you two to have another chat ... And you call me back, Fahwaz if you want me."

"Sure, boss. I'm sorry. I don't know what happened."

The boss rose and left, and I was left alone again with a very embarrassed-seeming Fahwaz. I did not want to meet his eye. I felt like a naughty child; I felt as though I was about to be told off, or to come in for some pressure of the 'third degree'; I felt as though I had deserved whatever I got because I had let Fahwaz down and got him into trouble. "I'm sorry Fahwaz," I began, "you explained yourself very well but it's just not for me. I'm sorry, I'm not a joiner. I don't join things like this." He looked hurt: "You made me seem a fool, Nigel. You said you understood."

I felt so bad at this point, and so foolish – about getting myself into this situation, about making Fahwaz seem a fool and getting him into some sort of trouble – that it almost seemed to me better to sign. At least that would give me a way out of this horrid situation. If I signed, if I spent some £5,000, £8,000, it wouldn't break me financially (my family and friends would always help out money-wise if the worst came to the worst), and I would be away from this interaction, this room, this afternoon – and Fahwaz's displeasure, dislike, vengeance. However, Fahwaz stayed silent for a few seconds more, wondering how now to proceed with me, and that breathing space gave me a moment mentally to regroup. I returned from the flight of fancy of surrendering my will and giving away my money. I would simply leave. Now. Prize or no prize. New Austin Metro car or no new car. It was simply not worth extending this debacle and this agony by another minute.

I told Fahwaz that I wanted to leave. He looked resigned. "Look: I don't care if you sign or not, Nigel; it's just my job. It's just that I thought you said it was a good deal." He now looked hurt, but I was determined to leave, and told him so again. Finally, Fahwaz pushed back his chair and stood up: "OK. I'll just go out and arrange your prize." He meandered through the tables and went through a door to the secretary's office.

As the minutes of Fahwaz's absence mounted and I was left to be stared at – like a pariah and a failure, sitting at my table clutching my coat and bicycle pump – as the buzz of conversation continued and as the rushing, smiling operators darted around, and the thump of disco music beat out, my worries returned. How long did it take to 'arrange my prize'? What needed to be 'arranged' anyway? What sort of welcoming committee would await me on the other side of the door? Would Fahwaz be wanting to get back at me? After seeming to lead him, his boss and organisation a merry dance only to end up refusing their offer, would they allow me to escape scot-free?

At last, Fahwaz reemerged and, without fully meeting my gaze, motioned me to follow him out. As I did I considered the fact that of the people who had arrived with me at 2.30, I was the first to leave. It was now after 4.30, but there were Mr and Mrs Singh still deep in conversation with their operator. How were they coping with the verbal onslaught? Did Fahwaz *et al*. normally get most people to sign up of an afternoon? By now we had reached the door and Fahwaz held it open for me: "This is where we say 'Goodbye', Nigel." It sounded ominous. It was clear that Fahwaz was now in a hurry to see me off. Why the rush? I wanted us to part friends; I wanted a sign from him that there were no hard feelings before we parted and I was left alone to be dealt with by other operatives (whom?) in the outer offices. I extended my hand to Fahwaz and he shook it, but only grudgingly. "No hard feelings, Fahwaz? Thanks. You were very good." I tried my best to bring him out of his huff, and to draw out our farewell, in order to calm myself. I had achieved some sense of routine in my dealings with Fahwaz, but who knew what was to come? However, Fahwaz withdrew his hand and closed the door, returning into the main room.

In the secretaries' office, I was beckoned to the desk of the woman who had first told me to 'Smile'. En route, I noticed that the security guard had left his ante-room and was now standing by the door to this office; he also appeared to be fingering a holster at his belt. Taking my postcard from me, the uniformed woman at the desk checked the computerised number on it against a printed list in front of her: "572835. That means you win a wide-screen colour television set." 'Oh well,' I thought, 'that's not bad! Not the car, but at least it's better than a karaoke set'. But then the woman continued: "Unfortunately, the batch we ordered has proved to be below British standard. So, like it says on the back of your postcard, we are replacing it with goods of equal value." She held up a small padded case for me to see: "These two gold watches, gent's and lady's, will be sent you in a few weeks." She finished her sentence and looked down, returning to her papers. I was left standing by the desk.

It all seemed so sudden, such an anti-climax, that for a second I didn't react. What could I do or say to show my disappointment, to protest. I took a step forward, to make a token gesture at inspecting the watches, a token gesture at least to verify that I was getting my money's worth for the time I had spent and discomfort undergone. They were not going to palm me off in complete silence. As I did so, the security guard took a step forward too and bristled, his hands at his belt, as if ready to deal with any real remonstrance on my part. "Can I see?" I said weakly, and the woman looked up, glared, and grudgingly handed me the box of watches. They were both of yellow metal, but they did not seem to add up to the worth of a television set. And they did not form a matched set. "You can't take these away with you", she said. "Yours will be sent you in ten days or two weeks." I didn't know what further I could do or say. The injustice seemed enormous and I was obviously being fobbed off with nothing. I may not have been under threat to my person, but they were making of me a complete fool. None the less, as far as they were concerned the exchange was over and I was to leave forthwith. And the security guard would make sure I did even if I wished not to, or wished to take away some material winnings with me now.

I felt sick but not able to mount a counter argument. I returned the watches to the secretary, mumbled "Right" as rudely as I could, and allowed the security guard to escort me out of the office and shut the security door behind me. In the elevator and walking to my bicycle I realised I needed the toilet desperately again but I decided to punish myself by cycling home with a full bladder: how could I have thought they would be giving away anything, never mind a new car! That was what, after all, the proudly belligerent business motto 'There's no such thing as a free lunch!' amounted to. How naive could I have been to think otherwise? What a waste of two-and-a-half precious hours. What agony to put myself through voluntarily. I could 'put it all down to experience', as they say, I could 'count my blessings' at having finally escaped with only my pride dented, but overall I felt sick at being such a gullible (and spineless) fool.

And that was what my family and friends told me over the next weeks as I recounted the tale – indeed, made a moral narrative out of it, after dinner and over lunch. "There's no such thing as a free lunch, Nigel! You should know that. How do you think they make their money?" "Why do you think they mail these postcards from Malaysia? Because the whole thing is illegal under British law. 'Cheaper postage!' Rot!" "You should have just gone in there and made the whole thing a joke from the start. And then finally said: 'Right. I want my prize now.'"

A few days after the encounter I received a standardised letter from Infostar Ltd confirming the secretary's story. "Dear Guest," it read, "due to unforeseen circumstances we are unable to supply the award which was originally indicated. As such, it is necessary that we invoke our right, as detailed on the reverse of your original card, to substitute it with an alternative award. Details of the alternative award will be forwarded to you shortly. We trust that your time spent with us was both entertaining and informative. Assuring you of our best attention at all times, Yours Sincerely," and then a scribbled name "For and on behalf of Infostar Limited."

The following week, there was another letter, this time from "Golden Awards Company (UK)", the "Redemption Certificate Distributor for Infostar". To redeem the certificate enclosed for one "His and Hers Pair of Designer Watches" – "This precious pair of His and Hers Designer watches boasts of hand assembled mechanisms with analog display; their gold plated materials are created with a high degree of quality and refinement. Both watches come with a calender. Ideal for you and your loved ones for use on any occasions" – I simply had to send £29.95 (banker's draft, money order or postal order) for shipping, handling, insurance and redemption fee, to Golden Awards in London, within 15 days of receipt of this letter. Not only, it seemed, had I undergone a most unpleasant encounter, but I would end up with absolutely nothing at the end of it. For the watches themselves did not appear to be worth more than £29.95, and upon telephoning Golden Awards Company I was informed that I could not pick up my prize personally and so get round the 'shipping, handling, insurance and redemption fees'!

Only by making my own narrative of the encounter – in spoken accounts, and now in this essay – in such a way as to place myself hopefully in a sympathetic light, have I been able to overcome the overriding feeling of being made to seem completely foolish, and of having absolutely no riposte against an organisation that had held out to me the carrot of a 'freebie', only to (seek to) use me entirely for its own profit.

A Goffman would no doubt find much of remark in the above encounter; not to mention a Garfinkel, a Bernstein or a Foucault.

Here, après *Goffman (1961:*passim*), is a quasi-'total institution' inculcating me into its encompassing, bureaucratic control, through an initiation process designed to 'disculturate' – to break down my confidence and mortify my conception of self (violate the erstwhile territory of the self through an invasive public knowing of what was once private) – and so programme me for a new moral career in a new world. Here,* à la *Garfinkel (1968:*passim*), is a 'status degradation ceremony' in which a social group employs certain organisational and communicational strategies so as to cause shame in one or more of its members or neo-members, transform their public identity into a lower type, for the purpose of effecting a certain group function, such as eschewing eccentricity and rebelliousness; I am shamed into accepting the definition of others in the room concerning the worth of what they propose, and feeling that my own lack of loyalty to it is a failing in me. Here,* à la *Bernstein (1972:*passim*), is a 'restricted code' of limited verbal resources and conversational manoeuvre which holds me in thrall for the benefits of social solidarity; I find no way to counteract or reroute the course of our exchange, no way to elaborate on its relations in more personal directions, and must abide by its formal terms or cause rupture and fear violence. And here,* à la *Foucault (1972:*passim*), is a 'discourse' at once verbal and behavioural, collective and coercive, which inhabits my body and habituates my mind. The discourse of organised capital and commerce devolves into the micro-social power of the salesperson over the potential consumer, whereby the pressure to buy and partake translates into all manner of sensate, psycho-social and mental pressures and reactions; I feel it is almost better to part with my money than to disappoint and distance the salespersons, and hence undergo further discomforts, corporeal and conscientious.*

'Almost better to part' . . . but not quite, and the difference, the distance, is surely crucial. I did not sign, I did not become embroiled, I did walk away. No great victory perhaps, but a significant enough one for my purposes here. For what I would emphasise in the encounter and in my narrating of it are the apertures, the puncturings, the interruptions which cause the process of the encounter (the ceremony, the code, the discourse) to be suspended and, however marginally, undermined. For these reveal to me the persons behind the role-players (the ceremonial officiants, the speakers of code, the discursive sites), persons who cannot help themselves from periodically standing back from the social routines in which they are

engaged and reflecting on them, making sense of them, in ways which may subvert the totalising effects of those routines and in ways which reveal those persons to be able to adopt, seemingly at will, positions wholly outside the domain and determinism of those routines. Whatever the order and sense propounded by the logic of the routines as such, the persons taking part in those routines, animating them by their mental and bodily, verbal and behavioural, presence in those routines, are able to stand back and write their own sense, compose their own personal narratives which enable them to say: 'Here I am partaking of a conversation (a language-game, an encounter, a ceremony, a code, a discourse).'

Of course, to theorists of social determinism such as those alluded to above, this sort of cognitive move is not possible. "There is no meta-language", Lacan would exhort; and Derrida: "There is no outside-text." All that is possible, Foucault would conclude, is a move from one discourse to another: the only transcendence is a playing off of discourses against one another, a subverting of one power relationship in terms of others; while there is always power (in every exchange in every relationship), there is always entrapment, there is always a coming to consciousness in terms of a particular system of social signification, a particular discourse or other, and there are always and everywhere "bodies totally imprinted by history".

None the less, it seems to me that what the above narrative elicits is an account of the interpreting person: the individual who stands outside the discourse, who is affected by it to varying extents but is in no measure the effect of it. For Fahwaz, then, there were moments when it seemed clear that he was aware of the playing-out of a language-game: a game he learnt and was paid to play, but now a game of his own instigation, a game from which he inter-mittently stood back, a game he at some times played better than others, a game which he was able to treat more or less lightly. Hence: "Naughty boy, Nigel", as I enquire about holidays in Russia; him taking a deep breath and then: "but how much did your last proper holiday cost?" as I prevaricate with accounts of cheap conference breaks; and his embarrassed reticence surrounding the episodic ringing of the ship's bell and the ritual announcements.

Moreover, if my account of Fahwaz's being affected by our language-game is only ever an interpretation, an empathetic account of what, to me, Fahwaz's behaviour seemed to say, I know what I thought and felt; and, of course, it is of this that the above narrative largely treats. And what I have tried to show is that there was no moment at which I did not experience the mixed emotions of both recognising what the language-game expected of me and knowing precisely where I stood – actually, personally – in relation to it. It was not always so easy a matter to know how to reconcile these positions – what to say, how to act, how to seem – and it was by no means an easy matter to know where my interlocutors, the chief perpetrators, stood in relation to their language-game, but it was never hard to see myself both present and absent: a conscious player in the game (however reluctant) but never unconsciously played by it.

The determinist theorists, of course, have one last string to their bow. This is the argument that I no more know my own mind than I know Fahwaz's, because: both are the playthings of unconscious urges which are closed to conscious retrieval and reflection (Freud, Lacan); or, alternatively, the interiority of mind is a fiction since it is constituted through public and shared systems of signs (Foucault, Levi-Strauss); so my mind and Fahwaz's are equally superficial and open to being read through collective procedures of interpretation (Goffman, Garfinkel). Either way, presence is no guarantee of authenticity (Derrida); being there – seeing, thinking, imagining, empathising, feeling, intuiting and knowing – provides no claim to any knowledge that is not the property of the language-game that is being played out: the language-game knows its speakers but they do not know it; the 'first-person point of view' is overdetermined.

Against this final ploy, this last play, there is no response. For this is the point where argument, as Rorty might have put it, dissolves into the tautology of metaphysics. Which is why I prefer at this point to stay mute, end this brief envoi *and hope the above narrational exposition of anxious interiority speaks for me.*

Chapter 9

Discourse and Creativity
Sheikh Alwan: Fathalla: Sid Askrig

> Mzeina culture, being under the continual threat of effacement, tells itself in an allegorical way that it exists, metonymizing private experience for the history of the collectivity, and conjoining the local poetics of storytelling with the global political realities of neocolonialism.

This is the conclusion to Smadar Lavie's book, *The Poetics of Military Occupation. Mzeina Allegories of Bedouin Identity under Israeli and Egyptian Rule* (1990). It is a study of charismatic and creative individuals. In this essay I want first to explain the paradox by which this theme can eventuate in these closing sentences – individual creativity and charisma affording agency to 'Mzeina culture' – before considering more broadly the place of individual creativity in the anthropological writing of cultural discourse.

If 'discourse' is understood, broadly, as ways of speaking commonly practised and specifically situated in a social environment, then the question becomes whether limits to the routine and conventional forms of what is said need similarly limit what is known (thought, experienced and imagined) by individual speakers. In this essay, in particular, I take issue with those who would in this way 'decentre' the individual from the analysis of discourse.

SHEIKH ALWAN

Over the past 45 years, the South Sinai (like a political football) has been passed between Egypt and Israel on some five occasions. Throughout this time, Lavie describes the Mzeina (5,000 from the among the 13,000 South Sinai Bedouin population) as pawns: helpless to influence the external processes and interests impinging upon their land (cf. Marx and Schmueli 1984:*passim*). Indeed, this continual disenfranchisement has precluded for the Mzeina a 'typical' Bedouin identity: whether or not it has ever been practised, the romance of fierce nomads on loping camels across a vast desert continues to be inscribed by traditional Mzeina folk narratives – just as it was by those of turn-of-the century travellers, not to mention contemporary mass media and tourist guides who frequent Mzeina encampments. But now the military occupation has penetrated local life so deeply as to permeate even the most delicate and intimate of intra-tribal discourses. Hence, defining themselves as 'Bedouin' in contradistinction to outsiders amounts to a crisis in Mzeina cultural existence; only compounded by the certainty that open defiance means beatings, jail, even death.

In this situation, it is to a 'symbolic reconstruction' of identity and community that the Mzeina turn (Cohen 1985:*passim*). They import Islam and welcome radio preachers from Egypt and Saudi Arabia against the Israelis, and they 'check out' Christianity and flirt with Hebrew against the Egyptians. Above all, they tell one another stories. To be precise, allegories: the vicissitudes, conundrums, ambiguities of life under military occupation are narrativised into allegorical outbursts of protest. Here are moralistic, multivocal narratives which replace the straight talk of the quotidian public domain dominated by the occupier and thus symbolically confront the spatial and temporal boundaries of the occupying state.

'Allegories', Lavie describes as texts which tell an individual story so as to convey a lesson, a moral example, for a group. From the fragmentariness of a personal experience is woven a public story which unifies, contains and heals all: the individual as metonym (or layer) of the collective. This layering of the allegorical narrative also allows the interweaving of the occult, the grotesque and fantastical with the mundane. Moreover, allegory plays with otherness and the oxymoronic, and includes voices of self-criticism.

Mzeina allegories take the form of variations on a traditional genre of Bedouin legends called *Kan Ya Makan*, meaning "It has or has not happened that . . ." These are fantastic and also didactic stories which deal with a range of themes and figures from a tribal pantheon; they delineate pristine Bedouin behaviour in an ideal setting. In the current, improvised form, however, the fantasticality pertains not to the realm of myth but to current experience:

the absurdities of daily life are likened to and conjoined with the legendary. Here, then, are personal experiences of frustration, physical discomfort and spiritual humiliation fashioned into impersonal, distant, and funny stories in a stylised, traditional oral literary form, and dealing, as per tradition, with inter-tribal agreements, legal disputes, migration cycles, folk remedies, hospitality protocols, kinship and marriage patterns, and the history of resistance to colonialism. The individual experiences of the present come to serve as metonyms for collective traditions from the past, the artistry and persuasiveness of the narration being to redeem the present by thus linking it with an ideal past, hence creating authentic legends out of contemporary realities.

Furthermore, the narration is such that in these individual stories the listeners hear their own; presenting personal accounts of the paradoxes of everyday life – the yearning to be free-spirited nomads while faced with the conflicting realities of encroaching foreign settlements, military bases, rock concerts, naked tourists and policemen – the narratives mirror the endemic cultural crisis of the tribal whole. Hence, the performance provides a catalyst and conduit by which discrete lives come into contact, as well as affording didactic examples of how to press the incongruities of the present into serving nomadic tradition. The lesson is that while this tradition may seem to be marginal to the tribe's everyday life it still acts to define every tribesperson's identity; daily life may entail a continual culture shock but the very grotesqueness of that shock is evidence of the continuing vibrancy of the cultural expectations (of fantasticality) which underlie it.

By means of local poetics, in short, world politics are overwritten and the tensions of a harsh quotidian existence released. At the least, allegory provides some form of restoration of tribal dignity and identity and an elevated feeling of *communitas* and composure, of essence not disjunction. Through creative allegorical explication and redefinition, everyday paradoxes are transformed and overcome, so that Mzeina identity as wholly Bedouin and vitally distinct comes to be reaffirmed; Mzeina life is freed from the hegemonic rationale of the occupier. However much politico-economic relations may appear the same, the tribe is again a whole-society not a part.

The invention of these stories does not take place at a regular or predetermined time, however. Nor does the performance belong to a formal occasion, a matter of institutional heralding or sanctioning. Nevertheless, such performing amounts to a 'ritual' process. For inasmuch as the allegories overcome the paradoxical and absurd by demonstrating a transcendant logic, imaging a meaningful whole which includes all, they represent a break with ordinary discourse and commonsense expectations – they take place in the interstices of the everyday – and in such a way as to complement that discourse and make up for its deficiencies of meaning.

Imagine this: an everyday scene, of routine interaction, where talk has turned to the circumstances of present Mzeina identity and the hybridisations forced upon it, *qua* Bedouin, through constant compromises with the occupier. Almost inevitably, the flow of the conversation comes to a halt; debate disintegrates into loud argument, into heated and hurtful recriminations. For the situation admits no ordinary, commonsensical solution. Yet it is here that a story-teller just might come forward, to provide a narrative which overcomes the differences in speakers' points of view and transforms the paradoxes of Mzeina existence.

What is to be stressed, however, is that the occurrence is spontaneous, and, Lavie assures us, like the precise script, "entirely improvisatory". Here is a ritual process which the individual story-teller both initiates and orchestrates. Furthermore, it is not the practice of everyone to allegorise; nor is it the province of official story-tellers or those necessarily in leadership roles. Rather, the allegories are the work of a few individuals, gifted with the skills of dramatic performance: individuals who have achieved reputations for story-telling. What is more, all are local 'characters', as we might phrase it. That is, the story-tellers embody the paradoxes of the present in an especially eccentric way; all possess a certain blatant oddness in relation to the conventional norms of Bedouin life. And just as the allegories are versions of a traditional, legendary form, so the story-tellers themselves come to be publicly tagged with the name and identity of a fantastic figure from the legendary tribal pantheon whom they are said to resemble: The Sheikh, for example, The Madwoman, The Fool, The Ex-Smuggler, The Symbolic Battle Coordinator, The Old Woman, The One Who Writes Us, and others. Individuals' eccentricity is thus borrowed to animate a stock figure of collective inheritance to whom the conundrums of their everyday lives are seen as most closely approximating. And particularly when these individuals create and narrate their allegories (and can be seen

most dramatically to imply a departure from an everyday commonsensical world), it is these fantastic figures who are seen as being
represented. The individual narrators are said to transform themselves, their identities merging with the traditional ones, their
particular voices becoming those of generalised, total personae.
For instance, meet the figure of The Sheikh. Stereotypically,
The Sheikh is a man upon whom everyday exigencies make many
dependent, as clients, and yet whom the Bedouin ideology of
egalitarianism causes many to disrespect. The Sheikh acts as
spokesman to external agencies (who may indeed be responsible
for his appointment) and yet internally he wields no real administrative power. Thus he straddles the divide between Those of
the Land (as the Mzeina describe themselves) and the outsiders,
Those of Politics; ("What can we do to affect the political processes
impacting upon our lives?" the Mzeina rhetorise, "We are The
People of the Land"). Inasmuch as he conjoins a Bedouin self
with the 'otherness' of the occupier, the Sheikh is liminal; there
is an oxymoronicism basic to the traditional figure and his routine
behaviour which will always divorce The Sheikh's experiences
from those of ordinary Mzeinas.

In one of the Mzeina encampments which Lavie frequented,
there was an elderly man, called Sheikh Alwan, whose eccentricity
achieved him identification by the group with the above ideal
persona. And while the opposition between Those of the Land
and Those of Politics rarely surfaced in daily discourse, it could
if Sheikh Alwan were present – his physical presence serving as
a catalyst. Invariably, as conversation turned into dispute, there
was then criticism of Sheikh Alwan's own position and a calling
to account of his actions. Sometimes the sheikh himself remained
silent until the argument reached an acrimonious stalemate and
the circle of feuding men broke up. Sometimes, however, Sheikh
Alwan spoke up, and, as the fantastical Sheikh of legend, would
tell the story of a mundane event from his life which overcame
the paradoxes of being *both* a present-day sheikh and a traditional
Mzeina. Let me abridge Lavie here (1990:104–111):

> "How wonderful Bedouin talk would be if it were not redun-
> dant," Sheikh Alwan's weary voice breaks a bitter silence.
>
> "Not long ago, when the crescent moon of Ramadan had just
> risen, the big boss of the Reserve in Sharm al-Sheikh, Hawaja
> Assaf [an Israeli], asked me to join him for a trip to the
> Highlands and their people ...", and the sheikh goes on to

recount an overnight trip into the desert with the young head of the Nature Reserve which the Israelis had set up in the area. All the time he is careful to juxtapose Bedouin assumptions, artefacts and habits against Israeli ones.

The crux of his account is that the Israeli is fearful for the survival of the glasswort bush which the Bedouin use for firewood, now that the Mzeina are encamped (for wage labour) permanently in one place: maybe he will have to forbid them from gathering it! Thus Sheikh Alwan remonstrates with him: "Ahh ... The days of the past ... Once we lived without all this mess," and goes on to describe, for the Israeli, Bedouin life at the time of his grandpa. In those days, the Mzeina would procure a livelihood by freely collecting and burning bushes and acacia trees and making charcoal; this could then be sold at Suez or Qantara three times a year – only unmarried men having to stay there any longer and sell their labour. But why did the bushes and acacia trees not all get consumed, the Israeli asks. Because the Mzeina moved around more, Sheikh Alwan explains; and because they respected the land and maintained agreements between different phratries and tribes about its use; there were agreements on pastures, on camels, and on charcoal. So why not another agreement between sheikhs now on the glasswort bush, asks the Israeli: that would be better than the enforcement of an Israeli law. But Sheikh Alwan explains it is the customary judges who make Bedouin agreements (the sheikhs are good only for talking with foreign governments); and besides, there could never be a Mzeina agreement on something like glasswort bushes, for they just grow and are not used for selling and making money.

So, the climax of the story is reached: "That guy really loves our land of mountains. He just doesn't know how. ... I said to him, 'Look, ya Assaf. You're as young as one of my sons, and it's really great that your government pays you for just playing "Nature" or "Reserve". ... And you even said that you put your money in the bank. But we have no bank. All we have ever had is this Sinai and that's it. And for our life, we have to take from it. Your government says it's hers, and the Egyptians may say it's theirs, but we are the people of the land.' ... So after I told him that, he started the jeep's engine, and lit himself another cigarette. We sat. He looked like his mind was working fast. He said, 'One pick-up truck load of

[glasswort] for a family twice a month would be OK?' And I
had to say OK. It's better than nothing. And ... that's what
happened."

All the men listening repeat Sheikh Alwan's traditional
refrain. 'Bravo', some add, and serve the sheikh some coffee.
A peaceful silence embraces all, before a new conversation is
born.

From one perspective, much in this utterance could be seen as
conventional, and as resonating with the collective. Thus, we find
a routine conversation between Mzeina, followed by a routine
dissolution into argument, and silence, when certain topics are
broached. Then we find this silence being broken by an habitual
stylised form of narrative, performed by a character of joint ascrip-
tion and traditional legitimation. Paradox, it would seem, is
resolved in conventional ways.

For Lavie, however, it is the very creativity of individual agents
which results in the possibility of such allegorical conventionality.
Cultural practice entails a movement from individual experience
to social text, she explains (à la Simmel or Schuetz, and also Leach):
a movement from subjective, diverse and multiple meanings to
formal, stylised and singular structural forms (conversations, narrations, exchanges, rituals). Moreover, between experience and text
there is a gulf and there is tension, for the textual possesses a
certain inertia: the fixity of the social object. To channel into its
forms the diversity and particularity of experience is a creative act,
then, also a political and a strategic one. Hence, it is the creativity
and charisma of certain Mzeina individuals – "powerful soloists"
gifted with "persuasive dramatic power" – which enables the continued writing of local daily experience into an acceptable and
accepted social text, affording Mzeina tradition a continuing
authority and relevance.

Here, therefore, is the irony (the meta-paradox of Lavie's text
of the Mzeinas) that the disguising of the paradoxes of the present,
the transforming of its idiosyncrasy, calls for precisely that: it is
idiosyncratic individuals who are responsible for the reconstitu-
tion of the texts (and agency) of a Mzeina collectivity.

FATHALLA

The researches of psychoanalysis, of linguistics, of anthropology
have 'decentred' the subject in relation to the laws of its desire,

the forms of its language, the rules of its actions, or the play of its mythical and imaginative discourses.

M. Foucault

In short, it is a matter of depriving the subject ... of its role as originator, and of analyzing the subject as a variable and complex function of discourse.

M. Foucault

In these sentences, sadly, there is no such ironic meta-paradox, no place for individual creativity. For here is the modish post-structuralist imaging of social life as the playing out of impersonal systems of signification which are responsible for, which constitute, the individual self, depriving it of any status as "source and master of meaning" (Culler 1981:33). Here is the notion of collective discourses or forms of life as causing to be true a certain construction of the world, and that of its component parts (their desires, language, actions, imagination), and as instituting a set of knowledge-practices with inexorable links to a mastery of power.

I find such imaging unhappy and unconvincing. In saying this, I am not concerned merely with its anti-humanism, for that would be to initiate a political argument, and invite the rejoinders that links between the humanist's Individual and the ethically, politically and economically Bourgeois are readily apparent; so that if the individual subject to be decentred and dissolved is the erst-privileged transcendent, autonomous, bourgeois self, then 'good riddance' (cf. Lukes 1990:123; Eagleton 1981:138). To circumvent the political, I would argue that such impersonal imaging of social life is primarily unconvincing because of its inaccuracy, its unsubtlety, its distance from the details of the ongoing work of social interaction: work by individuals in conjunction, creating themselves and their social relationships. (Indeed, if there were a political argument to be made, it would surely be that to miss reporting that individual work and substitute the dead hand of determinism – to replace, as would the Foucauldian, individual mentalities by conventional 'governmentalities' – is a travesty).

It is Foucault who imbues, in part, recent accounts by Lila Abu-Lughod of Bedouin discourse in Egypt's Western Desert. Here too, over the past few decades, Awlad 'Ali Bedouin have exchanged a nomadic existence of herding sheep, growing barley and riding pack animals on trade caravans, for a more sedentarised existence of houses and Toyota trucks, of tending orchards,

smuggling, speculating on real estate and supplying building material (cf. Abu-Lughod 1986). In her article, 'Shifting politics in
Bedouin love poetry', Abu-Lughod focuses specifically on a traditional Bedouin genre of oral lyricism known as *ghinnawa*, and
explores its status as social text (1990:29):

> I'd figured, oh beloved, that distance
> would be a cure but it only made it worse ...

Abu-Lughod's particular intent is to criticise 'mentalist models' of
individual thought and emotion – conceptions of individual
consciousness as private – and to argue that it is the discourse
which informs individual experience and constitutes the realities
and truths by which individuals live. Far from *ghinnawa* being an
expressive stage for individual emotionality, then, and far from
this representing an inner state, the formulaic poetry must needs
be seen as usage which constructs emotions as legitimate social
phenomena, as social facts; "emotion" is created by the conventions of discourse, and emotionality is routine discursive practice.
This being the case, it is of and about social–structural conditions
that emotional expression, and poetry about emotion, actually
talks. Formed in and by certain social ecologies and political
economies, the emotion of *ghinnawa* will reflect the form of society
(the hierarchical social structure, the relations of power) which
gave rise to the genre and for which its continuing expression has
practical consequences.

Fathalla, for instance, Abu-Lughod introduces as a young
Bedouin man whose plans to marry 'his beloved' are thwarted by
her father (his uncle). Hence, Fathalla resorts to expressing 'his'
feelings of love and regret in *ghinnawa*. For while this poetic genre
is very much part of daily life, and is often interspersed in the middle of ordinary conversations with intimates, the sentiments which
Fathalla may properly express in conversation and in *ghinnawa* are
very different. Thus, it is legitimate for him to express a feeling of
love (to feel love) in the poetry while continuing to express (and
feel) very different emotions in the conversational discourse which
precedes and follows it. For Fathalla, we are informed, appropriate emotionality and proper discursive practice are one.

Ghinnawa is not resorted to by all of Bedouin society
alike, moreover; it is primarily associated with young men and
women. For these are the disadvantaged dependents of the social
structure; and the sentiment of love which *ghinnawa* constitutes

represents a subversion of the sentiment of modesty and of the hierarchical status-quo. *Ghinnawa* is a conventional discourse of defiance to the authority of the elders. And yet, those, like Fathalla, who compose *ghinnawa* are not disapproved of, even by the elders themselves. In fact, cassette-tapes have been made of Fathalla reciting his poems in a 'moving and pained' voice, and it was on the Mercedes cassette-player of her (elder) host that Abu-Lughod was first introduced to them. Elders "clearly admired this young man for his passion and for his ability to express it in poetry. They were moved by his poems and awed by the power of his words" (1990:36).

This quotation could have come from Lavie; likewise the description of poetry as a highly cherished and privileged art-form, thought of as distinctly Bedouin and associated with a noble past of political autonomy, strength and independence; and likewise the argument that in people's approval of *ghinnawa*, in their discomfort with its emotions in ordinary conversation and their glorification of them in conversation's interstices, can be read a fundamental paradox in Bedouin life between the ideals of equality and the everyday practice of hierarchy. However, Abu-Lughod's conclusion is very different. The fact that the Western Desert Bedouin may be frequently 'moved' by *ghinnawa* poetry pertains in no necessary way to individual qualities or subjective states. Rather, it concerns the public construction and exchange of cultural behaviours and concepts: the playing out of an emotional discourse and a discourse on emotion. It is this discourse, moreover, which is the proper object of anthropological enquiry, for its very playing out constitutes Fathalla and his audience as social actors, tells them what (and when and how) they can 'think and feel'. Here are people, Abu-Lughod claims, far removed from Western habits of contemplation, interpretation, understanding: far from what Foucault characterises as the 'psychologising' projects of the Western 'individual'.

COMMENTARY

[B]y failing to extend to the 'others' we study a recognition of the personal complexity which we perceive in ourselves, we are generalising them into a synthetic fiction which is both discredited and discreditable.

A.P. Cohen

Obviously, for the Western Desert Bedouin the Red Sea never parted; only the Mzeina of the South Sinai sit securely ensconced in that Promised Land of Western Individualism. Hence while the creativity of Sheikh Alwan's allegorical tale 'metonymises private experience for the history of the collectivity' and provides a conduit by which discrete individual lives come into contact, Fathalla's creativity finds no place beyond the 'political deployment of discourse' and the 'play of putative referents' in which to be. Whereas we hear Sheikh Alwan speaking with an individual voice which is his own, in Fathalla we learn that what speaks is simply discourse. Informed by the discursive forms available to him, Fathalla can but portray the ultimate power of the system of traditional authority in Awlad 'Ali society and the futility of the resistance which love-poetry represents. Indeed, "Fathalla" is constituted by discourse – how he feels and thinks as well as speaks.

But then again, a bridge can be built between them (if not their interlocutors) simply by eschewing a Foucauldian conflation of Individualism and Individuality. The former may indeed pertain to a particular cultural conceptualisation of the self, to a particular style of expression (the pursuit of self-distinguishment), and be absent from the formal surface of certain discourse. But the latter, Individuality, pertains to our being-in-the-world courtesy of distinct interpretative prisms, whereby, to paraphrase Simmel ("A human being is fundamentally a differentiating entity." (1890:19)), each of us engages with the world as other; each of us inevitably represents an independent seat of consciousness.

Such pertinences of individuality remain actual, moreover, even when individual 'projects of contemplation and understanding' are publicly downplayed (as is claimed for Western Desert Bedouin), even when individuality is strategically denied (à la Foucault), and even when individual differences and division an enculturation into a fund of discourses does its darndest to overcome. Communication is never unmediated (socialisation, in this sense, is never 'completed' (Berger 1990:31)), because it is the agency of each individual which is ever responsible for animating discourse with significance, and so maintaining its role as the major synthesising process of social life, without which discourse would simply remain inert cultural matter. There is a discourse in shared cultural concepts and there is individual usage and interpretation.

Hence, discourse can be seen always as exhibiting a dual structure, a duplicity. As Steiner formulates it (1975:170–3): a surface
of common speech-forms and notations, of grammar and phonol-
ogy, in public exchange covers a base of possibly private meanings
and associations, meanings which derive from the 'irreducible singularity' of personal consciousness and sub-consciousness, from
the singular specificity of an individual's somatic and psychological
identity. So that:

> [t]he language of a community, however uniform its social
> contour, is an inexhaustibly multiple aggregate of speech-atoms,
> of finally irreducible, personal meanings.
>
> (Steiner 1975:46)

Such a formulation seems to me unexceptionable: shared discursive forms and individually interpreted meanings. How could
this duality possibly be sundered? how possibly could it be
compounded? Yes, there may be rules and routines of interaction,
which are concerned with the constitution of collective discourses
on 'emotion', 'charisma', 'creativity', 'allegory', 'poetry', and so
on, and which affect differentials of power. But when people
speak, when Sheikh Alwan and Fathalla create their persuasive
utterances, it is surely impoverishing of our appreciation to
suggest that the playing out of a language-game is the only thing
happening, or the only thing the anthropologist can or need
consider. Yes, emotion as a public and structurally situated
discourse provides a link between the individual and the collective and an avenue of social exchange, but it is surely unperceptive
to claim that its enactment is all or most that its individual users
are or can be engaged with. In short, engagement in a cultural
discourse need in no way translate as that discourse achieving
agency, determining or causing meaning, eliminating the interpretative work of the individual participant. Rather, in interaction
the individual can be seen both assisting in a continuing collective performance and, at the same time, creating and fulfilling,
expressing and extending ongoing agendas, identities and world-
views of his or her own; the individual makes sense in interaction,
alongside others doing similarly. Thus, there can be worlds of
difference between shared grammatic-cum-paradigmatic compe-
tency on the one hand and shared cognition or mutual
comprehension on the other. And even if the various senses made
of discourse by different individuals (or the same individuals at

different moments) are complementary, even possibly consensual, then this is something achieved through individuals' work, through creativity and charisma, rather than something carried in on the back of the discourse *per se* (cf. Harris 1981:177–8).

To repeat: Without a fund of discourses the individual would not have the means of making sense, but without this work of interpretation, this individual use, discourse would not achieve animation in public life.

SID ASKRIG

I have already introduced the individual and animating Sid Askrig in Chapter 7. Sid is an inhabitant of the Cumbrian dale of Wanet, in north-west England, and I have described before aspects of his life and my relations with him (e.g. Rapport 1986, 1993). He is a jack-of-all-trades and a father in his mid-thirties, and I spent a period of anthropological fieldwork employed as his builder's mate. I would serve him with a ready supply of concrete blocks and cement and he would supply me with a ready array of information on the sad ('darly') ways of the world.

"How are we doing, does thee think, lad?" was one of Sid's favourite rhetorical punctuations, stretching his back or lighting a cigarette in between sections of the building, before he would provide the answer: "OK so long as we don't get catched, eh!" As his young apprentice, it was appropriate for me to stay silent and merely grin or nod, while he repeated the phrase or simply chuckled. On occasion I thought about supplying the punchline myself – to show him how willing and able I was to learn, and how happy to be included in his 'we' – but I could barely, with honesty, subdue myself to the ungrammatical 'catched' – it was not my style. Whereas, if (as on occasion) I instead said "caught", it turned the phrase into a wholly different creature and Sid would look at me askance. The saying was a whole, and it was Sid's (it *was* Sid) through and through. Here was a man able to survive as freelance by crafting anything, staying tricky, taking his chances by playing both sides against the middle – and never getting 'catched'.

Sid was renowned for his mouth and for the word-play it engendered. Only Sid would tell tourists to the dale to "bugger-off home", whilst he was always there to proffer advice on how to maintain Wanet, its united people and traditional ways, in the face

of an influx of newcomers, an 'offcomer' invasion. It was no acci-
dent that Sid judiciously balanced his knowledgeable advice
concerning offcomers and 'offcomed-uns' by peppering his talk
with such emblems of old Wanet locality as 'thee', and 'yan' (one),
and 'bones' (dominoes), and 'darly' (dour). For it was his individual style, his capability, to be thus betwixt and between
discourses, and willing to say what others ordinarily would not.
Hence, in common appellation Sid was 'The Chief', 'The Gaffer',
in Wanet – something of a self-appointed gate-keeper – and few
were as ostentatiously knowledgeable about how to deal with the
outside world on its own terms, while remaining stalwartly local.

For instance, when the offcomer threat to local life took the
form of the National Park, its warden and committee (the body
to which the government at Whitehall has delegated many of the
rights and duties of County and District Councils in the Wanet
area), Sid would remind people that the Park was as much hated
in neighbouring dales as in Wanet (they were not alone).
Moreover, he would suggest strategy: locals should act dumb and
pretend they do not understand its petty rules (on planning,
tipping, footpathing); also, pretend the Park officials can teach
them something, for then the 'Little Hitlers' really come around.
Failing that, Wanet people should consider reporting the National
Park to the Strasbourg International Court of Human Rights
because, since the Park is more a quango than an elected body,
what it does is probably illegal.

Then again, when heavy-handed offcomer officialdom represented itself in Wanet in the form of the Police, Sid would proffer
other loopholes of escape. For instance, if a policeman were to
stop a Wanet car because it was not roadworthy, all the local need
say was: "I elect to have this decision deferred for 30 days"; for
then, Sid would explain: "They can't touch your car, and you
can have it fixed up by when they send the police mechanics
round."

To contextualise this latter strategy more closely, as Sid asserts
(and surely every other Wanet local knows), officialdom favours
the offcomer. Since it is the offcomer breed which runs the
country's bureaucracies, Wanet locals will always lose out to their
inscrutability and their wordsmithery. In the case of the police
force, while there may no longer be a village bobby in Wanet
(keeping rowdy local kids in check) there *are* squad cars pestering
adults for driving out to pubs of an evening, and pulling them up

for having bald tyres. (Meanwhile, offcomer drivers cannot cope
with Wanet's bendy roads, but still get away scot-free. Either they
hog the middle of the road where two tractors could otherwise
easily pass, or else they bounce their cars off the lining walls and
hedgerows, threatening everything else in sight.) In this situation,
it is clear that locals need some inside information – the alien
spells and charms of offcomer bureaucratic discourse – and this
is what Sid provides. Hence, he disinters a phrase which can hinder
the progress of the Police, and brings it home for local benefit.
True, some of the words ('elect', 'deferred') sound strange on the
local tongue, but this discursive borrowing (creolisation, bricolage), paradoxically as it may seem, is necessary, Sid recognises,
if Wanet traditionality is to be protected; the new must be used
creatively to maintain the old.

And others recognise Sid's charisma. 'The Chief' is a real local
character, they admit; 'The Gaffer' is the head of the (fabular)
Wanet Republican Army, ready to post sentrics on the fell-tops
and kick the offcomers out! It is not that his advice is 'taken seriously' or acted upon. The idea of the Strasbourg International
Court or the magical police spell is laughed at. But Sid intends it
to be. For it is laughter at the organisation and running of the
offcomer world, and laughter at the paradox of locals having, in
some way at least, to come to terms with it. Furthermore, this
laughter is from the standpoint of sanity – of Wanet tradition and
propriety – which Sid's words cause to be highlighted. There is
nostalgia implicated here, but also a determination that Wanet
people can continue to be themselves. Sid, in short, is a creative
and charismatic improviser of the conventions of collective
discourse.

In the parlance of the present discussion, his words tell a local
audience of allegorical independence from powerful outsiders.
They conflate the levels of the individual, the dale and the outside
world, symbolically reversing the direction of power so that
the world becomes a story locally narrated and underwritten.
Moreover, this is represented by Sid's very person. He is a liminal
figure who knows the enemy ways, who has worked both sides,
and can show the locals who and how they really are. At once,
he partakes of local rules and routines of exchange, takes part in
the continuing constitution of Wanet discourses (extending these
to encompass present circumstances), and he makes them his own:
"That's Sid for you. Only Sid would . . .".

In sum, it is such personalisation of discursive structures that helps keep them alive in the present. Here are verbal and behavioural structures granted contemporary relevance, validity, significance, by being imparted such personal purpose and meaning as the clothing and broadcasting of Sid's wit.

CONCLUSION

Bakhtin once famously described how language was irredeemably "heteroglot" rather than unitary (1981:288). Only if abstracted from 'the concrete conceptualisations that fill it' and from 'the uninterrupted process of its historical becoming' could language be considered simply as a grammatical system of normative forms; in its use, each word comes to "taste" of its socially charged life (1981:293). What may be added to this, in elucidation, is that this tasting of words is personal, and charging of sociality individual; words only lead socially charged lives courtesy of individual agency.

If we were truly to decentre the individual in favour of conventional and collective systems of signification – languages of action, desire, myth and imagination – we would deprive ourselves of the route to understanding how and why 'a culture' maintains itself or develops, how and why discourses 'take place' and change. Only by paying as full attention to 'psyche' as to 'culture', as Chodorow terms it (1994:2), can anthropology avoid reducing the dialectical nature of reality and producing an image of cultural or discursive determinism (cf. Rapport 1990:*passim*).

Nor does this seem to me a 'mentalist' or 'bourgeois' or 'Western' stance. Certainly it accords with what I know of myself (of being myself) using cultural discourses in different interactions. But then I have no other route to knowing others, nor any right to deny their personal complexity.

Chapter 10

Individual Morality
Between liberalism, anthropology and biology

No cry of torment can be greater than the cry of one man.
Ludwig Wittgenstein

Preachers or scientists may generalise, but we know that no generality is possible about those whom we love; not one heaven awaits them, not even one oblivion.
E.M. Forster

Forster, the novelist and atheist, spoke of the individual as a "divine achievement" on which he was prepared to place his faith, and which he would defend against any view which sought to belittle him (1972:66). On behalf of the individual, Forster also defended liberal democracy as a form of polity. For such representative government started with the assumption that the individual was important; it also gave onto the type of society which allowed individuals most liberty to express themselves – at least in terms of creativity and discovery, if not power – because it recognised that the aggregation of a myriad of different individual citizens is what makes for civilisation. Notwithstanding, Forster could only award democracy "two cheers" (one for its admitting of variety, and one for its permitting of criticism), and insisted on reserving the ultimate accolade of three for 'the Beloved Republic of Love': love between individuals was even better than the liberal tolerance of a democracy (1972:78).

But then the Republic of Love was not a form of polity within wide or easy human reach. Love might be the greatest of all things and it might act as the great force in private life, but love in public affairs did not widely or easily work. For it seemed that human beings were only capable of loving what they knew personally, whereas in societies increasingly large-scale and complex (in a world appallingly full of people), human beings could not know so much.

In public affairs, therefore, in the building of civilisation, something much less dramatic and emotional than love had to make do, namely, tolerance: "tolerance, good temper, and sympathy" (1972:75). Tolerance could accommodate the fact that most people whom an individual met he did not know, and some of them whom he did know he did not like – didn't like "the colour of their skins, say, or the shape of their noses, or the way they blow them or don't blow them" (1972:55) – never mind find himself able to love. What tolerance called for, above all, was imagination. It entailed the individual all the time putting himself in someone else's place – someone met in the street, in the office, at the factory; someone of a different social class, nation, race – and not doing them harm because he knew how much it hurt to be hurt. Tolerance was the public ethic of a liberal civilisation; it might represent a poor second to love, but it nevertheless afforded a compromise whereby public life could best nourish and harbour a diversity of private lives ('real lives') of individuality, personal relations and love.

I share Forster's views (cf. Rapport 1994:*passim*), and in this essay I wish to draw links, form a compromise, between them and the discipline of social science, between my personal self and my work as an anthropologist. For I wish to work out an ethic for anthropology which will condemn Nazism, religious fundamentalism, female circumcision, infanticide and *suttee* because of the hurt they cause to individuals, because of the harm which accrues in those social milieux where an ethic of interpersonal tolerance is not managed: the violation of individual integrity, the threat to individuals' conscious potential, the ideological prioritising of the community above and beyond the individuals who at any one moment constitute it. Instead of a relativistic making of allowances for different cultures maintaining different traditions – whatever the consequences to their individual members – I want to outline a liberal basis for social science which recognises individuals as universal human agents above whom there is no greater good, without whom there is no wider society, and in contradistinction to whom there is no cultural tradition.

POSTMODERN IRONIC LIBERALISM

I begin drawing links by tracing the steps of philosopher Richard Rorty (1986; 1992). Rorty first offers a long quotation from novelist Milan Kundera (1990:164–5), which I abridge:

> That imaginative realm of tolerance [where no one owns the truth and everyone has the right to be understood] was born with modern Europe, it is the very image of Europe – or at least our dream of Europe, a dream many times betrayed but nonetheless strong enough to unite us all in the fraternity that stretches far beyond the little European continent. But we know that the world where the individual is respected (the imaginative world of the novel, and the real one of Europe) is fragile and perishable. . . . [I]f European culture seems under threat today, if the threat from within and without hangs over what is most precious about it – its respect for the individual, for his original thought, and for his right to an inviolable private life – then, I believe, that precious essence of the European spirit is being held safe as in a treasure chest inside the history of the novel, the wisdom of the novel.

In Kundera's words, too, I find a credo which I should not only like to preserve, but also to advance in my work. And Rorty assures me I can. For he uses Kundera to say that the principle vehicles of moral change and progress in recent centuries have not been the philosophical treatise or the theological sermon or the scientific theorem, but novels and pamphlets and magazines and movies and histories and . . . ethnographies. In moral expertise and advocation, 'specialists in metaphysical universality' who write in theoretical genres have been replaced by 'specialists in particularity' writing in narrational genres; and in the latter number Rorty would include ethnographers as well as novelists (cf. Wilde 1914:57).

Rorty also terms this latter group "connoisseurs of diversity" and "agents of love" (1986:529–30). For what these writers do is extend the range of moral discourse of members of a society, expand the moral imagination, especially that of those in power, so that people notice and can conceive of having a conversation with – sharing a society with, employing the beliefs and traditions of, sympathising with the hurt of, empathising with the humiliation and suffering of – more and more different sorts of people.

This expanding, through narrations of particularity, of people's moral imagination has the effect of more and more different sorts of people being possibly included in 'our community': of strangers being regarded more as 'one of us'. In the detailed descriptions of a Dickens, then, we read about the suffering of people to whom we may not have previously properly attended; in the detailed redescriptions of a Nabokov, we learn of the cruelty we ourselves are capable of; and in the thick descriptions of a Geertz, we discover the humiliations felt by people we did not rightly recognise as people. (Here is the ethnographer, in E. Bruner's telling phrasing, writing as the 'Arab Jew' (1993:8)).

Only when the connoisseurs of diversity have begun to persuade of the humanity of otherness is the moral torch to be passed on to what Rorty calls "guardians of universality" and "agents of justice" (1986:529). It is they who can then ensure that once the alien has been admitted to the citizenry, it is treated properly and fairly. Guardians of universality are doctors, lawyers and teachers, as well as ombudsmen and civil servants, and their brief is procedural justice. Doctors seek to cure irrespective of patients' lifestyle; lawyers attempt to defend irrespective of guilt; teachers wish to foster learning irrespective of who will best use or most agree with what is taught.

The point to be appreciated, Rorty continues, is that a liberal democracy is the polity which expressly employs and empowers both connoisseurs of diversity and guardians of universality, which prides itself, indeed, on its embracing of diversity, on always adding more perspectives on the world, extending the range of its sympathies, adapting itself to what it encounters. For a liberal democracy, tolerance of diversity is the source of a sense of moral self-worth, and its test.

Furthermore, the passing on of the moral torch from agents of love to agents of justice (from ethnographers to civil servants) once the border of the civil polity has been crossed, gives to the society of liberal democracy a certain characteristic form. Here is a meeting of a diversity of individuals under the aegis of universalistic procedural rules – but no insistence on a necessarily closer meeting than this. A liberal democracy, that is, intends to offer a wide public civility, a procedural umbrella, under which a veritable bazaar of private diversity may maintain itself and flourish. Its institutions are to provide the practical benefit whereby individuals may live together without intruding on one another's privacy or meddling with one another's notions of the good. Indeed, this is a deliberate policy, born out of a recognition of the human truth known at least since the time of Kant (and forcefully recounted recently by Berlin) that "Great Goods collide" (Berlin 1990:17).

To amplify somewhat: the supreme values, the ultimate ideals, the true perspectives adopted and pursued by individual human beings almost inevitably (certainly inexorably) remain incompatible with one another. No single overarching criterion of arbitration is likely to be available, within a polity, to decide between or reconcile individuals' opposed moralities; they remain unharmonisable, without final synthesis. The liberal solution, therefore, is a universalistic procedural justice and a compromise: a curtailing of the final end of absolute liberty of each individual so as to make room for that of others, and also a curtailing of expectations concerning the everyday reach of deep understanding (outwith the procedural) or love. Courtesy of the agents of love, one may liberally admit many individuals into one's polity, but then one does not expect necessarily to share their sense of what is ultimately or even proximately meaningful, one does not seek to convert them to one's own perspective, and one does not wish to have them missionise either. All one expects is a common respect for the procedural institutions of the polity which seek to balance, in an *ad hoc*, concrete, case-by-case fashion, the competing demands of diverse perspectives while not serving the exclusive interests of any one. The practice of love (sharing the life and interests, thoughts and feelings of another) and the practice of justice (sharing the same universalistic procedures) are hard to reconcile, and in most cases a liberal democracy accepts that justice must be enough – even if this gives onto a situation where many human relations, untouched by love, must take place "in the dark" of a lonely publicity; within the bazaar of diverse perspectives there might only be rather small and exclusive clubs of 'lovers' who share ultimate ideals (Rorty 1986:528).

Liberal democracy, in sum, makes a firm distinction between public and private. It accepts that while justice must be the public face of the polity and guardians of universality its brokers, love might remain something of a private face only. And while a 'beloved republic' of individuality and understanding may remain a chimera, here, nevertheless, is a political compromise between public justice and private love, private narcissism and public pragmatism, which allows for a societal synthesis while championing personal relations and individual freedom. (One is reminded of Gellner advocating a "constitutional religion", along the lines of a constitutional monarchy, which might grant a society a legitimacy – a ritual coherence, a symbolic order – while people's real beliefs and the technicalities of their profane lives are enabled to run along very different and diverse lines amidst the "theatre" (1993:91)).

RORTY AND ANTHROPOLOGY

There are points of clear meeting between a number of Rorty's assertions and conventional writing within anthropology. Many anthropologists would see their project as essentially a 'moral' one, which extends the perspective of different cultures so that areas of overlap become clear. And many would feel that solutions to cases of dispute between perspectives must be sought "by hunch or by conversational compromise" (Rorty 1986:531) rather than by reference to final or absolute priorities, to stable canonical criteria. Parenthetic reference has been made to points of agreement with Bruner and Gellner, and a more extended overlap could be adumbrated between Rorty's picture of a liberal polity and what Leach describes as a "modern state": where a plurality of cultures is contained; where a centralised legal apparatus imposes an appearance of universal consensus so as to maintain the polity's status-quo; and where society reaches such a level of complexity that the same norms of customary behaviour translate into almost as many diverse yet distinguishable systems of moral interpretation as there are individuals (1977:*passim*). Indeed, Wallace (followed by others) famously extended this picture of an 'organisation of diversity' to include all human societies, modern or traditional (1964:*passim*). Even within 'a single culture', social structures of behavioural equivalence could be seen formally to disguise "the diversity of the interests and motivations of their members, the practical impossibility of complete interpersonal understanding and communication, and the unavoidable residuum of loneliness that dwells in every man" (1961:131; and cf. Goodenough, 1963; Szwed, 1966; Paine, 1974; Schwartz, 1978). Hann concludes by praising Rorty's "honest attempt" to breathe more universalistic life "into some of America's most attractive, democratic traditions" (1996:28).

However, I believe Rorty and conventional anthropology would diverge concerning the moral place and role to be given to the social–scientific elucidation of such a society and polity, to its advocation in the world today. Rorty would claim an awareness of this 'liberal state' to be of global appropriateness, and argue that the idea of such a state should be globally advocated and vindicated. Indeed, in a celebrated essay, 'Reply to Clifford Geertz' (1986), he explains to anthropologists why this should be so and how his claim can be distinguished from the ethnocentric project of the missionary. To precis this argument (which I find persuasive), Rorty makes crucial the distinction between procedural beliefs and substantive beliefs. The procedures over which a liberal polity calls for consensus, and which a liberal polity would advocate other parts of the world adopting, entail little substantive agreement. The same picture of private diversity covered by an umbrella of public civility accommodates cultural groups as well as individuals; here is cultural pluralism within a procedural environment which makes institutional but not substantive assumptions of a meeting of difference.

And this is the reason that liberal beliefs are morally exportable: worth pinning one's highest hopes to, worth remaining faithful to, indeed, worth fighting for. Even though today's liberal may possess a postmodern, ironic attitude to all beliefs, including his own – recognises their contingency, recognises that liberal beliefs pertain to no 'necessary rationality', tap into no 'common human nature', no 'absolute truth', and recognise that these beliefs are recent, local and unusual Western cultural developments, the manifestation of one particular form of life, which most other cultures, past and present, might abhor – still he believes that practically they provide "the best hope for the species" (1986:532; and cf. Gray 1994:*passim*). Hence, he is prepared to assert their superiority in a language he recognises inevitably to be a situated human creation, in terms of arguments which are circular and by reference to standards which are relative. He is prepared to accept, as Rorty puts it, that "in the process of arranging things so that relatively fewer people get hurt", some will get hurt – Nazis, religious fundamentalists, cultural traditionalists; and that "the cruelty and humiliation that paves the way for universal liberal democracy is a necessary evil, like the cruelty and humiliation involved in socialising a child" (personal communication, 4/vi/94). The way to substantive diversity passes through a procedural singularity – even an overweening one.

And there is more. For while the practicalities of liberal procedure say little substantively about the fundamentals of belief which
might be held within the polity, they do not say nothing (as
ideal types, the procedural and the substantive may be absolutely
distinguishable, but in practice they are mutually, ideologically,
implicated). First, as has been mentioned, they say that the procedures must be sacrosanct and take precedence even over the
absoluteness of freedom of belief (which might otherwise cause
an overthrow of the procedures and the freedoms of others).
Second, liberal procedures also presume a belief in human equality
which pertains not merely to cultural beliefs in the abstract but
to the individual carriers and users of those beliefs, indeed, to the
equality of individuals *per se*. Irrespective of culture and society,
quite independent of the contingencies of particular languages,
individual human beings are "equal in respect to their liability to
suffering", to feel pain; and on this basis alone, "there is something within human beings which deserves respect and protection".
(Rorty 1992:88). Truth may be lost as a criterion of value but
humane behaviour remains.

It is not simply, then, that a liberal polity is best because it
recognises and respects the diversity of cultures (and seeks to
manage their just interaction), but because it recognises and
respects the individual diversity by which these cultures are constituted, and upon which their formal samenesses stand. A liberal
polity allows and expects different individuals to flourish, to create
themselves, their own self-images: to make their own truths, to
weave their own webs of belief and desire, to work their own
private salvations, to fulfil their own idiosyncratic fantasies, to give
their lives a radically poetic character, to reach a diversity of
personal purposes, to attain autonomy. In short, for Rorty, the
liberal polity which is to be globalised is one which publicly
respects the right of the individual citizen to his [or her] own civil
freedoms *against* cultural prejudices, *against* social statuses, and
against the language embodied in their self-expressions.

This is to be brought about, Rorty concludes, by "maximising
the quality of education, freedom of the press, educational opportunity, opportunities to exert political influence, and the like",
attempting to routinise social mobility, literacy, peace and leisure,
so as to inculcate a "free and open encounter" between the citizens
of a polity engaging in undistorted, "domination-free communication" (1992:67–8). Given such open communication and free

discussion, Rorty is assured, individuals would not abide by (or expect others to abide by) concepts of the person or self, and of self-esteem, which ultimately cause harm to the individual; females would not agree to genital-mutilation nor males to suicide-bombing, and no individual would condone the absolute certainty of a religious fundamentalism and the cruelties which inexorably follow. Through these liberal procedures, in short, individuals can be expected to seek to make the "best selves" for themselves that they can, not allow this potential to be curtailed by cultural, social or linguistic norms (whether this curtailment is self-inflicted or imposed), and grant others the space to do likewise (1992:80).

INDIVIDUALS AGAINST CULTURES

A conventional anthropological response to the above – even granting Rorty's admission that his vision is utopian – might be the relativist one that not only are Rorty's ideas culturally specific but his ideas of other cultures are culturally specific also: that the notion that cultures might meet in a polity socially organised over and against those cultures, so that they find a way to respect one another (never mind respecting each other's 'individual actors') while maintaining some semblance of exclusivity and belonging, is a westernised conception of the relationship between culture and society (and individual). And that given this cultural specificity, there is no Archimedean point from which (Rortian) pragmatism can be measured or even conceived. Geertz, perhaps, would argue something like this. Gellner, meanwhile, might give the positivist-realist response that to expect ideas of a liberal polity to be met (and discussed, accepted, celebrated) as abstract ideas, as ideas alone, as ideas at all, is to fail to understand global real-politik. There are certain facts of our shared, global, human condition today, important amongst which are that the world is not one of balance, Western culture (and rationality and science and technology and liberal democracy) is the predominant meaning-system, and all other cultures are either in the process of peacefully accommodating themselves to the West or else, through reactionary measures as diverse as religious fundamentalism and female circumcision, ethnic militancy and romantic localism, are sporadically making war against the West as best they can. Liberalism wins out, therefore, where and when it does, because Western capitalism as an industrial–military complex wins out, and not because people come to see its idealistic and ideational characteristics and strengths.

A secondary elaboration of both of these anthropological arguments, then, is that it is societies or communities which are the real political actors in the world, which act as repositories of power and knowledge, and that it is cultures which mediate the lives, insights and rights of their members, which grant whatever notions of individuation may exist. Far from the fetishising of atomistic individual freedom of which liberalism is the political manifestation, and far from Rorty's concept of the individual person voided of the diversity of its actual cultural identities, its community attachments and historical inheritances, other societies and cultures will more likely celebrate notions of common interest, collective attachment, public good, patriotism, group loyalty, respect for tradition, and so on: the virtues of community and communitarianism. In the actual workings of most (if not all) of the world's societies and cultures, it is not a 'politics of individual rights' which is being played out, so much as a 'politics of common good'.

That is, conventional anthropological responses to Rorty's suggestions might be seen to come down (ultimately from Durkheim) to a reiterating of a brand of communitarian thought which emphasises the primacy of collective life over individual, and raises up as supreme the value of the community and its requirements over those of the individual. In this view, it is their deep and diverse collective attachments which give people their particular identities, it is their roles and group memberships which willy-nilly are constitutive of their persons. 'In the real world', people see themselves not as essential persons, not as partaking of societies of strangers, but as constituted by their particular histories and communities. Furthermore, their collective life is construed to be intrinsically good and valuable, not simply instrumental, and it is impossible to consider individuals as bearers of selves independently of such attachments. They assert themselves as peoples not individual persons, and their senses of injustice arise from their being people who are oppressed (whether religiously, locally, ethnically, nationally or whatever).

Whether etically or emically, then, to consider an 'I' is to elicit a 'they' who made and make the 'I' and continue to contextualise its being. Even where human rights and freedoms of individuals have come to be enshrined in the laws of a polity or an organisation (such as the US Constitution, or the UN Declaration), it is the individual in his cultural, national and spiritual environment which is being referred to, removed from which, "man loses his essential humanity" (Moskovitz 1968:169–70); human beings individuate themselves as members of historic communes not as specimens of generic humanity. As Sandel puts it (1984:5–6):

> the story of my life is always embedded in the story of those communities from which I derive my identity – whether family or city, tribe or nation, party or cause.

Finally, the conventional anthropological response might assert, even where individual rights and freedoms are validated, their full enjoyment requires certain rights to devolve upon groups. Hence, the right to freedom of expression, association and assembly call for the right to group security, public order and health; the right to join a trade union, to follow a religious conscience, to enjoy folk traditions, call for the right of the group to preserve its trades unions, its religious institutions, its folk traditions; the right to escape discrimination calls for the right of the group (ethnic, religious, political, racial, usually) freely to maintain its own membership, etc. And the preservation of these individual rights inevitably gives onto claims by their communities to distinct legal regimes and distinct laws, whether pertaining to sexual behaviour, dress codes, blasphemy or whatever. In short, in the face of a faceless, mass assault, individual freedoms are powerless outwith a coherent collectivity (cf. Sandel 1982:143; Triggs 1988:141–4; Raz 1990:251–4).

TOTALITARIAN COMMUNITARIANISM

And yet, to fight the faceless and impersonal with the same would seem to me but a recipe for legitimating a widespread, mass deindividuation. Hence, let me suggest a non-conventional anthropological response to Rorty. I have argued that criticism of Rorty's (or Forster's) liberal assumptions concerning the individual, and the treatment of individual difference, within a polity and a theory of society, may be seen as 'communitarian' in inspiration. In what follows, it is a counter-criticism of communitarianism as a social philosophy (including the above anthropological privileging of the collective over the individual) that, in brief, I offer.

A significant feature with communitarian critiques of liberalism is that, as Gray has pointed out (1992:15), however ostentatiously 'realistic' and dystopian they set out to be, the communities they present are invariably ideal ones: Salem without the 'witches' (cf. Himmelfarb 1996:13). Seldom taken as norms are actual communities with their histories of exclusivity, inequity and bigotry: communities dehumanising and treating inhumanely those deemed different and who do not belong – Jews (and Communists and Gypsies and homosexuals) in Nazi Germany; Armenians in Turkey; women ubiquitously; heretics in Inquisitorial Spain; slaves and barbarians in classical Greece – dividing to the same degree as uniting, casting shadows of enmity, and settling their boundaries by war. Alternatively, such actualities of community life are taken to be pathologies (in Durkheimian terminology) of a social system which is morbid, dysfunctional or otherwise out of its normal (teleological) equilibrium. In short, if liberalism is criticised for its historico-cultural specificity, then communitarian thought can be seen to be invariably imbued with what Phillips has referred to as a "mythic" search for that time in the past and the future when the modern ills of individualism and liberalism were and will be exchanged for an embodiment of cognitive and behavioural commonality (1993:149–56). Hence, its adherents run the risk of denying or marginalising myriad disastrous failures of social arrangement and everyday circumstance from which the institutionalisation of liberal thought has afforded an escape.

Indeed, communitarian thought is finally totalitarian, I would argue. Far from providing human beings with a sense of their basic selves and identities, it misrepresents their 'essential humanity' (à la Moskovitz et al., above): it generalises and categorises and stereotypes them, it defines and limits them, it deprives and impoverishes them. Communitarian thought would determine (over-determine) its subjects and, where this is not possible, it would deny them.

Furthermore, communitarian thought dehumanises not only those it seeks to exclude but also those it works to encompass. To take an extreme example:

> The Muslim community has been seduced, tricked and subverted into a disastrous relationship with the *Kafir* [disbeliever], the result of which has been the abandonment of our educational nexus for theirs, our moral nexus for theirs, our governmental nexus for theirs so that our anthropological

distinctness has been submerged and eradicated until all that is allowed to remain is a romantic appraisal of our Islamic past in Museums of Mankind and other Jew-designated mortuaries of wisdom.

This is extracted from a leaflet put out by an Islamic group, *Hizb ut Tahrir* (Party of Liberation), which seeks to recruit Muslim students from British university and college campuses (*Observer* 1994). The cause of the recruitment is to alert Muslims to the 'deceptiveness, dangerousness and unworkability of democracy', to celebrate the Koranic praise of fighting and killing, to proclaim 'the battlefield' as the only place for Muslims and Jews to meet, to regard the state of Israel intrinsically as 'criminality' and to advocate the creation of an Islamic state 'wherever there is a concentration of Muslims'.

Thanks to ethnographic 'agents of love', in Rorty's terms, I can understand (appreciate, imagine myself in the place of, sympathise and empathise with) these sentiments, albeit on the level of discourse. What I hear is the generalised voice of the immigrant and transnational from the relatively powerless inner-city margins of post-colonial Britain, from the underdeveloped and undercapitalised base of the Western-but-global market economy; I hear the voice of the 'orientalised' other whose control over the privileged writing and hegemonic representation of his culture and tradition and religion is usurped, even to the extent of having the latter marketed and commoditised by Western outsiders. As such, the sentiments, while extreme in tone, can be heard to express a justifiable outrage, even to the liberal ear.

However, what can also be heard is a return-orientalism. The outrage is expressed in terms of a reciprocal hegemonic denial, a reciprocal collective stereotyping, of what lies beyond the boundaries of a cultural community; it is mutually exclusive and exclusionary. As such, the 'argument' expressed is communitarian. It also accords, in principle, with an insistence on so-called "third generation rights" which spokespersons of Third World states and Fourth World peoples commonly enunciate today. These are 'cultural rights', based on a sense of group solidarity, 'the rights of peoples' and they include *inter alia*: the right to self-determination, to development, to peace and security, to protection from genocide, to permanent sovereignty over natural resources and to the preservation of lifestyle and cultural diversity (cf. Prott 1988:95–6).

But thanks to Rorty too, I can argue that the way of communitarian politics is the wrong way, is a way leading to widespread hurt, cruelty and humiliation, to mutual stereotyping and denigration, if not worse; (even where this stereotyping is sympathetic in intent, as mine is here with regard to the voice of *Hizb ut Tahrir*). Communitarian politics treats the group as a given, as *sui generis*, and individual members as derivatives therefrom; it will never accommodate the specificity (righful, inexorable) of the individual. And I can argue that there is a significant advantage to liberalism – to postmodern, ironic liberalism – which leads instead to a possible mutual accommodation of difference (cultural, religious, individual, whatever). For only in an ironic liberal attitude to all beliefs, in the ironising and the relativising of all substantive absoluteness, can difference be accommodated within an equalitarian procedural justice. Finally, I can argue that the humiliation of those who currently insist on a mutually exclusive absoluteness (cultural, religious, individual, whatever) is a necessary cruelty which paves the way to relative kindness – a cruelty, then, commensurate with the hurt I feel, as a Jew, treating the sentiments voiced in the above extract.

IRONISM AND 'TRIBALISM'

Rorty describes ironism as 'a reaction against the absoluteness of final vocabularies'; and ironists as those who recognise the relativity of their own consciences, their most central values, beliefs and desires. The ironist recognises that the vocabulary in which he states his highest hopes does not refer to a reality beyond the reach of time and chance: that today's truth was yesterday's heresy and tomorrow's superstition. And yet, Rorty goes on to say (1992:46), recognition of this contingency would be his definition of freedom. Furthermore, such recognition is the chief virtue of which the members of a liberal society can boast; the major aim of liberal society must be the substitution of contingency for what Berlin identified as the barbarism, the "moral and political immaturity", of absolutism (1969:172).

Ironism is also the key to liberal communities; for here are communities recognised as ideological constructs – happy communities, voluntary communities, just as much as imposed, imprisoning ones. However much communities may present an essential (and essentialised) singular face to the outside world – and to themselves – they are none the less composed of and constituted by a multiplicity of individuals who work to accommodate their diverse meanings and motivations in the form of common symbols and equivalent behaviours. The anthropologist should not confuse the rhetoric of metaphysical homogeneity with the reality of individual diversity – any more than should community members themselves or their neighbours; the anthropologist's appreciation (and publication) of how a community is worked by its members need not accord with a local model of the ('autonomous', 'traditional') workings of that community (cf. Rapport 1997c).

Within the ironism of a liberal democracy, then, the community is safe for individuals because here people may make and inhabit (ethnic, religious, local, occupational) communities as they wish while at the same time recognising their constructed, ideological nature: the contingency of community identity. Hence, the liberal community does not value itself, its culture, over and above the lives of its individual members, or those of its individual neighbours; the liberal community is an ironic community which ultimately denies itself and freely allows for the facticity of individuals and their agency.

Rorty's notion of ironism is distilled from the writings of Nietzsche, William James, Freud, Proust and Wittgenstein. But then the concept can be democratised by describing it in terms of behaviour which anthropologists have more widely recognised, albeit in the context of small-scale societies which they have been wont to claim demonstrate not ironism but an holistic (hierarchical) absolutism.

In *Other Tribes, Other Scribes*, James Boon reflected on the way that identities are constituted through comparison and contrast (1982:230–6). One achieves identity by saying what one is not, by 'playing the vis-à-vis': by reaching out to otherness and then holding it dialectically at bay. Identity, Boon surmised, is intrinsically comparative, in continuing antithetical relationship with the elements of its own negation: fundamentally beside itself, implicitly admitting its own negativity.

However, Boon continued, this 'nay-saying', this setting up of a dialectical other, has been historically of two types, themselves in a dialectical relationship with each other (a historical meta-dialectic). And the two types might be called "Tribal" and "Scribal": a Tribal or 'generalised' system of nay-saying, versus a Scribal or 'centralised' system of nay-saying. The Tribal/generalised system conceives of the relationship with an other as one between *mutual necessities*. Hence: sacred and profane; male and female; night and day; moiety 'a' and moiety 'b'. Moreover, there is the further balance crucially built into the Tribal system whereby *ego* and *alter* mutually recognise that, 'anything the other is to me, I am to it'. By contrast, the Scribal/centralised system of nay-saying conceives of this same relationship with an other as one between *mutual exclusivities*. Hence: good and evil; traditional and modern; communism and capitalism; Muslims and Jews. Moreover, this is a competitive system, often organised so that the winner completely overwhelms or destroys or co-opts the loser. Expanding into his space, the winner can ultimately hope to envelop the universe. In this way, the Scribal system is homogenising and totalising, eventuating in a 'spiceless, universal monoculture'. There is an absoluteness inherent in the Scribal – an intolerance of symbolic difference, a reaching out towards a contrastive other only to overcome its oppositeness – which the Tribal does not evoke. The Tribal is ready to relativise differences in a symbolic system containing all, to maintain more of a differentiated steady state.

It is an important aspect of the Tribal and Scribal, therefore, that they do not represent an evolution, and rather that Boon sees their relationship as dialectical. For this gives the anthropologist a vital role: the carrying forward of the Tribal, polytheistic flag. It is the task of the anthropologist, Boon says, to emphasise the virtues of ironism: of plural cultures, languages and histories in the one world, in the one global social space. It is his duty to eschew the definitive and decisive, the singular, absolute and totalising, from his descriptions and those of others. For only in this fashion can the anthropologist hope to exorcise the spectre of uniformitarianism, defeat the forces of Scribalism and their insistence on one substantive (as opposed to procedural) reality (cf. Geertz 1986:118).

In short, between Rorty's liberal ironism and the Tribalism which Boon identifies not simply as half of the world but as the only way forward for anthropology, I can read of a convivial overlap.

BIOLOGICAL INTEGRITY

If postmodern liberalism embodies ironism – teaches the way of ironism in opposition to absolutism – then it also posits individuality in place of community. Finally, then, it is to Forster's ironic reference to the 'divine' individual that I would return.

And I begin again with Rorty's philosophical ironist. What fires philosophers such as Kierkegaard, Nietzsche and Wittgenstein, Rorty suggests, is a sense of wonder at the individual human capacity for creativity. Rather than beings that one can describe accurately and conclusively – absolutely – human individuals are ever "generators of new descriptions", whether of themselves, others or the world; they are ubiquitous creators of "something new under the sun, something which is not an accurate representation of what was already there, something which (at least for the moment) cannot be explained and can barely be described" (1979:370,378). The ironist eschews the absolute not least because he wishes ever to keep space open for individual creativity – what in other terminologies might be described as 'divine'. Moreover, it is this creativity which, I would argue, provides the foundation for a liberal insistence on an 'individual morality'. For here is a creativity inextricably tied to the individual human being as a physically distinct, biological organism.

Rorty's definition of a liberal (borrowed from Judith Shklar (1984:43–4)), 'someone who thinks that cruelty is the worst of human acts', is grounded in the belief that other human beings warrant inclusion within one's polity, and equal treatment, because they can feel pain and suffer humiliation; (an echo, here, of Jeremy Bentham's: 'the capability of suffering pain confers rights.') I would likewise ground my belief in a liberal privileging of the individual human being in biological terms; in a biological theory of consciousness, as recently elucidated by Gerald Edelman (1992).

In terms of bodies, brains, minds and consciousnesses, Edelman begins, "each individual person is like no other" (1992:171). In particular, Edelman's interest in the evolution of the brain leads him to emphasise 'the enormous diversity and individuality of brain structure' – something which is specifically mammalian, more specifically primatal, and most specifically human. There are three main reasons for this. First, there is the early stage of physical development at which the mammalian organism is born; so that much of the brainy development of that organism (most, in humans) takes place while living in particular environments. Second, there is the enormous complexity of the brain wherein the potential connections between the different neurons and neuronal clusters (cells and cellular groups) of which the brain is composed is almost infinite, and whereby actual connections are made on an experimental basis through testing the value of those behavioural interactions with the environment which ensue from making one particular connection as opposed to another. And third, there is the superlative spontaneity of the brain's activity, its "extraordinary imaginative freedom" (1992:170), whereby new and unpredictable connections continue to be made in the brain throughout life so that the present and past of the brain's characteristics do not determine its future. The end-result is that the consciousness of each individual is unique to him or her: "unique to his or her body and individual history" (1992:136).

To elaborate upon this conclusion somewhat, much traditional thinking about the brain has been either "instructionist" – 'characteristics are produced in response to the environment' – or "programmatic" – 'characteristics are written into a computer-like program which is either in-born or learned'. Edelman's model is, instead, (*après* Darwin) "selectionist": 'characteristics originally appear in the brain randomly, irrespective of their usefulness, and are selected for there and then by an experimenting human organism exploring its environment.' In Darwin's theory of selection, diversity was the key: the diversity of species and the diversity of individuals. Variations occurred in species and individuals, Darwin argued, which were quite independent of those organisms' environment: the variations were self-generated, they were ongoing and they were random. Hence, diversity (and evolutionary development) was to be accounted for largely in terms of genetic drift. Moreover, it was such variation, tiny though it may have been in each case, which affected the viability of organisms *per se*. The environment, in short, did not directly shape the form of living things, it merely selected the best-adapted from pre-existing variants by encouraging their expression; and the story of evolution did not concern an unfolding so much as 'the play', in H.A.L. Fisher's phrasing, 'of the contingent and the unforeseen'. (Indeed, in the most recent appreciation of this contingency and diversity, the genetic uniqueness of each individual human being is seen to be their most salient defence against humankind's most dogged enemy: parasitical bacteria (Wells 1994:12)).

In Edelman's thesis, selection operates within the individual brain as within the individual body, but on a very different time-scale. Precisely, the brain adapts to the world, selects for new ideas and behaviours, in seconds. There is an initial diversity in the brain, spontaneous and intrinsic, generated independently of the environment and how it is changing: the brain has a hundred billion nerve cells with a possible million billion connections, each causing a different behaviour. The body causes a number of these variant forms to encounter and interact with the environment, and through sensory signals (visual, auditory and so on), the brain retrieves the result. In this way, some behavioural and ideational variants come to be seen as more 'successful' than others (pleasurable, interesting, gratifying), and are more or less strongly 'valued' as such; patterns of brain connections which produce favourable results are 'valued' more highly than the failures by cellular 'value systems' located in the brain stem which strengthen chemically one connection between cells over others. The valued, successful behaviours, skills and perceptions are thus 'learnt'.

But more than this, certain behaviours, skills and perceptions are thus 'made'. For what the brain is doing, by interacting with the world from the moment of birth (if not before), is actively generating information: making distinctions and categories, imposing boundaries and, hence, structuring the world. The 'real' world is open-ended, ambiguous; there is no absolute or correct description of the world which does not depend on the individual body and brain which is interacting with it: each individual constructs his or her own version of the world.

In this way, through activity in the world, we build up more and more abstract cycles of thought and action, every one suffused with value, with some goal that's achieved, as perceived by the individual organism. Thus motivated by its own system of 'values' – of what has worked 'successively' for it in the past – each brain comes to react to the world in a unique way. (It is through prolonged and repeated acts of inventing the self and its world, agency and epistemology, that, in Bruner and Weisser's conclusion, the 'mind' is formed (1991:145–6)). Not only this, but it is impossible to prescribe how an individual will behave in the future, even with the knowledge of his or her strong values in the present. For the inherent spontaneity of the brain's activity always throws up new variations for possible experimentation. Here is the creativity whereby each individual, each day, says and does and thinks things never done or said or thought before, by them or anyone else, comes to judge their success and value them accordingly.

Hence, the facts, for Edelman, speak ineluctably of individuality (individual variations in biological structure and experience) (cf. Mithen 1995:6). Also, of a more humane sense of human nature – undetermined, neither instructed nor programmed. Also, of an individual morality, whereby each individual's 'spirit' is precious *because* it is mortal (the derivative of a unique embodiment), and because it is unpredictable in its creativity – a creativity eventuating in the 'constant surprise' of 'extraordinary achievements' (Edelman 1992:164). (Here is an echo, perhaps, of John Stuart Mill's: 'the peculiar evil of silencing an individual opinion is that it is robbing the human race.') As Rorty ironically derived a picture of universalistic liberalism from an appreciation of the contingency of belief, so Edelman concludes that sexual relations, genetic drift and environmental upbringing can give onto the finite coalescence of a precious biological individuality.

Furthermore, the facts speak to me of a premium not only on the mortal individual human body, but also on its confidence, comfort, health and freedom from suffering. Since consciousness and creativity derive from a unique individual embodiment, a premium must be placed on the body's unique potential to interact with the environment in a non-circumscribed fashion. Which makes not merely murder immoral but also the unwelcome infliction of pain and withholding of succour. To attack the body of another in this way, to curb its potential for experience, is to threaten its innate and beautiful capacity to create what no-one else has or could: itself in the world (cf. Boulware-Miller 1985).

It is not that the individual's unique embodiment translates as something monadic, solipsistic, isolated or impermeable. Of course the individual's consciousness comes to be (and becomes) within a socio-cultural environment; of course his conscious individuality expresses itself in terms of activity in the world, in terms of cultural discourses or systems of symbols, in terms of social and environmental interaction and interdependency, in terms of all manner of substantive transfer (oxygen, bacteria, noise, babies, food, language and so on) over the boundaries which divide the physical organism of the brain (and the physical organism of the body it orchestrates) from what lies beyond it (cf. Geertz 1973:46–51). Nevertheless, an individual's being-in-the-world is universally mediated by the very particular interpretative prisms of body and brain which distance him from it. That is, individuals engage with their environments (socio-cultural and physical) by virtue of discrete sense-making apparatuses – discrete centres of consciousness in discrete bodies – which afford them distinct perspectives on the world around them. Hence, while intrinsically 'of the world', the individual inexorably comes to know the world as 'other'. And there is always an individuality, a differentiation, which their behaviour embodies, whether this is locally, culturally, recognised and validated (for example as a form of individualism) or not (cf. Rapport 1997a).

Inasmuch as the individual body and brain is the site of sense-making, of experiencing and interpreting, then, any morality which circumscribes or denies or threatens these processes on the basis of the value of a socio-cultural environment *per se* replaces a physical reality with a metaphysical one, and thereby mistakes the nature of consciousness. There can be no socio-cultural environment (no 'community') without individual consciousness of that environment, without individuality.

INDIVIDUAL MORALITY

Echoing E.M. Forster ("'a general feeling' and 'the great world' do not exist and never have existed" (1964:67–8)), F.R. Leavis once rhetorised: "what is the 'social condition' that has nothing to do with an individual condition? what is the 'social hope' that transcends, cancels or makes indifferent the condition of each individual? where is a condition, a life, to be located if not in individuals' lives – lives which cannot be generalised, averaged or compounded" (1972:53–4). Of course, largely due to Durkheim and his apologists, such generalising, averaging and compounding is precisely what social anthropology has attempted, is precisely the communitarian way (of hypostatised "society" and "culture") that social anthropology has trodden: 'social structure', 'social organisation', 'social function', 'social role'; 'cultural representation', 'cultural prescription', 'cultural value', 'cultural norm'. (How different if anthropology had followed Mill or Simmel, or even Weber: the individual is "the upper limit and the sole carrier of meaningful conduct", "collectivities must be treated as *solely* the resultants and modes of organisation of the particular acts of individual persons", and hence it is in the 'understandable acts' of such "participating individual men" that social science must, without exception, deal (Weber 1964:101)).

From such Durkheimian hypostatisation, I am happy to be an apostate. For there is little distance to travel, it would seem, from the absolutism of socio-cultural holism to the absolutism of religious fundamentalism – and other forms of totalitarianism. Here is not a procedural (liberal) accommodation of difference so much as a substantive (totalitarian) imposition of collective sameness. Sacrificing the individual to the commonweal, the public good, the culture or society, making the individual an instrument of deindividuation, of group needs, confuses the concrete with the ideological, and misconstrues the proper nature of the relations between the two. Individuals are attached to one another and to societies and cultures but they are not emanations from, or embodiments of, them.

Contra Durkheim, morality must begin with the biological individual and his or her needs and potential, his or her 'cry of torment'. It is individuals who are the corporeal constituents of the social world, the moving agents in history, the origins of culture. Moreover, it is individual bodies, the 'common embodiedness of our being-in-the-world' as Jackson puts it (1989:135), which gives onto a common ground between one individual and another. Finally, it is individuals who potentially suffer. Thus it is that individuals must be the measure of moral action, the benchmark of justice in society, the foundation of cultural value, and their bodiliness unite the world in a common liberal morality.

Bibliography

Abu-Lughod, L. (1986) *Veiled Sentiments: Honor and Poetry in a Bedouin Society*, Berkeley: University of California Press.
—— (1990) 'Shifting politics in Bedouin love poetry', in C.A. Lutz and L. Abu-Lughod (eds) *Language and the Politics of Emotion*, Cambridge: Cambridge University Press.
Appadurai, A. (1990) 'Disjuncture and difference in the global cultural economy', *Public Culture* 2,2: 1–24.
Appleyard, B. (1991) *Understanding the Present. Science and the Soul of Modern Man*, St. Albans: Picador.
Arshi, S., Kirstein, C., Naqvi, R. and Pankow, F. (1994) 'Why travel? Tropics, en-tropics and apo-tropaics', in G. Robertson *et al.* (eds) *Travellers' Tales. Narratives of Home and Displacement*, London: Routledge.
Ashley, K. (1990) 'Introduction', in K. Ashley (ed.) *Victor Turner and the Construction of Cultural Criticism. Between Literature and Anthropology*, Bloomington: Indiana University Press.
Auge, M. (1995) *Non-Places: Introduction to an Anthropology of Supermodernity*, London: Verso.
Babcock, B. (1993) 'At home, no women are storytellers: ceramic creativity and the politics of discourse in a Cochiti pueblo', in S. Lavie, K. Narayan and R. Rosaldo (eds) *Creativity/Anthropology*, Cornell: Cornell University Press.
Bakhtin, M. (1981) *The Dialogic Imagination*, Austin: University of Texas Press.
Barnard, A. and Good, A. (1984) *Research Practices in the Study of Kinship*, London: Academic.
Barth, F. (1969) 'Introduction', in F. Barth (ed.) *Ethnic Groups and Boundaries*, Boston: Little, Brown.
Barthes, R. (1982) *A Barthes Reader* (ed. S. Sontag), London: Cape.
Bateson, G. (1951) (with J. Ruesch) *Communication: the Social Matrix of Psychiatry*, New York: Norton.
—— (1958) 'Language and psychotherapy', *Psychiatry* 21: 96–100.
—— (1972) *Steps to an Ecology of Mind*, London: Intertext.
Benedict, R. (1932) 'Configurations of culture in North America', *American Anthropologist* 34: 1–27.

Berger, J. (1967) *A Fortunate Man. The Story of a Country Doctor*, London: Penguin.

—— (1975) *The Seventh Man*, Harmondsworth: Penguin.

—— (1979) *Pig Earth*, London: Writers & Readers.

—— (1984) *And Our Faces, My Heart, Brief as Photos*, London: Writers & Readers.

—— (1988) *The White Bird*, London: Hogarth.

Berger, P. (1990) *The Sacred Canopy*, New York: Doubleday.

Berger, P. and Luckmann, T. (1969) 'Sociology of religion and sociology of knowledge', in R. Robertson (ed.) *The Sociology of Religion*, Harmondsworth: Penguin.

Berlin, I. (1969) *Four Essays on Liberty*, Oxford: Oxford University Press.

—— (1990) *The Crooked Timber of Humanity. Chapters in the History of Ideas*, London: Murray.

Bernstein, B. (1972) 'A sociolinguistic approach to socialisation; with some reference to educability', in J. Gumperz and D. Hymes (eds) *Directions in Sociolinguistics*, New York: Holt, Rinehart & Winston.

Blake, W. (1975) *The Complete Poems*, London: Longman.

Bloom, H. (1975) *The Anxiety of Influence. A Theory of Poetry*, Oxford: Oxford University Press.

Boon, J. (1982) *Other Tribes, Other Scribes*, Cambridge: Cambridge University Press.

Boulware-Miller, K. (1985) 'Female circumcision: challenges to the practice as a human rights violation', *Harvard Women's Law Journal* 8 (Spring): 155–77.

Bourdieu, P. (1966) 'The sentiment of honour in Kabyle society', in J. Peristiany (ed.) *Honour and Shame*, Chicago: University of Chicago Press.

Briggs, J. (1991) 'Mazes of meaning: the exploration of individuality in culture and of culture through individual constructs', in L. Bryce-Boyer (ed.) *The Psychoanalytic Study of Society*, New York: Analytic.

Brittan, A. (1973) *Meanings and Situations*, London: Routledge & Kegan Paul.

Bruner, E. (1993) 'Introduction: the ethnographic self and the personal self', in P. Benson (ed.) *Anthropology and Literature*, Urbana: Illinois University Press.

Bruner, J. (1990) *Acts of Meaning*, Cambridge MA: Harvard University Press.

Bruner, J. and Weisser, S. (1991) 'The invention of self: autobiography and its forms', in D. Olson and N. Torrance (eds) *Literacy and Orality*, Cambridge: Cambridge University Press.

Burridge, K. (1979) *Someone, No One. An Essay on Individuality*, Princeton: Princeton University Press.

Butor, M. (1972) 'Le voyage et l'écriture', *Romantisme* 4: 4–19.

Campbell, A. (1989) *To Square with Genesis. Causal Statements and Shamanic Ideas in Wayapi*, Edinburgh: Edinburgh University Press.

Carrithers, M. (1985) 'An alternative social history of the self', in M. Carrithers, S. Collins and S. Lukes (eds) *The Category of the Person.*

Anthropology, Philosophy, History, Cambridge: Cambridge University Press.

Carter, P. (1992) *Living in a New Country. History, Travelling and Language*, London: Faber.

Chambers, I. (1994a) *Migrancy Culture Identity*, London: Routledge.

—— (1994b) 'Leaky habitats and broken grammar', in G. Robertson *et al.* (eds) *Travellers' Tales. Narratives of Home and Displacement*, London: Routledge.

Chesterton, G.K. (1936) *Stories, Essays and Poems*, London: Dent.

Chodorow, N. (1994) 'Reflections on personal meaning and cultural meaning', paper presented at the AAA Meetings, Atlanta.

Clifford, J. (1986a) 'Introduction: partial truths', in G. Marcus and J. Clifford (eds) *Writing Culture*, Berkeley: University of California Press.

—— (1986b) 'On ethnographic self-fashioning: Conrad and Malinowski', in T. Heller, M. Sosna and D. Wellbery (eds) *Reconstructing Individualism*, Stanford: Stanford University Press.

—— (1990) 'Notes on (field)notes', in R. Sanjek (ed.) *Fieldnotes. The Makings of Anthropology*, Ithaca: Cornell University Press.

—— (1992) 'Travelling Cultures', in L. Grossberg, C. Nelson and P. Treichler (eds) *Cultural Studies*, London: Routledge.

Cohen, A.P. (1978) 'Ethnographic method in the real community', *Sociologia Ruralis* XVIII,1: 1–22.

—— (1985) *The Symbolic Construction of Community*, Chichester: Horwood.

—— (1986) 'Post-modernism, interpretative anthropology and the two selves of the ethnographer', paper presented at the ESRC Field Studies Seminar, University of Warwick.

—— (1989) 'Opposing the motion that "social anthropology is a generalising science or it is nothing"', *Group for Debates in Anthropological Theory*, Dept of Social Anthropology, University of Manchester.

—— (1994) *Self Consciousness. An Alternative Anthropology of Identity*, London: Routledge.

Conrad, J. (1973) *The Nigger of the Narcissus*, Harmondsworth: Penguin.

Coy, P. (1980) 'Correspondence: Malinowski's diary', *Royal Anthropological Institute News* 41.

Crites, S. (1971) 'The narrative quality of experience', *Journal of the American Academy of Religion* XXXIX: 291–311.

Culler, J. (1981) *The Pursuit of Signs: Semiotics, Literature, Deconstruction*, Ithaca: Cornell University Press.

D.S. (1995) 'NB', *Times Literary Supplement* 4798: 14.

Dias, N. (1994) 'Looking at objects: memory, knowledge in nineteenth century ethnographic displays', in G. Robertson *et al.* (eds) *Travellers' Tales. Narratives of Home and Displacement*, London: Routledge.

Douglas, M. (1966) *Purity and Danger*, London: Routledge & Kegan Paul.

Drummond, L. (1980) 'The cultural continuum: a theory of intersystems', *MAN* 15: 352–74.

Dumont, L. (1985) 'A modified view of our origins: the Christian beginnings of modern individualism', in M. Carrithers, S. Collins and S. Lukes (eds) *The Category of the Person. Anthropology, Philosophy, History*, Cambridge: Cambridge University Press.

—— (1986) *Essays on Individualism. Modern Ideology in Anthropological Perspective*, Chicago: University of Chicago Press.

Durkheim, E. (1966 [1885]) *The Rules of Sociological Method*, New York: Free.

Eagleton, T. (1981) *Walter Benjamin. Or Towards a Revolutionary Criticism*, London: New Left Books.

Edelman, G. (1992) *Bright Air, Brilliant Fire. On the Matter of the Mind*, Harmondsworth: Penguin.

Eliade, M. (1954) *The Myth of the Eternal Return, or Cosmos and History*, Princeton: Princeton University Press.

Ellen, R. (1984) (ed.) *Ethnographic Research*, London: Academic.

Emerson, R.W. (1877) *Essays (second series)*, Boston: Osgood.

—— (1950) *Selected Prose and Poetry*, New York: Rinehart.

Fardon, R. (1990) (ed.) *Localizing Strategies. Regional Traditions of Ethnographic Writing*, Edinburgh: Scottish Academic Press.

Featherstone, M. (1990) 'Global culture: an introduction', in M. Featherstone (ed.) *Global Culture: Nationalism, Globalisation and Modernity*, London: Sage.

Feldman, C. (1987) 'Thought from language: the linguistic construction of cognitive representations', in J. Bruner and H. Haste (eds) *Making Sense. The Child's Construction of the World*, London: Methuen.

Fernandez, J. (1992) 'What it is like to be a Banzie: on sharing the experience of an equatorial microcosm', in J. Gort, H. Vroom, R. Fernhout and A. Wessels (eds) *On Sharing Religious Experience*, Amsterdam: Rodopi.

—— (1993) 'Ceferino Suarez: a village versifier', in S. Lavie, K. Narayan, and R. Rosaldo (eds) *Creativity/Anthropology*, Cornell: Cornell University Press.

Finnegan, R. (1977) *Oral Poetry*, Cambridge: Cambridge University Press.

Fire, J. and Erdoes, R. (1980) *Lame Deer: Sioux Medicine Man*, London: Quartet.

Forge, A. (1967) 'Malinowski's diary: a review', *New Society* August 17th.

Forster, E.M. (1950) *Howards End*, Harmondsworth: Penguin.

—— (1964) *The Longest Journey*, Harmondsworth: Penguin.

—— (1972) *Two Cheers for Democracy*, Harmondsworth: Penguin.

—— (1984) *Aspects of the Novel*, Harmondsworth: Penguin.

Foucault, M. (1972) *The Archaeology of Knowledge*, London: Tavistock.

—— (1991) 'What is an author?', in P. Rabinow (ed.) *The Foucault Reader*, Harmondsworth: Penguin.

Garfinkel, H. (1968) 'Conditions of successful status-degradation ceremonies', in J. Manis and B. Meltzer (eds) *Symbolic Interaction*, Boston: Allyn & Bacon.

Gatheru, R.M. (1965) *Child of Two Worlds. A Kikuyu's Story*, New York: Doubleday.

Gatrell, V. (1994) *The Hanging Tree: Execution and the English People, 1770–1868*, Oxford: Oxford University Press.

Geertz, C. (1967) 'Malinowski's diary: a review', *New York Review of Books* September 14th.
—— (1973) *The Interpretation of Cultures*, New York: Basic.
—— (1983) *Local Knowledge*, New York: Basic.
—— (1986) 'The uses of diversity', *Michigan Quarterly Review* 25 (Summer): 105–22.
—— (1988) *Works and Lives. The Anthropologist as Author*, Cambridge: Polity.
Gellner, E. (1959) *Words and Things*, London: Gollancz.
—— (1993) *Postmodernism, Reason and Religion*, London: Routledge.
Giddens, A. (1973) *The Class Structure of the Advanced Societies*, London: Hutchinson.
—— (1976) *New Rules of Sociological Method*, London: Hutchinson.
Gluckman, M. (1963) 'Gossip and scandal', *Current Anthropology* 4,3: 307–16.
Goffman, E. (1961) *Asylums*, Harmondsworth: Penguin.
Goodenough, W. (1963) *Cooperation in Change*, New York: Sage.
Goodman, N. (1978) *Ways of Worldmaking*, Hassocks: Harvester.
—— (1984) *Of Mind and Other Matters*, Cambridge MA: Harvard University Press.
Goody, J. (1977) *The Domestication of the Savage Mind*, Cambridge: Cambridge University Press.
Goody, J. and Watt, I. (1968) 'The consequences of literacy', in J. Goody (ed.) *Literacy in Traditional Societies*, Cambridge: Cambridge University Press.
Gray, J. (1992) 'Against the new liberalism: Rawls, Dworkin and the emptying of political life', *Times Literary Supplement* 4657: 13–15.
—— (1994) *Isaiah Berlin*, London: HarperCollins.
Grimshaw, A. (1994a) 'The eye in the door. Anthropology, film and the exploration of interior space', unpublished paper, Dept of Social Anthropology, Manchester University.
—— (1994b) 'The end in the beginning: New Year at Rizong', unpublished paper, Dept of Social Anthropology, Manchester University.
Handler, R and Segal, D. (1990) *Jane Austen and the Fiction of Culture: An Essay on the Narration of Social Realities*, Tucson: Arizona University Press.
Hann, C. (1996) 'One folk, one nation?', *Times Literary Supplement* 4863: 28.
Hannerz, U. (1992) 'The global ecumene as a network of networks', in A. Kuper (ed.) *Conceptualising Society*, London: Routledge.
—— (1993) 'The cultural role of world cities', in A.P. Cohen and K. Fukui (eds) *Humanising the City?*, Edinburgh: Edinburgh University Press.
Hardy, B. (1968) 'Towards a poetics of fiction: 3. an approach through narrative', *Novel* 2,1.
Harre, R. and de Waele, J-P. (1976) 'The personality of individuals', in R. Harre (ed.) *Personality*, Oxford: Blackwell.
Harris, R. (1981) *The Language Myth*, London: Duckworth.
Hart, K. (1990) 'Swimming into the human current', *Cambridge*

Anthropology 14,3: 3–10.

Haviland, J. (1977) *Gossip, Reputation and Knowledge in Zinacantan*, Chicago: University of Chicago Press.

Hayek, F. (1969) *Individualism and Economic Order*, Chicago: University of Chicago Press.

Herzfeld, M. (1992) *The Social Production of Indifference. Exploring the Symbolic Roots of Western Bureaucracy*, Oxford: Berg.

Himmelfarb, G. (1996) 'The unravelled fabric – and how to knit it up. Mixed motives among the new communitarians', *Times Literary Supplement* 4859: 12–13.

Hoebel, E. (1967) 'A review of Malinowski's diary', *Minnesota Tribune* May.

Hoebel, E.A. and Wallace, E. (1958) *The Comanches*, Norman: Oklahoma University Press.

Holy, L. and Stuchlik, M. (1981) "The structure of folk models', in L. Holy and M. Stuchlik (eds) *The Structure of Folk Models*, London: Academic.

Hsu, F. (1980) 'Malinowskiana', *Royal Anthropological Institute News* 39.

Huizinga, J. (1980) *Homo Ludens*, London: Routledge & Kegan Paul.

Humphrey, N. (1982) 'Consciousness: a just-so story', *New Scientist* 95: 474–8.

Huxley, A. (1964) *Those Barren Leaves*, Harmondsworth: Penguin.

Iser, W. (1989) 'Towards a literary anthropology', in R. Cohen (ed.) *Future Literary Theory*, London: Routledge.

Jackson, J. (1990) '"I am a fieldnote": fieldnotes as a symbol of professional identity', in R. Sanjek (ed.) *Fieldnotes. The Makings of Anthropology*, Ithaca: Cornell University Press.

Jackson, M. (1989) *Paths toward a Clearing. Radical Empiricism and Ethnographic Inquiry*, Bloomington: Indiana University Press.

Jackson, M. and Karp, I. (1990) *Personhood and Agency. The Experience of Self and Other in African Cultures*, Uppsala: Uppsala University Press.

James, A. (1993) *Childhood Identities. Self and Social Relationships in the Experience of the Child*, Edinburgh: Edinburgh University Press.

Jonas, H. (1954) 'The nobility of sight', *Philosophy and Phenomenology Research* 14: 507–19.

Jorgensen, D. (1994) 'Locating the divine in Melanesia: an appreciation of the work of Kenelm Burridge', *Anthropology and Humanism* 19,2: 130–7.

Jowett, B. (1860) *Essays and Reviews*, London: Murray.

Kearney, R. (1988) *The Wake of the Imagination. Ideas of Creativity in Western Culture*, London: Hutchinson.

Kelly, G. (1969) *Clinical Psychology and Personality. The Selected Papers of George Kelly* (ed. B. Maher), New York: Wiley.

Kerby, A.P. (1991) *Narrative and the Self*, Bloomington: Indiana University Press.

Kiberd, D. (1994) 'Wilde and the English question', *Times Literary Supplement* 4785: 13–15.

Kierkegaard, S. (1940) *Thoughts on the Present Age, and Two Minor Ethico-religious Treatises*, London: Oxford University Press.

Koscuiszko Foundation, (1961) *English–Polish and Polish–English Dictionary*, The Hague: Mouton.

Kundera, M. (1990) *The Art of the Novel*, London: Faber.

Laing, R.D. (1968) *The Politics of Experience*, Harmondsworth: Penguin.

Langer, S. (1964) *Philosophical Sketches*, New York: Mentor.

Larkin, P. (1990) *Collected Poems*, London: Faber, Marvell.

Lavie, S. (1990) *The Poetics of Military Occupation. Mzeina Bedouin Allegories of Bedouin Identity under Israeli and Egyptian Rule*, Berkeley: University of California Press.

Leach, E.R. (1967) 'Review of Malinowski's diary', *Guardian* August 11th.

—— (1968) 'Anthropological aspects of language: animal categories and verbal abuse', in E. Lenneberg (ed.) *New Directions in the Study of Language*, Cambridge MA: MIT Press.

—— (1969) *A Runaway World?*, London: Oxford University Press.

—— (1976a) 'Humanism', public lecture delivered at the Humanism Society, University of Cambridge.

—— (1976b) *Culture and Communication*, Cambridge: Cambridge University Press.

—— (1977) *Custom, Law and Terrorist Violence*, Edinburgh: Edinburgh University Press.

—— (1980) 'Malinowskiana', *Royal Anthropological Institute News* 36 and 40.

Leavis, F.R. (1972) *Nor Shall My Sword. Discourses on Pluralism, Compassion and Social Hope*, London: Chatto & Windus.

Lederman, R. (1990) 'Pretexts for ethnography: on reading fieldnotes', in R. Sanjek (ed.) *Fieldnotes. The Makings of Anthropology*, Ithaca: Cornell University Press.

Levi-Strauss, C. (1975) *The Raw and the Cooked*, New York: Harper Colophon.

Lewin, R. (1988) *In the Age of Mankind*, Washington: Smithsonian.

Lewis, I. (1968) 'Review of *A Diary in the Strict Sense of the Term* by B. Malinowski', *MAN* 3: 348–9.

Louch, A. (1966) *Explanation and Human Action*, Oxford: Blackwell.

Lukes, S. (1990) *Individualism*, Oxford: Blackwell.

Lyotard, J-F. (1986) *The Post-Modern Condition: A Report on Knowledge*, Manchester: Manchester University Press.

Macfarlane, A. (ed.) (1976) *The Diary of Ralph Josselin 1616–1683*, Oxford: Oxford University Press.

—— (1978) *The Origins of English Individualism*, Oxford: Blackwell.

—— (1989) *The Culture of Capitalism*, Oxford: Blackwell.

MacIver, A. (1961) 'Historical explanation', in A. Flew (ed.) *Logic and Language (second series)*, Oxford: Blackwell.

Malinowski, B. (1961) *Argonauts of the Western Pacific*, New York: Dutton.

—— (1989) *A Diary in the Strict Sense of the Term* , London: Athlone Press.

Mannheim, K. (1952) *Ideology and Utopia*, London: Routledge & Kegan Paul.

Marcus, G. (1986) 'Contemporary problems of ethnography in the modern world', in J. Clifford and G. Marcus (eds) *Writing Culture*, Berkeley: University of California Press.

Marcus, G. and Fischer, M. (1986) *Anthropology as Cultural Critique. An Experimental Moment in the Human Sciences*, Chicago: University of Chicago Press.

Marsella, A., DeVos, G. and Hsu, F. (eds) (1985) *Culture and Self: Asian and Western Perspectives*, New York: Tavistock.

Marx, E. and Schmueli, A. (eds) (1984) *The Changing Bedouin*, New Brunswick: Transaction.

Mauss, M. (1985) 'A category of the human mind: the notion of person, the notion of self', in M. Carrithers, S. Collins and S. Lukes (eds) *The Category of the Person. Anthropology, Philosophy, History*, Cambridge: Cambridge University Press.

Mill, J.S. (1875) *A System of Logic (volume II)*, London: Longmans, Green.

Minh-ha, T. (1994) 'Other than myself/my other self', in G. Robertson *et al.* (eds) *Travellers' Tales. Narratives of Home and Displacement*, London: Routledge.

Mithen, S. (1995) 'Understanding mind and culture', *Anthropology Today* 11,6: 3–7.

Mommsen, W. (1965) 'Max Weber's political sociology and his philosophy of world history', *International Social Science Journal* XVII.

Morris, B. (1991) *Western Conceptions of the Individual*, Oxford: Berg.

Moskovitz, M. (1968) *The Politics of Human Rights*, Dordrecht: Kluwer.

Mundle, C. (1970) *A Critique of Linguistic Philosophy*, Oxford: Oxford University Press.

Myerhoff, B. (1974) *Peyote Hunt*, Ithaca: Cornell University Press.

Nehamas, A. (1985) *Nietzsche: Life as Literature*, Cambridge MA: Harvard University Press.

Nietzsche, F. (1968) *The Will to Power*, New York: Random House.

—— (1979a) *Beyond Good and Evil*, Harmondsworth, Penguin.

—— (1979b) *Twilight of the Idols*, Harmondsworth: Penguin.

Nkosi, L. (1994) 'Ironies of exile: post-colonial homelessness and the anti-climax of return', *Times Literary Supplement* 4748: 5.

Ong, W. (1969) 'World as view and world as event', *American Anthropologist* 71: 634–47.

Observer (1994) 'Hitler's heirs incite Islamic students', March 13: 25.

Paine, R. (1974) *Second Thoughts about Barth's Models*, London: Royal Anthropological Institute, Occasional Papers No. 32.

—— (1987) (ed.) *Anthropology and Advocacy*, St John's: ISER Press, Memorial University of Newfoundland.

—— (1992) 'The Marabar Caves, 1920–2020', in S. Wallman (ed.) *Contemporary Futures*, London: Routledge.

Park, G. (1974) *The Idea of Social Structure*, New York: Doubleday.

Parkin, D. (1987) 'Comparison as a search for continuity', in L. Holy (ed.) *Comparative Anthropology*, Oxford: Blackwell.

Peacock, J. (1986) *The Anthropological Lens*, Cambridge: Cambridge University Press.

Pelto, P, and Pelto, G. (1978) *Anthropological Research: The Structure of Inquiry*, Cambridge: Cambridge University Press.

Phillips, D. (1993) *Looking Backward. A Critical Appraisal of Communitarian Thought*, Princeton: Princeton University Press.

Popper, K. (1965) 'Unity of method in the natural and social sciences', in D. Braybrooke (ed.) *Philosophical Problems of the Social Sciences*, New York: Macmillan.

—— (1966) *The Open Society and its Enemies (volume 2)*, Princeton: Princeton University Press.

Pospisil, L. (1971) *Kapauku Papuans and their Law*, New Haven: Human Relations Area Files Press.

Powdermaker, H. and Montagu, A. (1967) 'Malinowski's diary: a review', *New York Review of Books* November 9.

Prott, L. (1988) 'Cultural rights as peoples' rights in international law', in J. Crawford (ed.) *The Rights of Peoples*, Oxford: Oxford University Press.

Rabinow, P. (1977) *Reflections on Fieldwork in Morocco*, Berkeley: University of California Press.

Rapport, N.J. (1986) 'Cedar High Farm: ambiguous symbolic boundary. An essay in anthropological intuition,' in A.P. Cohen (ed.), *Symbolising Boundaries*, Manchester: Manchester University Press.

—— (1987) *Talking Violence. An Anthropological Interpretation of Conversation in the City*, St. John's: ISER Press, Memorial University of Newfoundland.

—— (1990) 'Ritual conversation in a Canadian suburb. Anthropology and the problem of generalisation,' *Human Relations* 43,9: 849–64.

—— (1993) *Diverse World-Views in an English Village*, Edinburgh: Edinburgh University Press.

—— (1994) *The Prose and the Passion. Anthropology, Literature and the Writing of E.M. Forster*, Manchester: Manchester University Press.

—— (1995) 'Migrant selves and stereotypes: personal context in a postmodern world', in S. Pile and N. Thrift (eds) *Mapping the Subject: Geographies of Cultural Transformation*, London: Routledge.

—— (1996) 'Thick description', in D. Levinson and M. Ember (eds) *The Encyclopedia of Cultural Anthropology*, New York: Holt.

—— (1997a) 'Individualism', in A. Barnard and J. Spencer (eds) *The Encyclopaedic Dictionary of Social and Cultural Anthropology*, London: Routledge.

—— (1997b) 'Gossip', in A. Barnard and J. Spencer (eds) *The Encyclopaedic Dictionary of Social and Cultural Anthropology*, London: Routledge.

—— (1997c) 'Community', in A. Barnard and J. Spencer (eds) *The Encyclopaedic Dictionary of Social and Cultural Anthropology*, London: Routledge.

Raz, J. (1990) *The Morality of Freedom*, Oxford: Oxford University Press.

Redfield, R. (1963) *The Little Community and Peasant Society and Culture*, Chicago: University of Chicago Press.

Riches, D. (1995) 'Dreaming as social process, and its implication for consciousness', in A.P. Cohen and N.J. Rapport (eds) *Questions of Consciousness*, London: Routledge.

Ricoeur, P. (1981) *Hermeneutics and the Human Sciences*, Cambridge: Cambridge University Press.

Riesman, D. (1954) *Individualism Reconsidered, and Other Essays*, Glencoe: Free.

—— (1958) 'The suburban sadness', in W. Dobriner (ed.) *The Suburban Community*, New York: Putnam.

Rorty, R. (1979) *Philosophy and the Mirror of Nature*, Princeton: Princeton University Press.

—— (1986) 'On ethnocentrism: a reply to Clifford Geertz', *Michigan Quarterly Review* 25 (Winter): 525–34.

—— (1992) *Contingency, Irony, and Solidarity*, Cambridge: Cambridge University Press.

Rosaldo, R., Lavie, S. and Narayan, K. (1993) 'Introduction: creativity in anthropology', in S. Lavie, K. Narayan and R. Rosaldo (eds) *Creativity/Anthropology*, Cornell: Cornell University Press.

Rushdie, S. (1990) 'The language of the pack', *Times Literary Supplement* 4572: 1239.

—— (1991) 'Imaginary homelands', *Granta* 9–21.

Sahlins, M. (1968) *Tribesmen*, Englewood Cliffs: Prentice-Hall.

Sandel, M. (1982) *Liberalism and the Limits of Justice*, Cambridge: Cambridge University Press.

—— (1984) 'Introduction', in M. Sandel (ed.) *Liberalism and its Critics*, Oxford: Blackwell.

Sanjek, R. (1990a) (ed.) *Fieldnotes. The Makings of Anthropology*, Ithaca: Cornell University Press.

—— (1990b) 'Preface', in R. Sanjek (ed.) *Fieldnotes. The Makings of Anthropology*, Ithaca: Cornell University Press.

—— (1990c) 'Fire, loss and the sorcerer's apprentice', in R. Sanjek (ed.) *Fieldnotes. The Makings of Anthropology*, Ithaca: Cornell University Press.

—— (1990d) 'A vocabulary for fieldnotes', in R. Sanjek (ed.) *Fieldnotes. The Makings of Anthropology*, Ithaca: Cornell University Press.

Sapir, E. (1956) *Culture, Language and Personality* (ed. D. Mandelbaum), Berkeley: University of California Press.

Sartre, J-P. (1972) *The Psychology of Imagination*, New York: Citadel.

Sassoon, S. (1983) *Diaries 1915–1918*, London: Faber.

Schopenhauer, A. (1969) *The World as Will and Representation (volume I)*, New York: Dover.

Schuetz, A. (1944) 'The stranger. An essay in social psychology', *American Journal of Sociology* 49,6: 499–507.

Schwartz, T. (1978) 'Where is the culture? Personality as the distributive locus of culture', in G. Spindler (ed.) *The Making of Psychological Anthropology*, Berkeley: University of California Press.

Shelley, P.B. (1954) *Shelley's Prose* (ed. D. Clark), Alburquerque:

University of New Mexico Press.

Sheringham, M. (1993) *French Autobiography*, Oxford: Oxford University Press.

Shklar, J. (1984) *Ordinary Vices*, Cambridge MA: Harvard University Press.

Shostak, M. (1983) *Nisa. The Life and Words of a !Kung Woman*, Harmondsworth: Penguin.

—— (1993) 'The creative individual in the world of the !Kung San', in S. Lavie, K. Narayan and R. Rosaldo (eds) *Creativity/Anthropology*, Cornell: Cornell University Press.

Shweder, R. (1986) 'Storytelling among the anthropologists', *New York Times Book Review*, September 20, I: 38–9.

—— (1991) *Thinking through Cultures*, Cambridge MA: Harvard University Press.

Sieburth, R. (1994) 'Narcissus at work', *Times Literary Supplement* 4775: 10–12.

Silverstone, R., Hirsch, E. and Morley, D. (1994) 'Information and communication technologies and the moral economy of the household', in R. Silverstone and E. Hirsch (eds) *Consuming Technologies. Media and Information in Domestic Spaces*, London: Routledge.

Simmel, G. (1890) *Ueber sociale Differenzierung*, Leipzig: Duncker & Humblot.

—— (1971) *On Individuality and Social Forms*, Chicago: Chicago University Press.

Sontag, S. (1967) *Against Interpretation*, New York: Farrar, Straus, Giroux.

Stanley, L. (1993) 'On auto/biography in sociology', *Sociology* 27,1: 41–52.

Steiner, G. (1967) *Language and Silence*, London: Faber.

—— (1975) *After Babel*, London: Oxford University Press.

—— (1978) *On Difficulty, and Other Essays*, Oxford: Oxford University Press.

Stock, B. (1983) *The Implications of Literacy*, Princeton: Princeton University Press.

—— (1990) *Listening for the Text*, Baltimore: Johns Hopkins University Press.

Stocking, G. (1974) 'Empathy and antipathy in the heart of darkness', in R. Darnell (ed.) *Readings in the History of Anthropology*, London: Harper & Row.

Strathern, M. (1981) *Kinship at the Core*, Cambridge: Cambridge University Press.

—— (1987) 'Out of context, the persuasive fictions of anthropology', *Current Anthropology* 28,3: 251–81.

—— (1990a) *The Gender of the Gift. Problems with Women and Problems with Society in Melanesia*, Berkeley: University of California Press.

—— (1990b) 'Proposing the motion that "The concept of society is theoretically obsolete"', *Group for Debates in Anthropological Theory*, Dept of Social Anthropology, University of Manchester.

—— (1992) 'Writing societies, writing persons', *The History of the Human Sciences* 5,1: 5–16.

Street, B. (1984) *Literacy in Theory and Practice*, Cambridge: Cambridge University Press.

Szwed, J. (1966) *Private Cultures and Public Imagery*, St. John's: ISER Press, Memorial University of Newfoundland.

Thornton, R. (1991) 'The end of the future?' *Anthropology Today* 7,1: 1–2.

—— (1992) 'The chains of reciprocity: the impact of Nietzsche's *Genealogy* on Malinowski's *Crime and Custom in Savage Society*', *The Polish Sociological Bulletin* 1: 19–33.

Thornton, R. and Skalnik, P. (eds) (1993) *The Early Writings of Bronislaw Malinowski*, Cambridge: Cambridge University Press.

Triggs, G. (1988) 'The rights of "peoples" and individual rights: conflict or harmony', in J. Crawford (ed.) *The Rights of Peoples*, Oxford: Oxford University Press.

Trzaska, Evert and Michalski, (1946) *English–Polish and Polish–English Dictionary*, New York: Brown.

Turner, V. (1969) *The Ritual Process*, Chicago: Aldine.

—— (1974) *Dramas, Fields, Metaphors*, Cornell: Cornell University Press.

—— (1983) 'The spirit of celebration', in F. Manning (ed.) *The Celebration of Society*, Bowling Green: Popular.

Velsen, J. van (1967) 'The extended-case method and situational analysis', in A. Epstein *The Craft of Social Anthropology*, London: Tavistock.

Wagner, R. (1991) 'Poetics and the recentering of anthropology', in I. Brady (ed.) *Anthropological Poetics*, Savage: Rowman & Littlefield.

Wallace, A.F.C. (1961) 'The psychic unity of human groups', in B. Kaplan (ed.) *Studying Personality Cross-Culturally*, New York: Harper & Row.

—— (1964) *Culture and Personality*, New York: Random House.

Watkins, J. (1953) 'Ideal types and historical explanation', in H. Feigl and M. Brodbeck (eds) *Readings in the Philosophy of Science*, New York: Appleton-Century-Crofts.

—— (1959) 'Historical explanation in the social sciences', in P. Gardiner (ed.) *Theories of History*, London: Allen & Unwin.

Weber, M. (1964) *Theory of Social and Economic Organisation*, New York: Free.

Wedgwood, C. (1932–34) Wedgwood Personal Archives, University Archives, University of Sydney.

Wells, P. (1994) 'Why are we not more like the water flea?', *Times Literary Supplement* 4774: 12–13.

Wiener, N. (1949) *Cybernetics*, New York: Wiley.

Wilde, O. (1910) *The Importance of Being Earnest*, London: French.

—— (1913) *Intentions*, London: Methuen.

—— (1914) *Selected Prose of Oscar Wilde*, London: Methuen.

—— (1954) *The Picture of Dorian Gray*, Harmondsworth: Penguin.

—— (1968) *Critical Writings of Oscar Wilde: The Artist as Critic*, New York: Random House.

Williams, R. (1983) *Writing in Society*, London: Verso.

Wittgenstein, L. (1978) *Philosophical Investigations*, Oxford: Blackwell.

—— (1980) *Culture and Value*, Chicago: University of Chicago Press.

Wolf, M. (1990) 'Chinanotes: engendering anthropology', in R. Sanjek (ed.) *Fieldnotes. The Makings of Anthropology*, Ithaca: Cornell University Press.

Woolf, V. (1944) *The Second Common Reader*, Harmondsworth: Penguin.

—— (1980) *Orlando*, London: Granada.

Yamba, C.B. (1992) 'Going there and getting there: the future as a legitimating charter for life in the present', in S. Wallman (ed.) *Contemporary Futures*, London: Routledge.

Index